Knitting Around the World

A MULTISTRANDED HISTORY
OF A TIME-HONORED TRADITION

Knitting

AROUND THE WORLD

**A Multistranded History
of a Time-Honored Tradition**

by Lela Nargi

Voyageur Press

First published in 2011 by Voyageur Press,
an imprint of MBI Publishing Company,
400 First Avenue North, Suite 300,
Minneapolis, MN 55401 USA

Voyageur Press titles are also available at
discounts in bulk quantity for industrial or sales-
promotional use. For details write to Special
Sales Manager at MBI Publishing Company,
400 First Avenue North, Suite 300, Minneapolis,
MN 55401 USA.

To find out more about our books,
visit us online at www.voyageurpress.com.

ISBN-13: 978-0-7603-3794-3

Editor: Kari Cornell
Design Manager: Katie Sonmor
Layout: Wendy Holdman

Library of Congress Cataloging-in-Publication
Data

Nargi, Lela.
  Knitting around the world : a multistranded
history of a time-honored tradition / Lela Nargi.
      p.cm.
  Includes bibliographical references.
  ISBN 978-0-7603-3794-3 (plc w/jkt)
  1. Knitting—History. I. Title.
TT820.N3685 2011
746.43'2—dc22

                                    2010047533

On the front cover:
Sweater courtesy of the Ostrobothnian
Museum, photo by Gunnar Backman; Socks
made and photographed by Tuulia Salmela;
Gloves courtesy of Museum of Fine Arts,
Boston Accession #38.1262a-b, gift of
Phillip Lehman in memory of his wife,
Carrie L. Lehman, 1938; Hat courtesy of
Victoria and Albert Museum #T.176-1958,
given by Pamela Sanguinetti.

On facing page: Norwegian Cross Country
Ski Socks, photo by Sue Flanders and
Janine Kosel

Contents pages: Knitting Around the World map,
photo by Sue Flanders and Janine Kosel

CONTENTS

INTRODUCTION

Vintage postcards and photos of knitters from around the world. *All images courtesy of Voyageur Press Archives, with the exception of center image: Library of Congress Prints and Photographs Division #LC-USZ62-106363; and bottom right image: Photo by J Peterson, #P03721, courtesy of the Shetland Museum and Archives*

*K*NITTING IS OLD—WELL, SORT OF. It's old compared to some handcrafts (rug hooking), but not so old compared to others (weaving). Beyond that, it's hard to get specific, since no one knows how old knitting really is. There's certainly been speculation through the ages, and plenty of confusion; for example, many ancient textile fragments once thought to be knitting have turned out to be  another textile craft altogether: *nålbinding*, an ancient form of needlecraft that is sometimes refered to as "single-needle knitting" (*see page* 121).

This book certainly doesn't pretend to have all the answers. It does, however, present some of the history of hand knitting and, in some instances, some of the conflicting opinions about hand knitting history in the various countries where knitting has found a toehold throughout the centuries. It also attempts to follow knitting's trail, from its purported origins in the Islamic world up through Spain, into Western Europe and beyond, and, eventually, across the ocean to our own shores. Mostly, though, it seeks to present the knitting traditions of these places in all their particularities. What makes the knitting of Sweden (or Estonia, or Peru) so distinctly Swedish (or Estonian, or Peruvian)? Herein lie answers—some old, some new, and, hopefully, all inspiring.

Chapter 1

THE ISLAMIC WORLD

"Study of Female Figure in Ciociaria Traditional Costume" by Angelo Pietrasanta,
watercolor on thin cardboard, 1851–1861.
DEA/VENERANDA BIBLOTECA AMBROSIANA/Getty Images

$\mathcal{K}$NITTING IS GENERALLY THOUGHT to have originated in the Arab world and, from there, spread with the Crusades into Spain. Aficionados of knitting history will be familiar with the blue-and-white patterned socks found in Egypt and dating to . . . well, more about that in a minute.

Here's what the ever-entertaining British knitwear designer James Norbury has to say on the topic, in *Traditional Knitting Patterns*.

"Arabic knitting is a generic term. It covers the earliest known types of knitting that were carried out by Nomadic people living in the desert places of North Africa who were, as far as we are aware, the first knitters and are probably antecedents of the Arabs of the present time. The earliest known specimens of this type of knitting were all worked on frames. The frames were either circular or narrow oblong ones; the circular frames being used mainly for knitting sandal socks, the narrow oblong ones for carpets, tent flaps, and possibly articles of clothing that were worn by the Tribal Leaders. The knitting action was similar to 'Bobbin Work' . . . Four nails were inserted round the hole at the top of a bobbin and a cord produced by making loops on the four nails and then passing the loops singly over a length of wool that had been wound round the inside of each nail. The wool was wound round in an anti-clockwise direction producing a twisted loop, and it was from this twisted action that 'Crossed Stocking Stitch' was formed that is the basic texture of all Arabic Knitting." (Herein lies the root of the theory that 'French' Knitting (*see page* 26) originated in the Arab world.)

Norbury's not done yet. "We do not know at what stage in the development of the craft of knitting the frames were dispensed with and the work done directly on hooked knitting needles," he writes. "We do know that up to the middle of the nineteenth century hooked needles were still used in many parts of Europe and that 'Crossed Stocking Stitch' was then known as 'Continental Stocking Stitch.'"

Earliest Surviving Knitted Items

Polish material culture scholar Irena Turnau has a bit to add to the above monologue: Some early surviving knitted items (though not the earliest; these were "small in size and usually of one color") of probably "Arab origin" are fragments of good-quality, multicolored wool socks in a stripe pattern, in shades of beige and green, "Coptic or Arab, kept in the Musées Royaux d'Art et d'Histoire in Brussels, in the section with Coptic and Arabian fabrics." The gauges were fine, anywhere from twelve to twenty stitches per inch and tightly knit.

In addition to wool, cotton was also used throughout the Arabian Peninsula, according to textile and design scholar, Ruta Saliklis, and this was commonly knit at a gauge of ten to fourteen stitches per inch. When cotton fragments are found, they are usually colored off-white and indigo. Patterns for all developed, in medieval times, into abstract zigzags, triangles, and diamonds.

Historian Richard Rutt also weighs in, in his celebrated tome A History of Hand Knitting, dating the "probably first examples of true knitting"— such as a fragment from Islamic Egypt—to the seventh to ninth century. He discovers blue-and-white Islamic socks from around 1200, also mostly hailing from Egypt, knitted in cotton from the toe up and festooned with Islamic motifs and script. From there, he picks up the thread quite a bit later. He finds mountain shepherds knitting wool leggings; townspeople knitting coarse woolen socks

with pointed toes (not unlike Turkish socks) using simple yarnover patterns and picot hems; caps, also with a picot edge and a flat top; and something he calls "trouser-girdles." Here's how Rutt describes the latter: "The tasseled girdles were 3–4 cm . . . across and 1.5 meters . . . long. Six or eight stitches were cast on. Each row was worked * over, knit 2 together. * The description of the method is not clear, but appears to mean that the work was slid to the blunt end of the needle and worked off, without turning—a simple method of knitting tubular cord. Earlier, true tubular girdles had been made in stockinette on five needles, using twenty stitches (five to each of four needles)."

Afghanistan has been classified in modern times as being part of Central Asia at least as often as part of the Middle East. Gail Ann Lambert, in her thesis for North Carolina State University, "The Taxonomy of Sweater Structures and Their Origins," identifies a knitted vest from this region, created by a group of Mongol origin called the Hazara. It is knit in the round of brown and beige wool, patterned with what Lambert terms "ancient horn designs and abstracted floral motifs." It seems to be the only one of its kind, although its mere existence, says Lambert, is proof that "sweaters have been produced in this region even though there is not much written documentation on the subject."

And finally comes an amusing and not exactly enlightening account from the New York Times in 1883:

> The Egyptians of the present . . . run about
> with bare feet. The ancient Egyptians, on
> the contrary, who are now only to be seen
> in dried condition in museums, possessed
> a very good method of knitting stockings,
> as is shown in the collection at the Louvre,
> in Paris. In the grave of a mummy there
> were found a pair of knitted stockings,
> which gave the surprising evidence, firstly,
> that short stockings, resembling socks,

were worn by ancient Egyptians; and secondly, that the art of knitting stockings had already attained great perfection in ancient Egypt. These curious stockings are knitted in a very clever manner, and the material, fine wool of sheep, that might once have been white, is now brown with age. The needles with which the work was done must have been a little thicker than we should choose for the same purpose, and the knitting is loose and elastic. The stocking is begun just as we make the design, only in the simplest manner, with single thread; but in the continuation of the work it is not simply plain, but fanciful. The usual border of the stocking which prevents the rolling up of the work is narrow, consisting of a row of turned loops; and the circle, the nicely shaped heel, which is a little different from our method, show a very skillful hand.

❊ A twelfth-century sock of white and indigo cotton, found in Egypt. Although the color and materials were common in Egypt at the time, this sock utilizes a knitting technique that was not common to the area. According to the Textile Museum in Washington, D.C., "The heel was made last and then attached to loops formed while knitting the leg. This ingenious practice allowed the heel to be replaced when it wore out without the necessity of making new socks . . . Egyptians at this time used a simpler method that started at the top of the leg and worked down towards the toe." This sock is thought to have originated in India. *The Textile Museum #73.698, acquired by George Hewitt Myers in 1953*

Dura-Europos Leaf Pattern

This interpretation of an elegant leaf textile design is derived from Barbara Walker's version in her 1970 masterpiece, *A Second Treasury of Knitting Patterns*. She based her patterns on textile fragments excavated in the 1920s and 1930s from the Roman fort Dura-Europos (300 BCE – 256 CE) set high on the banks of the Euphrates River in present-day Syria. To quote Walker: "Knitter, let your hands reach back twenty centuries into the past and touch the hands of your unknown cultural ancestor who made that ancient fragment . . ."

At the time Walker published her patterns, the fragments were assumed to have been knitted. It is now generally believed that true knitting with two needles did not originate until at least 800-1000 CE and did not become widespread throughout the Middle East and Egypt until the Middle Ages. The original fragment was created by the earlier art of *nålbinding*, where fabric is formed by sewing freehand rows of interconnected loops. The results are remarkably similar to knitting. However, this older method is phenomenally tedious. For example, during the height of Renaissance knitting in the fifteenth and sixteenth centuries in Italy and France (for women in convents and for men in the guilds), most knitted articles were constructed at the unbelievably tiny gauge of 28-12 sts to the inch. This pattern for a leaf motif, at 10 sts to the inch, is quite coarse in comparison.

MATERIALS

Cascade *Heritage* (75% wool/25% nylon, 437 yds/100g per skein): 2 skeins red #5607 Note: you will need only a small amount of the 2nd skein, if at all
2.25mm (US #1) and 2.75mm (US #2) double-pointed needles, in sets of five
Open-able stitch markers

GAUGE

40 sts and 50 rnds = 4 inches (10cm) in st st (worked through the back loops) on larger needles

PATTERN NOTES

Working Through the Back Loops: Every stitch, whether knitted or purled is worked through the back loop. The only exceptions are immediately after picking up sts from the cast-on edge and on certain decreases where it is more expedient to work a simple k2tog (see below). In order to streamline the pattern, it is written without indicating this technique for every stitch. Also note that the severe amount of twist created by this technique is to be expected.

Working Tightly: Especially at the needle intersections, increasing and decreasing, be sure to pull the working yarn tightly.

—Pattern from Elanor Lynn, *Knitting Socks from Around the World*

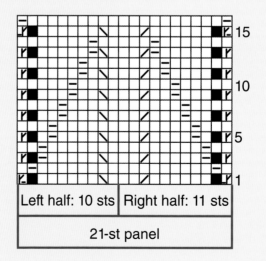

Left half: 10 sts	Right half: 11 sts
21-st panel	

These Dura-Europos socks, designed and knit by Elanor Lynn, feature the leaf pattern. The complete sock pattern instructions can be found in *Knitting Socks from Around the World*. *Photo by Sue Flanders and Janine Kosel*

Chapter 2

WESTERN EUROPE

Villanella, an engraving by J. Levasseur based on an 1874 painting by
C.H. Jalabert, depicts a young Italian girl, strolling and knitting.

OST EVERYONE SEEMS TO AGREE: knitting found its first toehold in Western Europe within the borders of Spain, thundering in through the Islamic world. Early examples from the region are silk, and knitted in the round; the back-and-forth knitting we know and love today didn't emerge until almost 1600. To wit: two small Arab-knit silk pillows, found in the royal tombs of Las Huelgas in Burgos, Spain, and a pair of bishop's gloves. French knitting project realized for Crafts Council (England) with the London-based Somali Women's Group. The cushions are remarkably beautiful, especially considering that they were made during a time when most knitting was entirely utilitarian. (Even several centuries later, common knitting of and for the masses would be perfectly serviceable, although hardly artful, socks.) Knitted stockinette stitch on steel pins, the cushions are intricate, consisting of filled diamonds and lozenges, rosettes, and fleurs-de-lis patterns.

From Spain, knitting swept through Europe, embraced by artisans for its ease and portability as, unlike weaving, it didn't require the use of any heavy equipment. The first European knitted items were small: There were relic purses for holding the remains of saints (from the thirteenth and fourteenth centuries), as well as liturgical gloves and the above-mentioned pillows, which were only eleven and fourteen inches square, respectively. There were also knitted stockings (emerging by the early sixteenth century to replace cloth stockings held up by garters, ribbons, and all manner of contraptions), knitted sleeves, purses, and a various pouches. Knitting writer Deborah Pulliam, in a 2007 article for *Piecework* magazine, describes certain fourteenth-century pouches that could be hung from girdles beneath the copious folds on both men's and women's garments, as well as drawstring bags of the sixteenth century known as "pokes." By the eighteenth century, knitted workbags for needlework projects were quite the rage, and by the nineteenth century, bags knitted with beads appeared.

Knitting Guilds

Knitting was the domain of the highly skilled, as evidenced by Irena Turnau's paper, "The Knitting Crafts in Europe from the Thirteenth to the Eighteenth Century." Knitting guilds, she writes—organization of craftsmen who were required to pass rigorous tests in order to gain membership—were set up in France as early as 1268, and by the fifteenth century, had also reached the Netherlands and Spain. Meanwhile, the peasantry took to knitting woolen caps and stockings for the gentry in order to supplement their meager earnings, and also to outfit themselves and their families.

By the eighteenth century, knitting was everywhere, and almost everything was knitted: trousers, shawls, even carpets, an essentially south German phenomenon of the seventeenth and eighteenth centuries (*see page* 29). Sweaters as we think of them today did not make an appearance until quite late. Their precursors were probably the elaborate Italianate silk jackets and vests that became popular throughout the continent in the seventeenth century, and the plain, undershirt-like garments of the fourteenth century. Their patterning, when present, notes knitting teacher and author Priscilla Gibson-Roberts, often paid homage to patterns from earlier sock knitting.

Frustratingly, though knitting was assuredly a strong and old technique in the countries of Spain, Italy, and France, far too little research has been conducted about the craft there; from the sixteenth or seventeenth century onward, the trail begins to go cold.

PATTERN

Open-work Stockings

On each needle cast on 52 stitches with fine cotton, knit the welts and raise one stitch for the seam. When you arrive at the narrowings, narrow every eighth row, and when you have 38 stitches on each needle, cease, and knit until the article is completed; then take half the stitches to form the heel, knit 23 loops, and narrow on each side of the seam for three rows. In forming the heel, narrow every row once the fourth loop from the seam, and then the loops must be taken up, the end one as close as possible. Take three stitches from each side of the fore foot needle to the other, and knit a round plain; after which, widen every fifth stitch on both sides of the heel. Alternate rows of the heel needles are then to be narrowed until only 36 loops remain on each. The stitches to be narrowed are the fifth and sixth from the ends. Knit the feet of a proper length, and then narrow at the ends of the needles every other row, until only ten remain on each; narrow every row until you have only three, which you cast off in the usual manner. The open pattern is produced by knitting every fifth round thus: take two stitches in one, and bring the cotton in front of the needle, that it may form a stitch before taking the succeeding two into one. The more open you desire the work to be, the fewer stitches and the finer needles you will require.

—From *The Ladies' Work-Table Book*, Anonymous, J. Winchester, New York, 1844
   (Project Gutenberg)

Spain and Portugal

In *Traditional Knitting Patterns*, James Norbury places knitting in Spain in the ninth century, even though he cites no material evidence to support this. (But consider, please, this compelling fact: The first Western European knitting was of the highly elaborate two-colored variety. How many years, or decades, or centuries would it have taken for the basics of knitting to evolve into such a sophisticated art form?) More supportable is Norbury's claim that most early knitting in Spain was liturgical—carried out for the Catholic church. Ruta Saliklis, author of *A Wealth of Pattern: Northern European and Middle Eastern Folk Knitting in the Helen Allen Textile Collection*, makes mention of the country's finely knit liturgical gloves, such as those from the thirteenth and fourteenth centuries, often stitched with gold and silver threads. Scholar Irena Turnau calls for more research.

According to Pulliam's "Early Silk Knitting," the first evidence of the purl stitch (as well as the first yarnover), c. 1562, appears on on a pair of stockings belonging to Eleanor of Toledo. Mary Schoeser, a writer and curator, identifies possibly another first for Spain: the knitting of silk garments. Barcelona, Toledo, and Málaga were most closely associated with knitting by the sixteenth century, Schoeser writes in her book, *Silk*, and it is these regions that produced luxury silk stockings for various English royalty. Irena Turnau writes of the knitting guilds that were already in evidence in the very late fifteenth century in Barcelona, and of the silk stockings knit in Toledo for the French court. Those stockings were ordered in sea green, red, sky blue, dark green, chestnut brown, the "color of a pigeon," yellow, white, violet, black, ash gray, fawn, and crimson.

❋ Pair of ecclesiastic gloves, probably eighteenth-century Spanish. Silk knit and measuring approximately eleven inches long, these gloves are similar in design and patterning to other gloves of their ilk dating back to the sixteenth century. *Museum of Fine Arts, Boston Accession #38.1262a-b, gift of Philip Lehman in memory of his wife, Carrie L. Lehman, 1938*

❋ Hand-knitted red silk cap, probably from late eighteenth-century Spain. Knit at a gauge of fourteen stitches to the inch, this cap features a pattern of chevrons and lozenges tapering toward its crown and is topped with a tufted silk tassel. According to the Victoria & Albert Museum, "Tasselled caps like this one were worn by men and women on festive occasions. A tapestry designed by the Spanish artist Goya shows a party of people on a picnic wearing similar headgear." *Victoria & Albert Museum #T.176-1958, given by Pamela Sanguinetti*

Turnau writes in *The History of Knitting Before Mass Production* of the magnificent silk waistcoats that were in vogue during the sixteenth and seventeenth centuries: "The oldest of the preserved relics point to Spain as an important but little investigated centre of knitting production using silk, which utilized the skill of the Arabs. The oldest of the preserved knitted waistcoats comes from the beginning of the sixteenth century and is kept in the Museo de Indumentaria Colección Rocamora [sic] in Barcelona. It is made of green silk with a gold metal thread. The design depicts eagles within a floral ornamentation similar [to] that seen on woven fabric of the same period."

By the seventeenth century, the industry had gone . . . industrial. In 1600, the knitting frame was adapted to silk, and it arrived in Portugal in 1678 and Catalonia in 1687. The nineteenth century saw knitting applied, thrillingly enough, to the trousers of toreadors. Small-scale hand knitting, what Irena Turnau identifies as "peasant knitting," certainly had—and continues to have—its place throughout the region. "I have myself seen local markets in villages or small towns . . . where peasants sit with the basket full of hand-made knitted stockings, socks, caps, gloves, or pullovers. This manner of marketing the knitted fabrics of domestic production in local markets is a very old

✳ Doilies from a sampler book, dating from 1875 to 1900, knit from *pita*, fiber from the Azores cactus plant seed and each showing a different pattern. "This type of small ornamental mat was placed under food on serving plates . . . Peasant knitters in the Azores islands, west of Portugal, used to specialise in making delicate lace items such as shawls and dresses . . . According to an article in *Harper's Bazaar* (1893), doilies like this one were knitted on 'five, very fine, slightly curved, barbed needles.'" *Victoria & Albert Museum #T.389-2001, given by Mrs. Mary Medlam*

✳ A pair of eighteenth century ecclesiastical gloves, silk knit, probably originating in Spain. *Museum of Fine Arts, Boston*

one." And later in *The History of Knitting Before Mass Production*, she remarks, "A very large diffusion of knitting sheaths in all regions of Catalonia, Spain, and Portugal testifies to the use of knitted parts of dress in peasant costume."

Lace knitted on the nine Portuguese islands known as the Azores has, since its inception in the 1840s, been known as pita lace, because of the aloe fiber—*pita*—commonly used in its production. It's most frequently been used in the creation of mats. A *Dictionary of Lace* calls it, unfortunately, tourist-oriented, "used to produce innumerable small mats a few inches across." In contrast, Rutt quotes this passage from an 1893 article in *Harper's Bazaar*: "The knitting of aloe lace has reached perfection, both in variety of patterns which, like those of open-work hose, are generally original, and invented by the knitters themselves; and in the delicacy of the fibre, which is split many times. Shawls, dresses, fichus, in fact anything for which lace may be properly used, are made in aloe."

Italy and France

Much has been made over the years of the so-called "knitting Madonnas" painted by various artists throughout Italy (and in at least one notable instance, in Germany) during the fourteenth century. They've engendered many assumptions and speculations about who knit them, and how early, and where. But Rutt cautions: "The evidence must not be over-interpreted. It shows that knitting was known in northern Italy before 1350 . . . It suggests that knitting was done at home by women, but does not tell us whether it was an occupation for ladies of leisure or a common pursuit, whether it was cheap or expensive."

Nevertheless, the knitting Madonnas—simply and literally, paintings that depict the Virgin Mary knitting—do tell us a few things about knitting in the Middle Ages, whether or not they tell us about knitting in Italy in the Middle Ages. One painting, by the Lorenzetti brothers, shows Mary knitting with variously colored bobbins of yarn, with

❋ An early seventeenth-century long-sleeved silk jacket, stockinette-knit in coral and gold in a stylized floral pattern, possibly from Italy; basket stitch borders the lower hem and cuffs. The jacket is composed of five rectangular panels: one each for the back, two fronts, and two sleeves, stitched together with silk thread and lined with blue linen. The gauge is seventeen stitches to the inch and it was once thought, according to the Victoria & Albert Museum, "that these jackets were produced on the early versions of the knitting frame. However research has shown that the frame was not developed enough in the early seventeeth century to produce purl stitches or such a fine gauge." Incredibly, such jackets were part of informal dress of the time, worn by both men and women. *Victoria & Albert Museum, #807-1904*

four needles "held under the palm" and the yarn carried over her right forefinger. Other Madonna paintings Rutt mentions (works by Vitale degli Equi and Tommaso da Modena) also show Mary knitting in the round with multiple needles—although what she could be knitting remains a mystery. Rutt recaps the evidence: "Knitting was done in the round on four needles . . . the working needles were held under the palms of each hand . . . the needles were not hooked . . . the yarn was carried in the right hand . . . and . . . more than one yarn could be used." Not a bad collection of evidence, after all.

Irena Turnau, in *The History of Knitting Before Mass Production*, makes a plea for more study on the matter of Italian knitting history and cites an iconographic depiction of a sixteenth-century Italian knitter making stockings from two-colored threads. She lists these items as indispensable to the Italian Renaissance attire: close-fitting knitted stockings, doublets, gloves, berets, and children's frocks, knit on from two to five needles.

Skip ahead two hundred years, and you'll find a pair of complexly patterned silk knee stockings worn by the wife of Cosimo I de'Medici. Were they knit in Italy? No one knows. But Rutt's description

❋ A pair of elegant, seventeenth century knitted silk mitts, from Italy. So little is known of the history of knitting in this country, leading textile scholar Irena Turnau and others to call for more research. *Museum of Fine Arts Boston*

of them gives a little taste of what may have been quintessentially Italian knitting of the time: "The pattern of these turn-over tops . . . consists of a narrow band of plain knitting with two zigzag lines of purl running round the stocking, divided by two purled rounds from the broad central band of the turnover. The broad band has a trellis of purls two purls wide, with plain lozenges between the trellis purls. Each lozenge contains four eyelets. The turnover is completed by a second narrow band with zigzags." Lucky was the lady who got to wear these (however, they were found in said lady's tomb, a circumstance which does seem a bit less than lucky).

Stockings abounded in these centuries. The *Encyclopedia Americana* mentions that Henry VIII wore Italian knitted hose in 1539. An article from an 1847 issue of *Godey's Magazine* makes this charming claim: "The invention of knitting is claimed by the Spaniards. Certainly it was known and practiced in that country before it was understood in England. It is said that one William Rider, an apprentice on London Bridge, seeing at the house of an Italian merchant a pair of knit worsted stockings from Mantua, took the hint and made a similar pair, which he presented to William, Earl of Pembroke. This was in 1564."

Norbury calls knitting in Italy "self-conscious" and "sophisticated," although he, too, has a difficult time finding any "continuity" to the story. He discovers that in the fifteenth and sixteenth centuries, it has lost its "primitive" Arabic influence (possibly as a result of visits from Spanish nobility to the country) and found an ornateness in the form of coats and jerkins: "Bright-coloured silk, silver and gold threads, even semi-precious stones are all at times used in the creation of floral and symbolic patternings that in many respects resembled the woven brocades of the same period."

As for France: "The village of Barège, situated on the French side of the Pyrennes [sic], at the foot of those lofty mountains, is celebrated for that peculiar description of knitting, where various coloured wools, and sometimes gold and silver,

are introduced to form most elegant patterns." So expounded Miss F. Lambert in 1846, in her *Handbook of Needlework*. But once again, in Rutt's history, it's stockings that take up most of the conversation (silk stockings were worn by the members of Charles IX's court in the late sixteenth century).

In *Traditional Knitting Patterns*, James Norbury states, "The French specialized in the knitting of stockings whose elaborate lace patternings made them one of the marvels of Europe." High praise indeed. Rutt goes on to describe the more common wool socks and stockings knitted and worn by average French citizens. In *History of Handknitting*, he recites this anecdote from 1793: The curate of Ars "and his little sister Marguerite went out every day to graze the family donkey, cows, and sheep. They took their knitting with them, since it was the custom of both sexes to make stockings while looking after their beasts."

Despite these lyrical details, France, as Turnau makes abundantly clear in her research, was a powerhouse of knitting, and much earlier than many other European countries. The first knitting guilds, which, as she writes "related to the increasing demand for knitted fabrics which could not be satisfied by domestic workers," date to the mid-thirteenth century, though their importance vis-à-vis the rest of the country's craft guilds was pretty marginal at first. Yet, by 1514, the guild of the *chapeliers de gants et de bonnets* (literally, "milliners of gloves and caps") was one of the most important in Paris. And France was one of the most important centers of knitting in Europe. Caps and stockings were made, as well as socks, gloves, mittens, and overcoats.

Tchanguès Knitting: The Shepherds of the Landes

The story of this strange, almost wholly extinct tradition among shepherds of the Landes begins in the early eighteenth century. Residents of the once-marshy region along France's southwest coast began using stilts to get around and became

used by the old Arabs; and can still be found in use round the Mediterranean and in places where Arab influence penetrated. The hooked needles . . . made by a shepherd of Landes, in the South of France, from old umbrella ribs . . . [a]re hand filed and shaped as they always have been made in this district, though earlier needles of this type were made from the young shoots of briar bushes. Five needles make a set. These shepherds are great knitters, and spin their own wool, which is mainly gleaned from the straggling tufts left by the sheep on hedge or bush, for wool-gathering has yet a real meaning in these parts. They knit as they watch their sheep, erect on stilts the better to keep guard over their straggling flocks . . . the knitting is kept in [a] pouch [called a *potche à tèche* in the dialect], which is worn slung about the neck with a long leather strap, to which is affixed a hook in the front. In knitting, the yarn is passed over this hook . . . and then round the left thumb, and in and out the fingers of the left hand, for these shepherds operate the wool with the left hand, in what we might assume was the orthodox method used when hook needles were in vogue.

known as *tchanguès,* from the regional term for "big legs." In addition to keeping feet dry, the stilts had another use: from up high, the residents—pretty much all shepherds, whose flocks fertilized rye crops that might otherwise never have flourished in the bogs—could keep track of their far-flung sheep. They adapted their entire lifestyle to the stilts. They cooked meals on high, on stoves they carried around with them, and they knitted.

Wrote Mary Thomas of the *Tchanguès* in her 1938 *Mary Thomas's Knitting Book:*

The earliest knitting needles were made with a hook at one end, like crochet hooks, and these, fashioned of copper wire, were

What were they knitting up there? Mary Thomas reports: "Socks and berets, the latter being felted, as in the fifteenth century." Other reports support especially the ever-present beret, worn in summer to protect against the sun and in winter, against rain. And, in some regions in winter, hooded wool capes.

The need for stilt-walking, and indeed sheep and shepherds, was virtually obliterated by the beginning of the twentieth century, by which time the Landes swamps had been overtaken by a forest of maritime pines, which were planted by the government in order to halt erosion.

The Beret

The beret, according to some, has its origins in the Middle Ages, in the former Béarn region of France (the place in southern France, in and below the Pyrenees, that brought us sauce béarnaise). A French history site makes mention of sculptures of men wearing berets on the church in Bellocq (dating from the thirteenth century) and on a monastery in the Aspe Valley (dating from the eighteenth). Mary Thomas reminds us that in the heyday of the knitting guilds, an apprentice would have to complete four masterpieces in thirteen weeks, including one of these disk-shaped caps.

Not surprisingly, if we take a cue from the *tchanguès*, berets were worn by shepherds and, of course, knitted by shepherds, to protect them from the elements. They were constructed in the round from undyed wool, on boxwood needles, then felted. Says Mary Thomas of the matter: "The last surviving use of felting, as applied to knitting, can be seen today in the French beret and the Eastern fez, both of which carry in the middle of the crown the knitter's end of wool, showing how it commenced. In early days it was the custom to knit the article in the natural colour of the wool, and then dye and felt it in one process by leaving it to soak for some four or five days. When the wool had thickened, the hat or cap would be blocked to any shape, brushed with a teasle brush, and even cut, since there was no fear of the knitting unraveling."

The fact that berets are almost exclusively thought to be Basque garments is said to be attributable to peddlers, who eventually brought them to that region, as well as to the Landes. Today so commonly associated with military garb, the beret was not used as such until 1891, when it was adopted by the elite mountain infantry of the French army, Les Chasseurs Alpins.

Les Tricoteuses

Literary knitters will no doubt be familiar with Les Tricoteuses of Robespierre, who make a notorious appearance in Charles Dickens's A *Tale of Two Cities*, most notably in the form of the nefarious Madame Defarge; she ceaselessly knits, secretly stitching up the names of intended Revolutionary victims as she goes.

Les Tricoteuses existed in reality too, of course, during the French Revolution of the eighteenth century, which saw the end of the absolute monarchy. Writes Suzyn Jackson in *Knit it Together* about this grisly circle of knitters, "While knitting was still common among the lower classes at the time, the real Tricoteuses were a small group. The Commune of Paris organized and paid these sadistic women to attend tribunals and beheadings. Their job, in the words of the Commune decree, was 'to greet death, to insult the victims, and to glut their eyes with blood.' They did their job well, jeering and shrieking as the upper classes were led to their death, knitting through it all."

What on earth could they have been knitting all that bloody time? John Gideon Millingen, in his 1848 account of the affair, posits that Les Tricoteuses were knitting stockings and garters as they stood watch over the scaffolds at the Place de la Concorde, although it's possible that they also knitted phrygian caps.

Paul Hanson, in his *Historical Dictionary of the French Revolution*, describes these symbolic bits of headwear thusly:

> Phyrgian caps, also known as Liberty caps, are amongst the most well-known symbols of the Revolution. They were floppy knit woolen caps, typically red in color, with a tri-colored cockade often attached to the tip. They appeared at least as early as the first Festivals of Federation in the summer of 1790. The name "phyrigian" was an allusion to the freed slaves of Roman times, who were given similar caps as a symbol of their liberated status. During the Revolution, the caps came to symbolize freedom from the despotism of the Old Regime, and the

🌿 PATTERN

Child's Bath or Bedroom Slippers

Length of sole, five and one-half inches. It is well to have the soles before beginning to sew. They can be secured at any store.

Each slipper requires two and one-half yards of round web. Start at the back of the heel . . . and make the first two rows three inches high, then gradually shorten the next three rows, and keep each row this height until the instep is finished. The first row on the vamp . . . is made one inch higher than the side. Each row is then gradually shortened, the last row being three-fourths of an inch high . . . This will complete one-half of the slipper.

The other half is made in just the reverse way by continuing the sewing from the toe . . . back to the heel, taking care that each row is exactly the same height as the corresponding row on the opposite side.

Join the back of the heel and sew to the soles before closing the vamp in front. Sew vamp up the center by catching corresponding loops together. Make cord and tassel to go around the top, as in illustration of finished slippers.

—*Spool Knitting* by Mary A. McCormack, 1909, A.S. Barnes & Company, New York. (Project Gutenberg)

newly gained liberty of all French citizens. They appeared frequently on the heads of female figures of Liberty, and became one of the defining aspects of dress of the *sans-culottes*. By 1793 they had become a virtually mandatory element of dress for those attending sectional assemblies.

Still, such grandiose sentiment and knitterly posturing was probably a little farfetched for the average Tricoteuse. It might have belonged more to the class of knitters (or perhaps, more accurately, the class of women who were knitted *for*) that emerged after the Revolution—the demimonde of *Les Merveilleuses*, or the Marvelous Women, who barely survived the Jacobin regime with their heads intact. After the Terror and the unseating of the French monarchy, they adopted a brazen and extravagant fashion meant to affect the form-fitting, transparent drapery of a barely clad Greek statue—dresses were dampened to get just the right cling, and hair was clipped short to emulate the haircuts given to victims of the guillotine, pre-chop.

What did this fashion mean for knitting? Apparently, Les Merveilleuses had some sense of decorum: knitted, knee length knickers, stays, and stockings were worn under what little existed of their ensembles.

"French" Knitting

The simple wooden spool around which children (and grown-ups such as artist Françoise Dupré, *see page* 30) have been wrapping wool for ages has more names than you can count on three hands: Knitting Nancy, Knitting Jenny, Knitting Nelly, Knitting Nana, Knitting Knobby, Knitting Noddy, Bizzy Lizzy, Corker, *Strick Susel* (German for "Knitting Susie"), Knitting Bob, Knitting Doll, Mushroom, Flower and Bee, Toy Knitter, Peg Knitter, and of paramount interest to us here, French knitter. Whatever the moniker, the tool accomplishes the pretty little function of creating a tube of wool as long as you choose to make it, which, somewhat

✳ French knitters have even more guises than names—here, just a small assortment of home- and factory-made varieties. *Photos courtesy of Françoise Dupré*

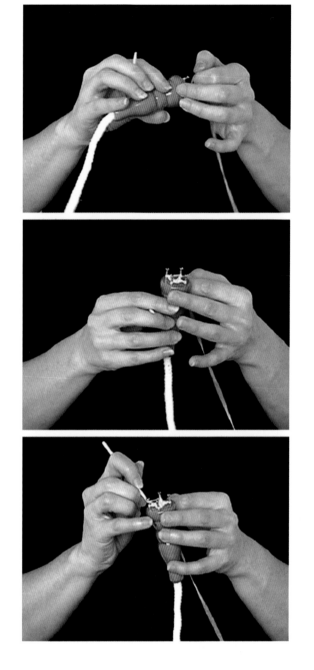

❋ How to use the French knitter: loop yarn around each of the pegs, then pull the stitch over and off with a crochet hook.

Photos by Françoise Dupré

wound once clockwise in a figure eight around each of the (usually) four nails hammered into its top. Once the cast on round is complete, says Vermont Yarn Shop owner Carrie Herzog, the yarn is then wrapped clockwise around the outside of all four pegs (not around each individual peg as one did on the first round). With a needle or crochet hook, the initial four loops are pulled up and over the yarn that was wrapped around. This is done continuously so there is always yarn to pull a stitch over. More nails can be added for larger tubes (say, for socks and hats). Mary A. McCormack's 1909 book titled, fittingly enough, *Spool Knitting*, sought to show child knitters how to create flat webbing (work with two nails at a time) as well as tubes, doll clothes (sew tubes together in various formations), and jump ropes (use jute or cotton in place of wool).

The I-cord (short for "idiot cord"), what must assuredly be seen as the "adult" version of spool-knitted cords, was adapted to needle knitting by the famous knitting teacher and author Elizabeth Zimmermann. This was despite childhood disdain for the output of the French knitter, which she deemed good only for "reins for playing horsey."

But, as you might expect of the grande dame of knitting, EZ didn't stop there. Writes her daughter, Meg Swansen, in *Piecework* magazine in 2008: "Elizabeth expanded on basic free-standing I-Cord and came up with I-Cord Casting-On and Casting-Off, Built-In and Applied Cord, I-Cord Belts of varying widths, I-Cord Glove Fingers and Corners plus I-Cord Buttonholes: Hidden, Looped and Tab." From there, she adds, "Other designers have picked up the baton: Joyce Williams discovered how to obviate the annoying blip that peeks through in Applied Cord in a strongly contrasting color; she also came up with Twisted and Braided I-Cord. Kathy Lynch is responsible for Intarsia I-Cord, which can only be worked in the round. I found 3-Needle-I-Cord-Cast-Off, Free-Form and Square Cord, plus Cord upon Cord to prevent stocking stitch from curling."

surprisingly to contemporary back-and-forth knitters, has an enormous variety of uses.

Some historians have postulated that the knitting spool has its origins in the Middle East; others that it owes its existence to the forklike lucet of the Viking era. The term *French knitter* is supposedly a reference not to the tool's country of origin, but to the spool-knit hats worn by some participants in the French Revolution.

Here's how spool knitting is done: Yarn is threaded through the middle of the spool, then

A sampling of French knitting spool kits from the 1920s through the 1950s.

Germany and Austria

James Norbury, in what seems a surprising lack of tact, lumps together the knitting traditions of Germany and Austria in his book *World Knitting Patterns*. But, as he points out, the Hapsburg rule of various parts of Western Europe (bits and pieces of latter-day Austria, Hungary, Germany, Italy, and other countries) may have forced a little cross-cultural influencing. Norbury is also quick to maintain that regional differences in knitting remained very much intact: lace knitting in Vienna, embroidered motifs in the Austrian Tyrol, heavily patterned Bavarian knitting (*see page 39*), austere knitted fabrics in northern Germany.

Knitting designer and writer Nicky Epstein dates knitting in Germany and Austria to the thirteenth century. Stockings and hats were the first knitted creations in the regions, as they were already pretty much everywhere else. Master Bertram of Minden's painting "Buxtehude Madonna," one of the now-famous knitting Madonnas, was completed in 1390, a sure indication that knitting had already stitched itself to the fabric of society by this time. What we now think of as "traditional" Bavarian stockings, in cream-colored wool with intricate patterns of cables and ribbings, became something of a rage in the seventeenth century, followed up by "traditional" Bavarian and Tyrolean sweaters.

Richard Rutt in *A History of World Knitting* makes some discussion of knitted carpets from the end of the seventeenth century to the latter end of the eighteenth century (*see page 38*). Writes Irena Turnau (with K.G. Ponting) in *The History of Knitting Before Mass Production*, "The production of a knitted carpet was the most important and most complicated of

Françoise Dupré

Françoise Dupré is a French-born sculptor and installation artist whose professed interest in the "art of the everyday" drew her to hobby kits and, more specifically, French spool knitting kits, the latter of which strongly inform her work today. Beyond serving as a medium for her art, spool knitting is also used by Dupré as a communal activity—like knitting itself—a means to collaborate with knitters both new and practiced in the creating of work that Dupré calls "trans-cultural."

"I was trained in sculpture and have always been interested in the physicality and materiality of the art object. I am concerned with the relationship we have as humans with the physical world around us, and the sensory experience we have with objects. This has prompted me to think about not only art objects, made in traditional sculptural materials, but also everyday objects that people fabricate to make their daily lives easier, through bricolage—a practice that is sadly disappearing in the developed world.

"My concern is with the everyday and the 'art of the making in the everyday' concept developed by the sociologist Michel de Certeau. For de Certeau, the world is full of 'small wonders'—objects made by people. I am also interested by the concept of 'making special' and 'joie de faire' (joy of making), a term used by American scholar Ellen Dissanayake when discussing the role of art in human society. For her, humans have an inherent *joie de faire* and pleasure in art making.

"All these concerns have brought me to work with textile materials and processes, and in contexts where the practice of making objects continues to be an integral part of the individual and community sense of identity. My aim is not to preserve skills that have in the past been associated with the feminine, but to give them a different and subversive life. In many of my collaborative-participatory projects, I have worked with women who have extraordinary knitting skills. These were used to

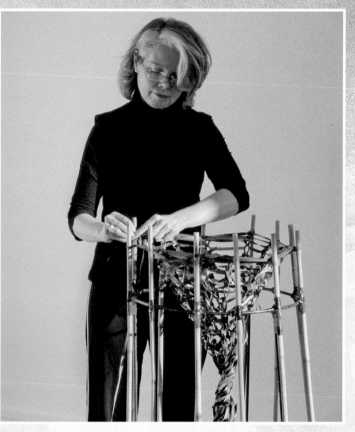

Above: Dupré performing "French Knitting with Rubber" for the installation la résidente at the Irish Museum of Modern Art, Dublin. *Photo by Claire Bracken*

develop installations and artwork. I have never met a participant that had a problem with shifting contexts from the craft/wearable object to the art object and installation; on the contrary! The problem always seems to come from the art world!

"Two examples of my collaborative installations are:

"Fil en aiguille . . . snáth nasc (Ireland, 2003–2004). This was a collaborative knitted project and exhibition I led while I was an artist in residence at the Irish Museum of Modern Art in Dublin. The knitting was used to create a floor installation inspired by the museum's formal garden. It brought together different kinds of knitting: French (spool) knitting and Irish knitting stitches used in the traditional Aran sweater.

"Fujaan (London, 2005). This was a collaborative French (spool) knitting project with the London-based Somali women's group Back to Basics and their group leader, Rakhia Ismail. Here the French (spool) knitting was used by participants to create small vessels/baskets which were then joined together to make a totemic sculpture, a Brancusi textile version of the Endless Column. Wire was threaded through the hollow knitted tube to strengthen it. Then, the tube was woven into 3-D spirals. For the Somali women, the concept of 'art for art's sake' was rather alien, and they were keen to make an artwork with strong utilitarian references, and the

Far left and left: details from exotic mk, 2009, a collaborative project with Milton Keynes Gallery's Offsite Education Program, and three women's groups. It was exhibited in a Barrow, UK shopping center in summer 2009. *Photos by Françoise Dupré and Nyla Elahi.*
Above: Fujaan, 2005—a collaborative French knitting project realized for Crafts Council (England) with the London-based Somali Women's Group. *Photos by Françoise Dupré*

basket/container was therefore chosen. As work progressed, the group made a visual connection with a particular type of stacked vessel: the *fujaan* used in traditional Somali weddings.

"My aim is to create projects that engage with participants' identity, and tap into their experience and history. I believe I cannot do this in a short event. Integral to the process is the production of some kind of tangible object/sculpture/installation where individuals and community can, through the making and experiencing of the object's physicality and materiality, translate emotions, desires, experiences; create new meanings and shape their identity. Again, this needs time and appropriate private spaces like a community center or a workshop space. Between all knitting sessions, participants knit at home, again creating another link to this wonderful web.

"I am very aware of the restorative and therapeutic value of knitting. French (spool) knitting is a simple activity, easy to learn and practice. It is a highly accessible art form, and its practically universal association with childhood makes it a perfect group activity where participants can talk and engage with the artist and each other. Many comments go as follows: "Oh! I do remember my grandmother teaching me!" Of course, not all participants have done spool knitting before, but it is easy to learn.

"Knitting is a time-consuming activity; it encourages long-term commitment, and the end product always brings a sense of self-worth and pride. As a group activity, it strengthens the existing groups with which I have worked and fosters new connections within new groups. When participants come together at the start of a project, there is always a short moment where there is a little bit of doubt about how a simple knitting technique can be used to create an ambitious installation.

"But knitting is used in industries, like the building industry; it's never called *knitting*. It all comes back to *context*."

all the tasks that the aspiring master craftsman had to accomplish before receiving full master status in a guild." The word *carpet*, though, is somewhat misleading: Large pieces of knitted fabric were used as wall hangings, tablecloths, and possibly bedcovers. They employed the use of stranded knitting to accomplish their intricate (and heavy!) styling, and some of them display cartouches filled with other decorative elements—flowers, animals, people—at, says Rutt, "a tension of 28 stitches to 10 cm (4 in.)," in stockinette stitch in as many as twenty different colors. Liturgical subjects were popular (and of course, leave it to Bishop Rutt to speculate as to whether the carpets were knitted by Protestants or Catholics), as were the imperial double-headed eagle (which features on the German Confederation's coat of arms) and lion rampant (a feature of the Kingdom of Bohemia's coat of arms). Rutt calls such carpet knitting an essentially south German specialty, although the craft did take hold in the seventeenth century in Alsace (given over to France) and Silesia (under Austrian rule at this time). According to Rutt, the largest of all the carpets are Silesian; the Alsatian feature lighter colors than the others, as well as floral borders and central motifs.

The area of the Upper Rhine was an important center for hand knitting beginning in the late sixteenth century. In 1599, writes Turnau, there were between 210 and 220 workshops in the towns of the region, and by 1653, there were twenty-eight towns occupied with knitting in Alsace alone. Austria wasn't far behind, which isn't surprising considering the "large herds of sheep in the mountains [that] provided much rough wool for cloth."

Pattern Books

The knitting pattern book as we know it today was a long time in the making. A reasonable facsimile of the contemporary variety emerged in the nineteenth century, but its roots are much longer-standing. And they begin in Germany.

This first pattern book of any kind at all was the *Modelbuch*—according to Charlotte Paludan of the Kunstindustrimuseet in Copenhagen—a printed pattern collection specifically for embroidery and lace. It emerged, incredibly enough, at the beginning of the sixteenth century, about two centuries earlier in Germany than in some other countries. The very earliest of these was from 1524, by a book and textile printer named Johann Schönsperger the Younger, who probably used the same woodblock engravings for his textiles as he used for his books. While his book covered only the craft of embroidery, books for bobbin lace were soon to follow (1557, and in Venice, illustrating how far and fast the craze for pattern books spread). But many of these patterns were assuredly adapted to knitting as well by handcrafters of the

era, "primarily amateurs within the higher social circles," as Paludan writes in 98 *Pattern Books for Embroidery, Lace, and Knitting.*

By the mid-seventeenth century, patterns specifically for knitting were emerging within the pages of some of the books. Rosina Helena Fürst's 1676 *Model-Buchs Dritter Theil* (Third Pattern Book), which was primarily a book of patterns for filet lace, advertised new vine patterns and flowered borders "in the Baroque style;" naturalistic patterns for flowers, birds, and fruit; and stocking knitting. If all was of a piece, those would have been some stockings. A full century later, in 1761, Susanna Dorothea Riegl came out with *Strikkemostre* (Knitting Patterns). The first of its kind? No one dares venture a guess; so few of the truly old pattern books survived, says Paludan, as "patterns were frequently ruined through pricking or tracing, sheets [being] removed and scattered or worn out." What is certain, however, is that Riegl's charted pattern samplers, of various checkerboarded motifs and woven-like basket-stitch crossings (which seem to a modern knitter's eye to have more in common with wood parquet work than yarn craft), would have been accomplished by the most fastidious of needle crafters.

Ladies' Work-Book pattern booklet, late 1800s.

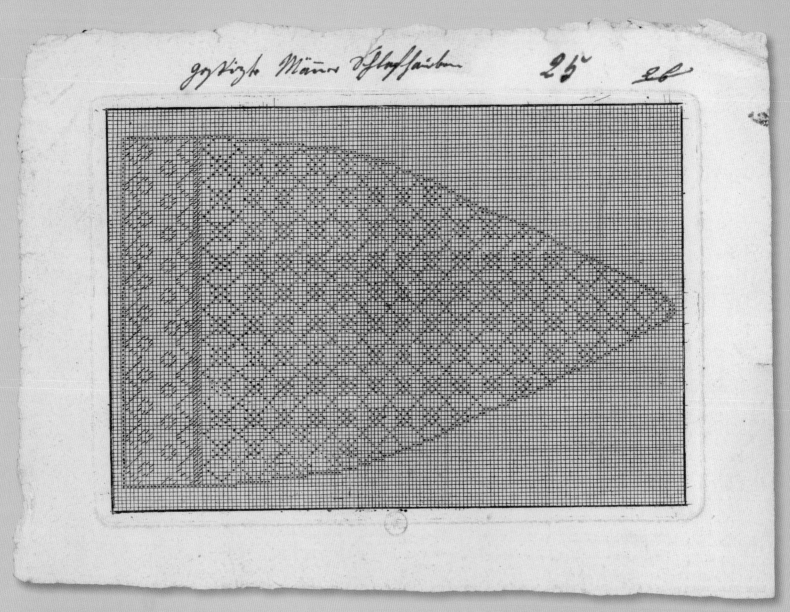

✳ An engraved pattern for netting or knitting a panel of a child's cap.
Victoria & Albert Museum Prints, Drawings, and Paintings Collection, #2007BM0169

More pattern books began to appear as the decades wore on, featuring motifs that were used interchangeably for knitting or cross-stitch (and which probably were greatly adapted from cross-stitch patterns). As Rutt describes them, they show "no understanding of design derived from the nature of knitted fabric. They include clocks, borders, friezes, and pictures of fruit, flowers, birds, emblems, urns, and neo-classical fragments of architecture. They are intended for multicolored stockinette. Subtle shading by knitting two differently colored yarns into one stitch is suggested."

In late nineteenth century Austria, Thérèse de Dillmont was working on her *Encyclopaedia of Needlework*, which was to contain a significant passage on knitting. It was published in German, French, English, Italian, and Spanish, and enjoyed many reprintings, in numerous editions.

Kunstriken—Viennese Lace Knitting

Eventually known as Kunst lace and "modern" lace knitting, the Austrian and German craft of *kunstriken* (literally, "art knitting") derives from the bobbin lace of the eighteenth century that was so popular in those regions at the time. Rutt dates knitted lace to the mid-nineteenth-century publication of the book *Anweisun zur Kunst-Strickerei*, which featured Victorian England–derived patterns in profusion.

Says Marianne Kinzel, herself an accomplished lace knitter and designer, in the *First Book of Modern Lace Knitting*, "The knitter of those days used the finest lace thread and extremely fine needles to achieve open lace patterns." She calls the making of lace in this fashion "very tedious"—no wonder it went out of style.

But between the two world wars, a mania for lace knitting was revived, thanks in large part to the published patterns of Herbert Niebling, called by lace aficionado Mary Frances Wogec the "acknowledged master." According to Rutt, in the 1920s Niebling began to "revive and develop the designs of the Biedermeier period (1820–1848.)" Amazingly, the man wrote no books, but rather published patterns in various periodicals, based, says Kinzel,

> upon the old technique of medallion knitting, in combination with well-known lace stitches . . . This revived craft was generally known as "round art knitting" and very large lace cloths of one or even two yards diameter were worked in one piece without any joins . . . Soon we were taught how to design flower and leaf-shaped forms suited to the technique of knitting, and their application into lace-stitch background. Materials used were medium-fine linen thread or crochet cotton, but the wire-like needles were replaced by sock needles. Due to the comparatively thick knitting pins, the result was a cobweb-like product which grew rapidly in the hands of a skilled knitter in contrast to the slowness of the old-fashioned craft.

Oddly and delightfully, Niebling's work was discovered by a Japanese knitter, Kazuko Ichida, who published his designs in two books of her own, thereby spreading this technique to her home country.

Wogec is more generous about Niebling's accomplishments than Rutt. Of Niebling, she remarks that he had "a remarkable ability to translate the most intricate designs into a chart format that accurately represented the knitted fabric, thus making it available to knitters everywhere."

There was also Christine Duchrow, a German knitted lace designer of the early twentieth century, who published about one hundred four-page pamphlets of lace patterns between the years 1900 and 1940. Each of her pamphlets contained patterns, largely in chart form, for four to six objects: narrow strip patterns, collars, jabots, doilies, tablecloths, medallions "possibly suitable for a pieced tablecloth or bedspread," camisole tops, lace fingerless gloves, baby bonnets, tea warmers, octagonal lace boxes, altar cloths, and petticoats, all of which were heavy on geometric patterns of triangles, diamonds, and squares. Rutt finds her designs reminiscent of Azores lace (*see page* 21.).

Marianne Kinzel was also instrumental in spreading the craze for so-called Viennese lace knitting to the United Kingdom and the United States. Of her work, Rutt has this to say: "Her designs have a personal style that is notably different from the work of other designers, and are of great beauty." It is she who gave the epithet "Viennese" lace knitting to this particular craft.

Curiously, Viennese lace turns up in, of all places, the Catalan region of Spain. Barcelona-born knitting writer and historian Montse Stanley, in an article for *Threads* magazine, documents her family's tradition of knitting (and perhaps even more excruciatingly, starching and blocking) lace mats, which were worked "from the center out, in a spiral of rows, increasing all the time. The pattern emerged from a combination of lace stitches and increases," she writes. Extremely fine cotton at a gauge of 1 mm was used, with fine, 0000 needles.

At one point, Stanley realized that a family treasure, a mat that had been in her family's possession for fifty years, was identical to one featured in Tessa Lorant's *Hand and Machine Knitted Laces*. "Clearly," says Stanley, "the pattern was too complex to have been created by two designers from such different

✳ A sampling of knitted lace patterns from the August 1894 issue of *The Delineator* magazine.

backgrounds." Stanley was finally able to trace the origin of the pattern to a book titled *Kunstricken*, published by Otto Beyer, who employed none other than Herbert Niebling to create patterns for him. How the craze for Viennese lace knitting, which began to die down in the fifties, ever reached the shores of Spain, is yet another of the great, transient mysteries of knitting.

Twisted-Stitch Knitting

Twisted-stitch knitting, also called Alpine knitting, is mostly associated with the adjoining mountainous regions of southern Germany and northern Austria. Although a tradition of sweater knitting emerged in the 1800s, sock knitting was its antecedent. In most of the Alpine regions of Austria, Germany, and Switzerland, folk costumes required intricate socks, and it was the pride of every girl to have the most complicated patterns on those she wore with her *dirndlkleid* and *loden* costume. Lisl Fanderl, who meticulously documented patterns of the mountainous regions of Austria, writes of a "revived" stocking, knit with white cotton on size 1 needles (U.S. size 5/0, or 1 mm, which even

An example of Austrian twisted stitch knitting.
Spectrum Photofile

in the late 1970s, when she wrote her first book, the classic *Bauerliches Stricken*, she identified as difficult to find). Fanderl's book shows these socks with patterning only down the outer side of the stocking, although fancy, allover openwork was also in evidence in certain places at certain times. Women's all-wool cardigans for wearing with *Dirndls* are tight-fitting to the waist and feature a distinctive inverse bottleneck shape down the back and a narrow braided border.

Men also wore traditional stockings, called *Stutzen* (a word that has no literal translation), which Maria Erlbacher, who accomplished a documentation similar to Fanderl's in her *Uberlieferte Strikmuster* (re-released by Schoolhouse Press as *Twisted-Stitch Knitting*), identifies as being worn specifically with lederhosen. These amazing socks, which appear in the late eighteenth century in the Enns Valley and Ausseerland (Austria), were knit primarily in white, gray, blue, or green wool—light-colored wools tend to show twisted-stitch knitting to its best advantage. A variety of patterns would be used, chosen from the samplers each woman knit to keep track of her favorite and/ or the most popular regional patterns, with such evocative names as Little Bell (*Glöckerl*), Mur Valley Pattern, Forgotten Love (*Vergessene Liebe*), Plum Pit (*Zwetschkenkern*), Thunder River Stocking Pattern

(*Donnersbacher Strumpfmodel*), and Triple Small Alpine Path (*Dreifaches Almwegerl*). They were inset with calf gussets, lozenge shaped, and replete with their own series of patterns. Fanderl discusses more generally *Mannerstrümpf*—men's stockings—knit in the nineteenth century of 100 percent wool (and in more contemporary times of 75 percent wool and 25 percent synthetic yarn), on U.S. size 1 needles (2.5 mm), with 80–90 stitches around the widest part of the leg.

Women in the Enns Valley wore kneesocks similar to the men's *Stutzen* described above by Erlbacher, only the calf gusset was of a slightly different shape (flat at the top rather than tapered), and shaped only with decreases, rather than increases and decreases.

Twisted-stitch knitting is usually achieved by knitting in the round and working knit stitches through the back loop. This produces patterns that "pop" off their garter-stitch backgrounds. Writes Erlbacher in *Twisted-Stitch Knitting*, "Motifs are created by crossing twisted knit stitches to the left or right over other stitches. These stitches can travel over purls or over other twisted knit stitches." Pattern stitches are worked on every row rather than every other row.

Alsatian Carpets

In the seventeenth and eighteenth centuries, knitting guilds throughout Europe imposed rigorous exams on those who desired to receive full master status. A craftsman would be required to knit a profusion of objects in a short time, the most important and complicated of which, according to Irena Turnau, was the knitted carpet. Up to twenty colors of wool were used, and the largest of the "masterpieces," as they were called, measured about six-and-a-half feet by almost ten feet. Upper Rhineland, especially, was acclaimed for these carpets. Knitting author Donna Druchunas in *The Knitted Rug: 21 Fantastic Designs* describes them as ranging from the "beautiful to the bizarre, each one an elaborate example of color work the like

---

TECHNIQUE

Twisted Knitting

Cast on 12 stitches, knit and seam alternate rows for 8 rows; the 3 first and last stitches of each row are always knit.

Ninth row:—Knit 3 stitches, take a third pin and knit 3 more, knit the remainder of the stitches with the first pin.

Tenth row:—Knit 3 stitches, seam the 3 stitches on the third pin, seam the other 3, knit the 3 edge stitches. This completes 1 twist, and is repeated after every 8 rows.

—From *Exercises in Knitting,* Cornelia Mee, London, 1868 (Project Guternberg)

of which we will never see again. From flowers and Bible scenes to scripture texts and portraits of nobles, these carpets provide clear evidence of the advanced skills of the knitter."

Following is an excerpted description of one such carpet, as it appeared in the 1925 article "An Unusual Alsatian Carpet" by Malvine Rubner in *The Burlington Magazine for Connoisseurs:*

> In 1918 I noticed when in the collection of Dr. Angst, formerly director of the Swiss National Museum, a carpet dated

❋ A hand-knit wool carpet made in Strasbourg, 1781. According to the Victoria & Albert Museum: "This carpet or hanging of multicoloured stocking stitch was made on needles, or possibly a peg frame. We do not know who made it. Adam and Eve appear beneath a central panel depicting Jacob's Dream, from the Old Testament, with the inscription 'hilfe wirt gott ferner schicken meinen feinden zum verdus.' God will continue to send help in despite of mine enemies." *Victoria & Albert Museum Textiles and Fashion Collection, #2006AN9286*

1705, measuring 2.4 m. by 2 m., having a technique till then unknown to me. Against a white background is a pattern composed of exotic flowers and fruit, peacocks in blue and yellow, small birds and golden brown squirrels sitting in the most natural postures among the branches. The centre, set against an indigo background, is occupied by a medallion with the lamb of God and the initials of the maker of the carpet, H.C.W., i.e., Heinrich Christof Wagner. Under the medallion is a shield with the coat of arms of the King of France, six golden lilies on a royal blue background. Both sides of the shield are flanked by lions in russet brown holding a blue lily in their paws . . . [A] flower border completes the happy design.

. . . The carpet was so intriguing as an unusual expression of religious sentiment and as good an example of clever craftsmanship that I contrived to acquire it . . . [I]n September, 1923, I received to my agreeable surprise a copy of an excellent study by Mr. Haug, the director of Strasbourg Museum . . . [H]e discovered, after prolonged research, that the knitters belonging to a special knitters' corporation, called at that time "Baretlimacher" and "Hosenstricker," were the actual makers of these carpets . . .

[A]nother Museum Director, Mr. Masner of Breslau . . . mentions the carpet here published among others in his study "Aus Schlesiens Vorzeit in Bild und Schrift, Band VIII" (Breslau), but does not altogether agree with Mr. Haug about the native town of the maker. Mr. Haug favours the town of Beblenheim in the Prostestant Duchy of Montbéliard, whereas Mr. Masner favours some town in Alsatia.

The Netherlands

Simple and austere. This is how James Norbury categorized Dutch knitting in his book *Knitting Patterns from Around the World*. He saw this predisposition as a direct reflection of the somberness of Dutch households. Dutch knitting author Henriette van der Klift-Tellegen concedes that Dutch knitters "knit differently from others" and cites decorative patterns in low relief in one color, with no crossed stitches, as an example. And indeed, the mostly blue or gray fisherman's sweaters from villages all over the country, depicted in her excellent book *Knitting from the Netherlands*, show an absolute starkness in their regimented knit-purl patterning, if you have read Norbury first and have his words "simple and austere" in mind. Later, charted, two-color knitting patterns show a predilection for simple, repeating motifs of squares or diamonds, perhaps a nod to the Dutch quilting proficiency Norbury also references. Even the knit-purl stitch patterns he chose to sample in his book follow a strict grid that is reminiscent of quilt squares.

Craft guilds were established in the Netherlands in 1429, and by 1550, according to van der Klift-Tellegen, Dutch stocking knitters were so adept they were hired by the king of Denmark to teach their techniques to his own knitters. By the seventeenth century, Dutch knitters were specializing in embossed knitting—"twisted stocking stitch on a reverse stocking-stitch ground," van der Klift-Tellegen calls it—intricate renderings of plants, birds, and other animals. By the eighteenth century, "white Eastern muslins," in the words of Mary Thomas in her *Knitting Book*, were being imported into Europe; no cotton yarn had been available there before 1740. This set off a general European white knitting craze. Knitters of white cotton aspired to knit openwork lace, according to Thomas, and "so fine and open in pattern did it grow that the finest lace thread was used, knitted upon needles known as 'wires.'" And while white knitting was the rage throughout Europe, Thomas

continued on page 46

Veronika Persché

Veronika Persché is an Austrian textile designer whose often eye-boggling fabrics take the concept of machine knitting in all-new, thoroughly unexpected directions—including a whole category of 3-D. Her work is used by fashion designers and fine artists, some of whom she collaborates with; costume designers for the theater and opera; and, in the case of some fabrics, used herself, as shades for a series of what she calls "light objects" of her own design. Shall we call her Bavarian? Or Tyrolean? Or something else altogether?

"I do textile design because I am fascinated by fabrics, materials, and patterns. I choose to work with knitted textiles because it's a way to construct a fabric and pattern at the same time; structure is often immanent in the pattern. And, compared to other textile techniques—especially weaving—knitting doesn't need a lot of preparation. Because knits basically are constructed by one single thread, all you need is to thread in and get going. That's what I like most, working directly on the machine, experimenting, and the possibility of making quick changes. During the design process I don't think of any possible application. I'm always asking myself, 'Could this work out?' and then sometimes getting the most stunning surprises. I design textiles only for the beauty in it.

"I work in two ways. One way is that I design fabrics that I then show in sample collections. These fabrics can be varied and ordered by the meter and are mostly bought by professionals who use them for clothes, costumes, interior design, art objects. Very often designers and artists show me a more or less detailed sketch of a piece they want me to knit. Then we discuss what it should look like and what kind of materials and techniques could work out best. Some clients have, of course, no idea how knitting works and want me to realize the most incredible pieces. This can be quite challenging, and it pushes me toward (and beyond) the borders of the technique. I like that way of working very much. During these cooperations I get a lot of new ideas from people who are not bound to the theme. This is a wonderful source of inspiration for me!

"During my training, after all I knew about hand knitting and other textile crafts, it was amazing to learn about what knitting machines are able to do. All the double bed-jacquards, for example, are amazing. If you want to use a lot of colors and difficult motifs, it's really tricky to do it by hand. Also there are some 'special effects' you can only achieve with the knitting machine.

"But, on the other hand, there are many patterns, especially tricky cables and nupps, which are practically impossible to knit on the machine. Some knitting mistresses do amazing work and are probably able to machine-knit such things, but it affords a lot hand-manipulating, and I myself am not patient enough to do that.

"I was taught to knit by my mother. She always dreamt [of working] as a crafts teacher, but somehow her life went a different way. So she put a lot of energy into teaching me and my older sister and brother knitting, crocheting, sewing. In fact, she did not only teach me the skills, but shared her enthusiasm for being creative and 'inventing' or designing clothes and other things. I am glad to know the principles of hand knitting very well; I like to try new patterns and techniques. Traditional Austrian knitting showed me that knitting is a universe itself, because you can find so many different styles. In the rural regions of Austria, every valley has its own traditional costume with knitted socks. I like the complexity of these patterns—it's perfect brain training.

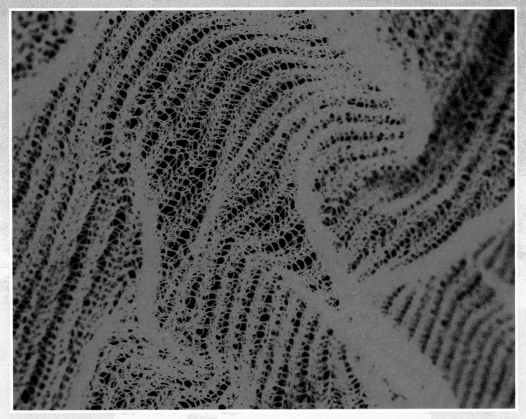

Above left: *Droptupf* in a red acetate/cotton/polyamide blend; Bottom left: *Dracherl*, in pink merino; Above: *Luckerl*, in glowing fluorescent polyester. *Knit fabric designs by Veronika Persché, photos by Jens Lindworksy*

"I love the possibility of knitting to do sculptural work. I did a small accessory using one of my 3-D designs to create a little sculpture. It was very surprising to see a sculpture evolving out of the fabric design itself. It looks like a small ram, which I find funny because of its relationship to the material wool. I also had a wonderful collaboration with the Belgian jewelry and objects designer Heidewinne. She did quite a big object in her collection called "Quand les corps se parlent" using one of my fabrics. It looks like a huge animal on which one can sit or lie. Of course I would like to do more sculptural projects and probably go into a bigger scale.

"There's one thing I realized in the very beginning of my knitting career: It seems that I am best when I focus on creating the fabric itself. I don't find my tries to do fashion very successful; I personally find it extremely difficult to drape my fabrics around the human form. I like to work in collaborations, and somehow fashion seemed to be the most logical thing. I see also in the clothes fashion designers create that they are using my fabrics in a very different way than I would and that's fantastic. But I am also happy to work with fine artists, like Erwin Wurm. He likes to use knitted fabrics and pullovers to 'dress' his sculptures. I like this approach and would love to do more 'nonfashion' projects.

"My textiles are the visible realization of my style, which I find difficult to describe because it evolves out of my personality. Some people say they like the way I combine and use colors, my love of playing with textures and materials, but also my preference for geometric patterns. Probably the designers also feel my passion for knitting! My textiles are somehow special and extraordinary, something you don't get in the fabric stores. I think they can provide a variety of qualities: Some show dramatic and sculptural surfaces, some are delicate and sophisticated, and some even glow in the dark. And there could be many more; I have some ideas and interesting materials on stock, I only need some time to make my experiments!

"The first reaction I get when I tell somebody 'I am knitting' is 'How strange, a young woman doing such an old-fashioned thing.' In Austria in particular, society is still quite shaped by the after-war period. My parents' generation grew up in very poor circumstances; everyone tried to survive through their own handwork. So for them, hand-knitted clothes were necessary, and the skill therefore was essential. In my school time, it was usual to learn knitting, crocheting, and sewing, and I think it is quite common also today. Besides that, Austria's society is very conservative and Catholic, so obviously it takes more time to change gender roles. In consequence, there are still a lot of people (mostly women), who are well-trained in knitting and know the most incredible traditional patterns. But in the last years I see there are some initiatives, like craft circles and lectures, also some craftivists are active and getting more and more interest. So it seems knitting here is catching up to modern times!"

❋ Dutch flower seller, c. 1900: Woman dressed in Dutch-style costume standing and knitting next to a stone wall and a large display of flowers. *Frances Benjamin Johnston Collection, Library of Congress Prints and Photographs Division, LC-USZ C2-6078*

✲ Hand-knit petticoat, possibly made in the Netherlands, 1700–1750. Says the Victoria & Albert Museum: "This petticoat is an extraordinary feat of knitting skill unparalleled in any known collection. We do not know exactly how it was made. It seems too large to have been produced by or on a knitting frame . . . [It] is knitted in two-ply wool, with surface decoration of animals, birds, and trees. Among the more exotic creatures are an elephant, a lion, an ostrich, and a rhinoceros. The motifs are knitted . . . in the round with no seams and [it] has a circumference of over three metres at the widest point. Despite the large surface area, the pattern does not repeat . . . Approximately 2,650 stitches were cast on and worked in a gauge of twenty-two stitches per inch." Damask knitting is, according to amateur knitting historian Susette Newberry, "textured through simple purl stitch patterning, and is technically (but not visually) reversible, like woven damask fabrics. Damask knitting of the sixteenth and seventeenth centuries imitated aristocratic garments knit the same way, only of silk and much finer, which were an expensive English export."
Victoria & Albert Museum Textiles and Fashion Collection #2006AC7142

Continued from page 41

posits that the countries not previously "engaged in the making of needlepoint or embroidered laces" were the ones that truly excelled at it—the Netherlands perhaps chief among them.

"The Dutch," writes Irena Turnau in "The Knitting Crafts in Europe from the Thirteenth to the Eighteenth Century," "were certainly known for their knitting. In the sixteenth century, England imported knitted gloves from the low countries and, according to one authority, it was from Holland that the art of knitting was carried to Scandinavia."

As was true in other countries, the advent of the knitting machine saw the end of the hand knitting of luxury goods in the Netherlands. No longer a profitable trade for men, hand knitting moved into the realm of necessary household craft for women. Dutch women, like others of their ilk elsewhere in Europe, were sometimes able to supplement meager household incomes with hand knitting, and for long generations knitting was associated for many with work.

Later on, Dutch knitting moved beyond its supposed "austere" roots. One cheerful example: Mittens from Groenlo show eight-star patterning surrounding an Eye of God atop a checkerboard field, worked in three-color patterning (navy or black, white, and a smattering of red) that is reminiscent of the intricately patterned two-color Sanquhar gloves that originated in Scotland.

An intriguing tidbit: some historians theorize that the English word for knitting comes from the Dutch word for knotting, *knutten*.

Gelderse Gebriede Mutsen—Knitted Bonnets from Gelderland

By Henny Abbink, Anke Grevers, and Connie Grevers

Grandma, Henny's mother-in-law, was a maker of traditional bonnets from the Achterhoek, a region in the east of the Netherlands surrounding Winterswijk. Grandma chose the profession because it was something she could do even with her hip defect, which prevented her from doing any heavy work. It was either sewing or making bonnets, and given that her older sister was already a seamstress (and the matter of whether she would ever get married, given her handicap), there was nothing left for her but to learn the craft of bonnet making. Grandma learned the craft from her mother-in-law, and Henny was always interested in the bonnets she made. She did not get to see many of them, however, as Grandma was of the opinion that they had gone out of fashion and were therefore useless. Then some local festivities were organized in 1979, featuring old traditional crafts. It was at that time that Grandma taught a group of women the craft of bonnet making. Henny Abbink (b. 1937) is the only member of this group still alive, and she has truly mastered the craft.

We, her daughters Anke and Connie, were introduced early to the bonnet-making profession. Gradually, Henny became more and more immersed in the craft; her daughters brought books home from the library, and it was in this way that we all became infatuated with traditional dress from the Achterhoek, in particular the bonnets.

Our first interest was in lace bonnets, and later knitted and crocheted bonnets captured our attention. Initially, we mainly came across the crocheted variety (of which many more examples have survived), and later on we found several knitted examples. Since knitting had been in our family all our lives, we began to copy the bonnets, first in their true (adult) dimensions; later on, Henny started making smaller versions for dolls.

Knitted bonnets were worn by farming women. These were mostly women who could not afford to buy an expensive lace bonnet, but also included those who desired headwear for working. Women who could afford it had a lace bonnet for feast days (weddings and church) and wore knitted and crocheted bonnets during their work. They even wore bonnets in bed!

✳ A charming hand-colored postcard of a young Dutch girl knitting.

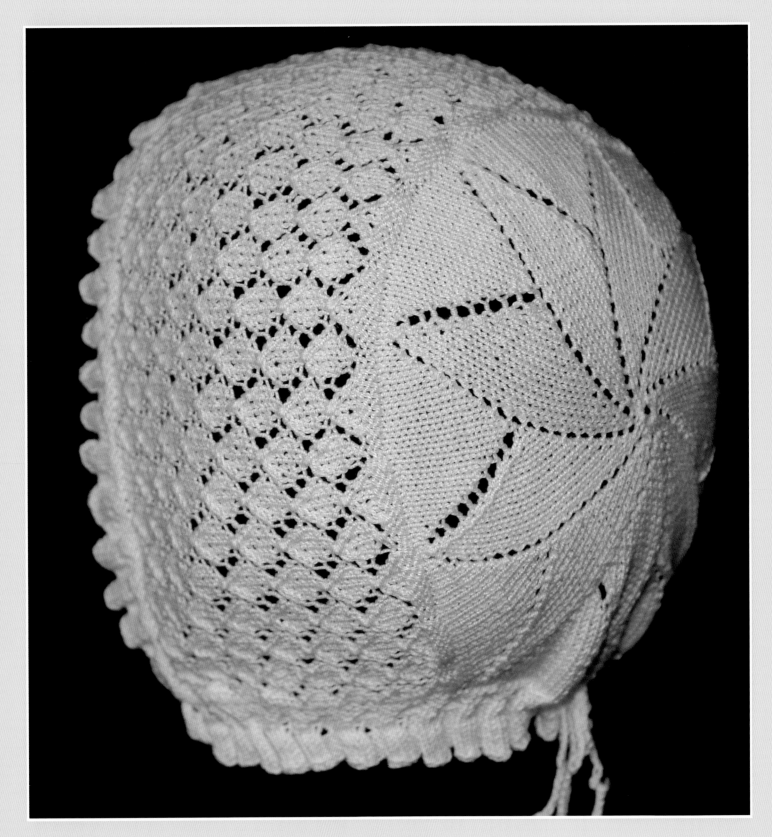

❋ An example of a *gebreide mutsen* (knitted bonnet) from the Grevers' family collection.
Photos by Anke Grevers

Lace bonnets need to be washed and pleated by the bonnet maker, an activity for which the wearers of the bonnets possessed neither the tools nor the skill. Because making the creation and washing it was a relatively costly process, women sought out a more affordable alternative: simple knitted or crocheted cotton bonnets. All women had their own preferences for both design and handcrafting technique. People reproduced bonnets they saw others wearing, and in this way the patterns were passed from mother to daughter, neighbor to neighbor.

The traditional bonnet was most popular around 1900. After World War II, traditional dress disappeared in the Achterhoek, partly because the production of lace and other materials had come to a standstill. The exact time when people began knitting the bonnets in Gelderland remains a mystery; however, we do know that women made them as a home craft and for personal use. The bonnets were always knitted in white cotton (editor's note: which would put their advent no earlier than the mid-eighteenth century, when cotton yarn became available in Europe); other materials did not make for comfortable headwear.

Over the years, the bonnets became smaller. Although at first they were very large with long flounces, these became shorter and shorter until they disappeared altogether. This made the bonnets more wearable—long neck flounces were uncomfortable and rubbed against the back of the smock (or blouse), causing both to wear out more quickly.

Although the stitch pattern used was up to the knitter's own imagination, the eight-pointed star was very common, and there was always knitted lace involved. The patterns used in the bonnets are still in use today, only nowadays they appear in cardigans or shawls.

Dutch Knitting Sampler M

By Carla Meijsen, Founder, Stitch 'n Bitch Netherlands

In the 1970s, teachers stopped teaching knitting in Dutch schools. I was in one of the last shifts, being seven years old when I started school. But even then, the way of knitting was getting more modern, so I used larger needles and acrylic yarn in bright colors to knit my *harlekin* doll. In those decades, the way of knitting was mainly modern, not very much traditional stuff, and in the 1990s, almost nobody knit. I think that we lost a lot of abilities with all crafts in this period. For example, in knitting, we don't use the very thin needles anymore; we knit with yarns that are easier to use in comparison to the thin cotton [of previous eras], and we don't use lots of intricate patterns. Also, I think most of us lost the ability to work quickly. We are proud to knit a pair of socks in a week, but in earlier days people seem to have knit longer hours, and speed was an issue. But, well, they didn't have TV or the Internet.

Compared to the old ways of knitting, all kinds of aspects have changed. The knowledge and sharing of patterns, books, and techniques are not local anymore, but international. Materials have changed too, and we now use materials from all over the world, which we can order with our credit card through the Internet: soy, metal, qiviut, camel, silk of all kinds. This is also an easy way to order books, even from Estonia, Russia, and Japan. Nowadays most Dutch people speak English, and many of us are capable of more or less speaking French and German. This makes the Dutch a people who are not afraid of unknown languages, even Japanese.

There are lots of patterns that feature truly good designs. The new ways of distributing patterns stimulate good design too. But even

though the knitting can be very contemporary, traditional knitting is still highly appreciated. Estonian lace knitting is very popular here at the moment, and often knitters try to find the original materials and prefer the more difficult traditional way of constructing a shawl above the modern, easier way.

On June 17, 2006, my husband Jan bought me this wonderful old cotton knitting sampler at an antiques market in Delft. He bought it from a woman who bought it from a minister's wife who was cleaning out her attic in the eastern part of the Netherlands. The patterns come from a knitting book published around 1900. The yarn is very fine, unbleached cotton, probably Durable. It is thinner than the kind of Durable cotton you can still buy in Dutch yarn shops and on the Internet, which has a very old-fashioned looking label on it, but it still looks very much the same. The knitting needles used were 1 or 1.25 mm. The knitting was probably made by a schoolgirl during crafts lessons in school at the beginning of the twentieth century.

In the sampler, there are either several knitted initials or a single initial, but which? When I held the sampler upside down (it starts with a picot border, as for a stocking) it was clear to me that the letter M was knitted. So I named it "sampler M."

Intrigued by the beautiful knitting, I tried to replicate the twenty-eight stitch patterns of

✳ All twenty-eight of the sampler's patterns.
Photo by Carla Meijsen

the sampler, a big job indeed! The patterns are as follows:

1. the letter M
2. Snowdrops
3. Cord
4. Zippers
5. Roman Arches
6. Pyramids
7. Waves
8. Clivia
9. Falling Leaves
10. Wickerwork
11. Twin Leaves
12. Drops
13. Rockefeller
14. Wybert
15. another version of Zippers
16. Cubics
17. another version of Wybert
18. Twisted Oak
19. Peacock
20. Beehive
21. Tricycle
22. Scales
23. Brioche
24. Cloche
25. Torch
26. Sugarscoop
27. Lily of the Valley
28. Finale

Believe me, you do not want to know how many times I had to rip out the knitting and start over because it was not quite the same! Sometimes I came across stitches that were clearly incorrectly knitted. In order to preserve the authenticity of the sampler, I chose to replicate these little mistakes. In this way, I contributed to conserving the art of knitting from the beginning of the last century.

You can find the sampler, and written patterns in Dutch and English, at groups.yahoo.com/group/KnitalongSamplerM.

❋ A charming Dutch postcard of a young girl knitting. *Voyageur Press Archives*

Chapter 3

THE BRITISH ISLES AND IRELAND

Woman knitting a Fair Isle jumper, wearing a makkin belt, c. 1940.

Photo by J. Peterson, #P03721, courtesy of the Shetland Museum and Archives

THE BRITISH ISLES AND ENGLAND in particular certainly kept pace with some of their European counterparts. Knitted liturgical gloves, akin to those found in Spain and France and dating from the fourteenth or fifteenth century, were part of the inventory of St. Paul's Cathedral in London; cap knitting was well-established by the late fifteenth century; and by the beginning of seventeenth century, as Turnau quotes J. Thirsk, "stockings were made in Wales, Cheshire, Gloucestershire, Cornwall, Devon, Westmorland, and Durham."

In other parts of the British Isles, distinctive styles of knitting would eventually take hold. With fishing as an important part of everyday life on the islands, many regions developed their own interpretation of the fisherman's sweater. Perhaps most popular are the intricately cabled sweaters of the Channel Islands, called either Ganseys or Jerseys, after two of the islands in the chain. Aran sweaters, the Irish version of the fisherman's sweater, also featured stitchwork patterning, but originated in the 1930s—much later than Ganseys. Aran sweaters were sold to tourists as a way for families to make money during the potato famine.

Interestingly, some of the same patterns traditionally used in Aran sweaters make an appearance in Scottish kilt hose, the richly textured, thick knee-high socks that were typically worn with kilts. Off the coasts of Scotland and Norway, the Shetland Islands have long been home to several defined knitting traditions. Whereas the fishermen's sweaters of the Channel Islands and the Aran sweaters of Ireland feature detailed stitch patterns that are knit using one color, elaborate colorwork distinguishes the sweaters of the Shetland Islands, commonly known as the Fair Isle sweater.

England

England is known for one of the most significant developments in the history of knitting: the invention of the knitting frame. This fantastical creation, invented in 1589 by William Lee, was to allow for the mass production of knitted articles. The frame was said to be composed of more than 2,000 workable parts, and was, according to Irena Turnau in *The History of Knitting Before Mass Production*, "the most complicated mechanism introduced into industry in the seventeenth century,"

But it's the knitting of stockings, beginning as early as the fourteenth century, that really seems to define England for much of its knitterly existence. From its inception, it didn't take long for the whole sock business to take off.

Queen Elizabeth was given her first pair of black knitted silk socks as a New Year's present shortly after the beginning of her reign; a few years later pretty much everyone in England was wearing knitted wool ones (a dramatic turn from the cloth ones that preceded them). In 1588, the first knitting schools, meant to teach the poor a viable skill, began to open nationwide, and by the end of century the sock industry was employing an estimated two hundred thousand people a year, engaged in the making of twenty million pairs of socks.

As is the way with knitting everywhere, it was bound to change. Socks gave way to waistcoats—damask ones were popular in Elizabethan and Jacobean times—then waistcoats gave way to knitted silk brocade jackets in the seventeenth and eighteenth centuries, at least for those who could afford to have such things made. For the poor, knitting went on much as it had before: practical items such as caps, hats, gloves, and yes, socks, were knit of wool.

A "white knitting" craze hit England, as well as the European continent at large, during the nineteenth

✻ Vocational knitting, taught at schools on both side of the Atlantic.
Library of Congress Prints and Photographs Division, National Photo Company Collection, LC-DIG-npcc-00279

❋ Almost anything could be—and was—knitted in England of yore. Here, a pair of knitted brown silk breeches, c. 1790. *Colonial Williamsburg, #1968-106*

Red Cross Gloves

MATERIALS

4 oz. Heavy Red Cross Service Yarn Set of 4 No. 11 Steel Knitting needles (points at both ends) Colours: Khaki, Navy, Airforce

MEASUREMENTS

Width all around hand at thumb 8 ins.

Tension: 6-1/2 sts.=1 inch

Check your tension—see inside back cover.

RIGHT GLOVE

Cast on 48 sts. Loosely (16, 16, 16), Work 3-1/2 ins. Ribbing (K2, P2). Knit 6 rounds plain knitting. Proceed:

To make gusset for thumb: 1st round: P1 (inc. 1 st. in next st. K1) twice. P1. Knit to end of round *Next 2 rounds:* Knit, purling the sts. which were purled in previous round. **4th round:** P1Inc. 1 st. in next st. Knit to the 2 sts. before the next purl st. Inc. 1 st. K1. P1. Knit to end of round. Repeat from * to * until there are 16 sts. **Next 2 rounds:** Knit, purling the sts. which were purled in previous round. **Next round:** K1. Cast on 4 sts. Slip next 16 sts. onto a thread and leave for thumb. Knit to end of round. Knit 13 rounds. Proceed:

To make fingers: 1st finger: Knit first 4 sts. Slip all but last 10 sts onto thread. Cast on 2 sts. Knit last 10 sts. Divide these 16 sts. on 3 needles. Join in round. Knit 2 ins. Plain knitting. **Next round:** (K2tog) 8 times, Break wool. Thread end through remaining sts. Draw up and fasten securely.

2nd finger: Knit next 6 sts. of round. Cast on 2 sts. Knit last 6 sts. of round and pick up and knit 3 sts. at base of 1st. finger. Divide these 17 sts. on 3 needles. Knit 3-1/2 ins. **Next round:** (K2tog) 8 times. K1.

3rd finger: Knit next 6 sts. of round. Cast on 2 sts. Knit last 6 sts. of round and pick up and knit 2 sts. at base of 2nd finger. Divide these 16 sts. on 3 needles. Knit 3 ins. **Next round:** (K2tog) 8 times.

4th finger: Knit remaining sts. from thread. Pick up and knit 4 sts. at base of 3rd finger. Divide these 14 sts. on 3 needles. Knit 2-1/2 ins. **Next round:** (K2tog) 7 times.

The thumb: Knit the sts. which were left for thumb, and pick up and knit 4 sts. at base of thumb. Divide these 20 sts. on 3 needles. **Next 2 rounds:** knit, dec. twice over the sts. which were picked up at base of thumb. (16 sts. in round). Knit 2-1/2 ins. **Next round:** (K2tog) 8 times.

LEFT GLOVE

Work as given for Right Glove until fingers are reached. Proceed:

To make fingers: 1st finger: Knit first 14 sts. Slip remaining sts. onto a thread. Cast on 2 sts. Divide these 16 sts. on 3 needles. Join in round. Finish finger and work remainder of glove as given for Right Glove, beginning at back of glove to knit up sts. for remaining fingers.

century. Cotton yarn had just become widely available, as Veronica Patterson writes in a 1996 *Piecework* article, due to "[t]he spinning machinery of the Industrial Revolution and a lively cotton trade with India." All manner of home goods were stitched up by knitters of this era; counterpanes, or cotton coverlets, were especially popular and impressive. The average bedspread, reports Patterson, was constructed of between eight and nine pounds of knitting cotton, featured both lace and solid stitchery at an average gauge of about ten stitches per inch, and when completed measured approximately 114 by 98 inches.

World War I saw a shift to knitting for the troops, which led to a postwar craze for sweaters (never much in fashion for regular, nonseafaring folks until this point), bathing suits, designer knitwear, knitting for charity . . . until anyone who chose to could knit anything at all, even socks.

Dales Knitting

In the Dales of Yorkshire, the cottage industry of sock knitting enjoyed a long tradition from the late sixteenth century right up to the early twentieth century. Men, women, and children got in on the action, originally spinning yarn from local sheep before knitting it up. However, as textile collector Sue Leighton-White notes, demand eventually overtook even the most dedicated efforts of the spinners, and thus began the practice of buying yarn from "stockingers" who also paid knitters for their completed goods. Lesser-known products of the Dales were fancy-patterned gloves, strand-knitted in two colors of fine wool.

Common knitting practice in the Dales was to use four curved needles and a knitting sheath at the waist. Knitters "swaved," or pumped, their right arms as stitches were carried out, which ensured incredibly swift accomplishment of projects. A thropple—"the windpipe of a goose filled with a few dried peas and bent into a circle," as Leighton-White describes it— would be wound inside the ball of wool, the noise of which would make the ball easy to find in the dark should a knitter drop it.

Scoggers and Hoggers

What are these? You may very well ask, as these archaic words for knitted sleeve coverings, in the first instance, and footless stockings in the latter, have certainly passed out of fashion. Although so-called hoggers are back in style for yet another go-round, it's difficult to fathom that any self-respecting teenager would wear legwarmers today if she were forced to call them by their sixteenth-century name.

The oldest evidence of knitted scoggers, at least, seems to be from 1545, the year the warship *Mary Rose* sank in battle off the coast of Hampshire. Among the artifacts found when she was recovered four hundred years later was a twelve-inch-long knitted stockinette tube of black wool. Richard Rutt is eager to point out that it was knit on four needles, evidenced by the large, evenly spaced decreases around the body of the work. His excitement about such a seemingly mundane fact stems from this interesting fact: decreases mean that shaping, at least among some accomplished craftspeople, was already occurring in knitting at this early date.

Similar scoggers have been excavated from sixteenth-century sites in London, and these have decorative purl-stitch borders at each end. While simple wool scoggers were worn by commoners and sailors to keep their arms warm, and by farmers to "protect their arms during salving or corn-stacking," according to the English Dialect Dictionary, more ornate decorative scoggers were also worn by the well-to-do. "Records show that Queen Elizabeth I wore knitted sleeves," writes Rohese de Fairhurst in an article on the subject for *The Fibre Guild of Lohac*, "both simple ('garnsey knit slevis') and ornate ('a peire of slevis of whit knit work with braunches of gold')."

Quaker Knitted Pinballs and Pincushions

A goodly amount of interest has been whipped up in recent years over these minute items dating to the eighteenth century. Measuring two inches

❄ A young girl wearing a hand-knit bathing suit knits on a deserted beach in at North Berwick, UK.

Fox Photos

in diameter, such pinballs and pincushions were knitted first, it's thought by some historians, by girls attending Quaker boarding schools at Ackworth and York. (Belgian stitcher Erica Uten disputes this: one pinball featured in her *Piecework* article, "Tokens of Love: Quaker Pinballs," "clearly bears the place name Bristol . . . [and] is dated to 1775, four years before the founding of Ackworth School;" and the model on the following page dates to 1759). They show a marked similarity in their geometric patterning to needlework medallion samplers of the same era, from which, in fact, their patterning hails. Yet while the samplers are brightly and variously colored, the pinballs and

⁑ A pinball, c. 1759, with geometric patterning similar to those found on later Quaker pinballs. This one, of brown and natural silk, shows a design of an eight-pointed star and triangles, along with the initials EP and the date.
Colonial Williamsburg, #1971-1315

Quaker knitting, and which surely did not stray too tremendously from the English: "In those days everybody wore woolen stockings, usually home-made, and knitting stockings was one of the most conspicuous employments . . . of our grandmothers. They seldom went visiting, even for a call, without taking a bag with them in which they carried the knitting needles and balls of yarn." Yes, there are those ever-practical socks again.

And yet, these exquisite, small items represent something quite different. An article on Ackworth medallion samplers in *Sampler & Antique Needlework Quarterly* claims that "[K]nitting fancy goods was considered a more genteel activity than knitting for necessity. Although Ackworth began as a school for students from more humble backgrounds, as more prosperous students began attending Ackworth, knitting was a skill shared by all."

Highly decorated, rather contrary to the standard Quaker simplicity, pinballs and pincushions "reflected the high value placed on the pins themselves," according to Kimberly Smith Ivey, a textile curator and historian. And as Uten points out, they kept pins in good condition "when houses did not benefit from central heating to keep damp at bay."

They are constructed on tiny needles, using fine silk at a gauge of about twenty-two stitches and twenty-five rows per inch. They are not at all unlike pinballs and pincushions being knitted in fine homes throughout England at this period—a period Rutt catalogs as giving over to "drawing room knitting," the polar opposite of the unrefined necessities of wool stocking knitting. He muses that while most of these items were probably used by the knitters themselves, or given as gifts, some were probably made by ladies (emphasis on *ladies* here) in reduced circumstances, "for more or less surreptitious sale." And he loops back to the Quakers. He writes of a navy blue and beige pincushion inscribed with the words "From the Retreat, near York," and remarks that the Retreat "was the first hospital in England for the cure

pincushions tend to be knitted up in two colors and two colors alone—brown and cream was a common combination.

Sampler historian Carol Humphrey calls knitting an "essential craft" to Quakers on both sides of the ocean, a description bolstered by this passage from the book *Quaker History*, which describes American

of mental disorders, opened by William Tuke, a Quaker tea merchant of York, in 1792."

For Quakers and non-Quakers alike, such knitting in the late eighteenth and early nineteenth century is a herald of the more refined, gentrified knitting ways to come all across England. It also marks the beginning of a phenomenon we cannot imagine living without today: the pattern book (see, Jane Gaugain, page 65).

Fishermen's Sweaters

Adrift in the English Channel, between southern England and northern France, the fourteen Channel Islands may have offered little to the dialogue on the history of knitting if it weren't for one critical garment: the fisherman's sweater.

Finding their way onto the backs of hardworking seamen who knows when, jerseys, or guernseys (the two names deriving from the two largest of the islands), certainly were not the first knitted items ever to be sported by fisher-folk—there were mittens and hats and, in the Faroe Islands, funny little outer shoes called *skolingar*. Some historians, Rutt included, remark that the type of knitting favored for stockings (namely stockinette) was known as "jersey" and was the precursor to the simple styling of the first fishermen's sweaters.

It's been argued by others that "jersey" refers to fine-wool sweaters knitted in sections and sewn together, while "guernsey" signifies a sweater made of thicker, coarser wool knit in the round. According to Madeline Weston, an authority on traditional knitting traditions, a guernsey sweater is almost completely unpatterned, and although it's knitted in the round, its sleeves are sewn into place; a fisher gansey has no seams and is similar

✳ A pincushion from 1733, hand-knitted on fine steel needles with cream-colored silk and silver gilt thread; its "formal and symmetrical decoration" is of flowers, birds, and eight-pointed stars. *Victoria & Albert Museum Textiles and Fashion Collection, #2006AC7428*

Lincoln Longwool

The fleece from the extremely . . . how can I say this? . . . wooly native Lincoln Longwool is a favorite blending wool among hand spinners. It's strong, long, has great luster, and can be spun very finely. Says Clara Parkes, author of The Big Book of Yarn, *"It can be a bit on the scratchy, brassy side, although I've seen folks add a dab of it to a finer wool because it's so strong and lustrous that it has a similar effect to nylon and/or mohair." But alas, this gorgeous breed, the largest of the English breeds, finds itself on the "at risk" list of the Rare Breed Survival Trust's Register. Veteran breeder Louise Fairburn, who in 2009 was married in a stunning dress made of Lincoln tresses, explains a bit about the breed's history and special qualities.*

"Lincoln wool was traditionally sold to the carpet manufacturing industry due to its great strength and, consequently, hard-wearing properties. I don't know of any commercial brands of yarn today that contain Lincoln, but we have some pure Lincoln 50-gram machine-spun balls of our own wool, and a small mill called the Natural Fibre Company offers this service to small producers. But the fleece is very popular with hand spinners. The main benefit of hand spinning Lincoln fleece is its length. I'm told it takes a little getting used to, but once you have the technique, it is a dream to spin, and of course, it's beautifully lustrous, which is more apparent in the hand-spun product. Like most wool and other natural fibers, it accepts dye readily.

"The Lincoln Longwool is an 'at risk' breed. This is a result of a couple of factors. First, the Lincoln is primarily a wool breed, and with no demand for wool, there is no incentive for farmers to breed or keep them. Second, the Lincoln produces fantastic meat from both lamb and mutton; however, it's a slow-maturing breed, and Lincoln lambs cannot compete with their commercial cousins who are bred for fast growth and with low bone-to-meat ratio. Mutton (meat from sheep over eighteen months old) was once a very popular cut of meat in Britain both pre- and postwar, but by the 1960s, it seems to have fallen out of fashion.

"Any farmer producing wool in Britain was always obliged to send all their wool clip to the British Wool Marketing Board, who are responsible for selling all our country's wool clip across the world. In recent years, due to the declining wool industry, the price of fleeces in general has fallen dramatically, and the 'grower's' wool check is only likely to cover the cost of the shearer. However, as a result of the precarious position of some of our native rare breeds (including the Lincoln), this rule has recently changed, allowing farmers of a registered rare breed to sell and market their wool independently. The rest of the country's farmers still have to send all their wool to the BWMB or apply for a license to burn it! Sadly, wool has actually become a byproduct of sheep farming.

"The Lincoln Longwool Sheep Breeders Association is still in existence today, although it was founded in 1891 under a very different set of circumstances than which it now operates. The fortunes of wool in the 1700s were great; it was being exported all over Europe as the main raw material of almost all garments and furnishings. The Lincoln Longwool was the 'darling' of the East of England, producing a heavy weight of wool and also providing a large carcass value (consumers were not as fussy in those days!). The association was originally formed by a bunch of wealthy gentlemen whose families' fortunes had been made from the magnificent Lincoln Longwool, with a desire to document a breed standard and administrate a pedigree registration for the breed. This is still the rubric of the association today, except that we also have the daunting task of preventing the breed from becoming extinct. Quite a responsibility! We still have classes at some of the agricultural shows, which keeps them in the public eye, but we need the breeders to breed and show, which is easier said than done.

"There are fewer than five hundred breeding ewes left in the United Kingdom (about fifty flocks in all—mostly small, say six ewes per flock). The other risky aspect on top of the low numbers is that they are concentrated in one region (Lincolnshire—their home county). Should we experience an outbreak of any serious sheep disease in this region, it could decimate the main Lincoln population. The renewed interest in historic fibers doesn't seem to have filtered through to us yet. Hand spinners are also a rare and dying breed in England."

Louise and Ian Fairburn just after their May 2009 wedding in the Lincolnshire Wolds. They led two eighteen-month-old shearling ewes in full wool, neither of whom had ever been sheared. Says Fairburn, "This, in essence, is a full Lincoln fleece with staples as long as eighteen inches. After their first shearing, they would then be clipped at twelve-month intervals. Fleece at first clip would be around twelve to fourteen kg (26–30 lbs) of wool; thereafter about eight to ten kg (17.5–22 lbs)."

On the left: Lincoln ewe Risby Ruby with her first lamb, Risby Honeymoon, born in 2009. On the right: Shearling ewe Risby Ariel, Supreme Lincoln Longwool Champion 2009. *Photos by Louise Fairburn*

to earlier garments like the fine silk knitwear imported from Italy in the seventeenth century.

British knitting author Rae Compton disputes these opinions. "Throughout the British Isles," she writes in *The Complete Book of Guernsey and Jersey Knitting*, "the fisherman's garment is known in some places as a guernsey, in others as a gansey, and in others it has always been and still is a jersey." Simple as that. However, she adds a small wrinkle: "[T]here are still old knitters who can recall when it was known as a jersey-frock, which would seem to contradict any claim that it originated from the island of Guernsey."

Well then, on to things we know a bit more definitively, leaving off any further confusing discussion of spelling, etymology, or origins. "The fisher gansey represents the most widespread form of traditional knitting in the British Isles," say authors Alice Starmore and Anne Matheson in their book, *Knitting from the British Isles*. "It is practiced in virtually every fishing community from the Hebrides in the northwest, around the east coast ports of Scotland and England and reaching as far south as Cornwall and the Channel Islands of Guernsey and Jersey." Origins of the sweaters are considerably older than their popularity. Exactly when they originated remains a mystery, but they were adopted as part of the uniform of the Royal Navy during the Napoleonic Wars, worn in 1805 at the Battle of Trafalgar, evidence that supports the theory that sailors up and down the English seacoast had been wearing such sweaters for any number of decades before. Its popularity traveled as the fishermen themselves did, from its native port to ports as far-flung as Norway and the Netherlands.

Traditionally, a fisherman's sweater was tightly knit in the round on five fine "wires" out of a durable, three-, four-, five-, or six-ply twisted wool known as "seaman's iron." (Eventually, only five-ply would become available.) It was identical front and back, for even wearing, and colored blue, although around 1900, reports author Sabine Dominick in

Cellardyke fishermen, replete in their jerseys, in a local photographer's studio. Although Anstruther was an important fishing port, the fishing community lived in the adjoining village of Cellardyke. *Photograph courtesy of J. Smith/D. McArthur via the Scottish Fisheries Museum*

This photo was taken in Campbeltown and is dated to 1908, when flat caps were coming into vogue among the younger fishermen. The original photograph was owned by D. McArthur of Campbeltown. *Photograph courtesy of J. Smith/D. McArthur via the Scottish Fisheries Museum*

her book, *Cables, Diamonds, Herringbone*, gray became a popular color choice in England. The sleeves were knit slightly short for practical purposes—namely, keeping off the wet. They featured underarm gussets for ease of movement, as well as for extending the life of the sweater—arms could easily be reknit and replaced. Explain Starmore and Matheson, "The shoulder stitches were cast off together, and the sleeve stitches picked up from the armhole and knitted in the round to the cuff, thus creating a perfectly seamless garment." The neck could have received various treatments: picked up and ribbed to the desired length; open at the shoulder seam with a two-button closure; a turtleneck that could be folded down. (Proponents of the theory that guernseys and jerseys are distinct from each other would say a jersey neck would have to be square.) These sweaters would have replaced the gathered smocks previously worn by fishermen, and the first of them closely resembled smocks, with cables and other stitches arranged in such a way as to give a gathering effect.

According to Starmore, possibilities in patterning, all based on configurations of knit and purl stitches, would have been practically infinite. To Compton, this suggests an origin in older silk brocade shirts, which also relied on knit-purl for simple patterning.

Sabine Dominick archives some of the most common patterns: Indian Corn, cables, diamonds, Herringbone, Zigzag, Steps and Ladders, Tree of Life, hearts, anchors, crosses, Chicken's Eye, and Rice, plus an enormous number identified only by region of purported origin. (Although Compton warns: "It is unwise ever to claim that any detail or pattern proves that it was made in one area. It has been written that all English cables are edged with purl stitches, but Scottish cables may have stocking stitch or moss stitch worked up to their edges. This leaves Norfolk and Cornwall in some other land altogether.")

Patterns typically were not written down, but passed on from knitter to knitter. Often they appeared most densely on the yokes of work sweaters, for extra warmth, while sleeves were kept plain, both to conserve yarn and to allow for easy repair and replacement. Allover patterns were reserved for Sunday-best sweaters.

Henriette van der Klift-Tellegen, in her excellent *Knitting from the Netherlands*, has traced the origins of Dutch fishing sweaters, and this too gives a clue as to the development of fishermen's sweaters generally. She remarks that as early as 1500, Dutch whalers were trading food for Shetland "sweaters" to wear as underwear—Shetland being their home base during the fishing season. The Shetlanders themselves wore these garments as outerwear, a custom Dutch fishermen adopted beginning in the early nineteenth century. The structure of the Dutch sweaters was similar to guernseys, although absent underarm gussets. Patterns in the Netherlands, she says, were highly localized, either by home port or by family. In Bretagne, they varied between families and often indicated the number of sons.

Poor-quality yarn called *sajet*, dyed black or blue and tightly twisted, was commonly used until World War II, when better yarns became affordable. Patterns in some cases mimic those from other fishing heritages: God's Eye (in the Netherlands made with purl stitches, as opposed to England, where it was made with knit); flags, as in Scotland; Tree of Life; arrows; garter stitch bands at the neck; Braidstitch; blocks.

The Faroe Islands were not without their own fishing sweater tradition. They are identified by knitting designer Madelynn Fatelewitz in an article in *Knitting Around the World from Threads* as "white, with two other colors for the pattern. Faroe women sometimes use a dark wool for the main color and lighter-colored wools for the pattern." Susanne Pagoldh, who researched all manner of textiles for her comprehensive book *Nordic Knitting*, elaborates that the yarn for Faroese fishermen's sweaters was "thick and hard and spun mostly from the sheep's outer coat of long, thick hairs."

While it is charming to think of fishermen's wives knitting up the sweaters that would keep their men warm during months away from home, in truth, quite a number of sweaters were also *purchased* by fishermen. Conversely, some women knitted guernseys for extra cash while their husbands were at sea. Here is a description from Mary Wright's book *Cornish Guernseys and Knit Frocks*: "In Looe, knitters regularly organized collections of guernseys from their group, packing about eight or ten each upon their backs, they walked over the cliffs to Plymouth—'about twelve miles, if you know the shortcuts'—to deliver them to 'W. Johns and Co., General Drapers in Old Towne Street,' and other agents." In Sweden, according to Pagoldh, sweater merchants in the nineteenth century began "distributing wool for knitting sweaters . . . Women knitted the bodies of the large fishermen's sweaters, and men and children knitted the sleeves . . . The Nordic Museum in Stockholm has an old Halland fisherman's sweater with the *jyske* design knitted in purple on a natural white ground. *Skak og teinur* (slants and sticks), a similar pattern from the Faroe Islands, has also been knitted in that colorway." Iceland had a long, fruitful export business, with fishermen's sweaters making up the bulk of that country's export knitting.

A final point about fishermen's sweaters—they weren't just for fishermen. Knitting designer Elizabeth Lovick, in an article for *Interweave Knits*, has documented the activities of Scotland's herring lasses, or gutter girls, who sailed each June to Orkney to work the herring catch. Not only did they knit salable guernseys in their spare time, but they wore them as well. Lovick calls them "close fitting sweaters usually knitted at about seven stitches per inch. Many of the sweaters . . . used five-ply worsted spun wool that they purchased—typically, navy yarn in England and black yarn in Scotland." But the gutter girls took much greater liberties with their own garments than they were inclined to for the fishermen. Their guernseys were sometimes knit in "baby blue, pink, teal, raspberry, pistachio, fawn, lovat (a dusty green), and more." Some have short sleeves and V-necks that can be pinned shut to keep out the cold. A photo from the 1920s shows a gutter girl wearing a classic guernsey, only with this unexpected and happily referential detail: a band of Fair Isle across the yoke.

Scotland

"In Scotland the order of knitting has always been high, and at one time it was reputed the Scottish lay claim to its invention, St. Fiacre, the son of a Scottish King, being adopted as the patron saint of a Guild of Stocking Knitters formed in Paris about 1527. But knitting began earlier than this, though the beautiful lace knitting of Scotland has, like their openwork embroidery, ever been a source of wonder and admiration." So writes Mary Thomas in her *Knitting Book*, summing up Scottish knitting in fanciful, pithy, and somewhat unenlightening style.

As for when "earlier" may have been, Richard Rutt asserts that bonnet knitting was well established in Scotland—in the lowlands, at any rate, according to an article in *Am Foghar* by Vicki Quimby—by the fifteenth century, enough so that the bonnet makers of Dundee had set up a trade guild for themselves by 1496. Bonnets (blue ones) were knit in one piece and heavily felted. They were worn by servants in the sixteenth century, says Rutt, and by virtually all Scottish men in the seventeenth century. By the eighteenth century, they were ornamented with red and white checks on the headband. They had

CHILD'S SCOTCH CAP.

BY MRS. JANE WEAVER.

This cap is knitted in brioche-stitch, and is the most simple way of making these useful caps. Use needles No. 8 and single zephyr. Cast on No. 2 stitches, and knit a depth of ten inches. Cast off your stitches, make the brim or head of the cap double by carefully sewing down a hem two inches deep, join the two sides of the work carefully together, then draw up the stitches round the other edge together, and set securely; cover the sewing over with a tassel of silk. With a crochet-needle, work the following row round the edge of the hem: Join to the first stitch three chain, miss a rib, *, one treble on the next rib, two chain; repeat from the *, join neatly at the end to the first stitch. Second row: Seven chain, *, one double long or a treble with the wool three times round the needle between the next treble, two chain, repeat from * at the end, join with a single to the fifth chain, and fasten off. Through this last row, a ribbon is run, which fastens with a pretty bow-and-ends. Another small bow of ribbon is placed on the other side of the brim, and the head-part is lined through with silk.

disappeared from the hand-knitting landscape by the mid-nineteenth century. They resurfaced, in a manner of speaking, in Victorian times with the tammy, or tam o' shanter, a relative of the beret that shows up all over England and Europe beginning in the sixteenth century and that found favor among the young ladies of the last years of the 1800s.

Knitting in Scotland, though, was a matter for covering not only heads, but also, critically, feet. "Upwards of three centuries ago the wives of Scotch peasants knitted all the stockings they and their families required, and used the bark of the alder tree to dye their yarn," wrote economic historian David Bremner in his book, *The Industries of Scotland*, in 1869. "In the beginning of the last century many persons in that country were engaged in the making of stockings, which were chiefly exported to Holland, and thence dispersed throughout Germany. The spinning and knitting were done by hand in the homes of the people, and a number of merchants were established in the town of Aberdeen, who gave out the wool and

received the stockings ready for the market. The extent of this branch of industry . . . may be judged of by the following passage in 'Pennant's Tour of Scotland': 'Aberdeen imports annually £20,800 worth of wool . . . Of this wool are made 69,333 dozen pairs of stockings.'"

The socks started out humbly, and coarsely, but by the mid-nineteenth century, peasant women in the parish of Gairloch were found learning to knit from a Lady Mackenzie, and so began the manufacture of fancy stockings for men, some of which, perhaps, were festooned with the first knitted argyle patterning. The hand-knit hosiery trade dwindled in the late nineteenth century, replaced by machine knitting, and from then on, caps, the odd nightcap, glove, or article of underwear, composed the bulk of hand knitting in Scotland.

At around this same time, in the capital city of Edinburgh, hand knitting was undergoing a miraculous transformation. As reported by Kate Davies in her 2009 article for *Twist Collective*, well-to-do ladies were coming around to the knitting of

fancy articles—"lacy tippets and elegant muffatees." It was a trend facilitated at first, and later driven by, the amazing Scottish entrepreneur Jane Gaugain, who not only sold the materials necessary for knitting in her shop, but devised beautifully colored and openwork patterns as well. She published her first collection of them in 1840, under the title *Lady's Assistant in Knitting, Netting, and Crochet*, using "her own unique system of pattern notation— the first to be devised and widely used in Anglo-American knitting," according to Davies. Among her subscribers was Queen Adelaide, although no records indicate whether the monarch ever attempted Gaugain's patterns for shawls or caps or purses. (However, she was a known needleworker; an embroidered portfolio made by her hand was sold at auction in 2008. Perhaps knitting was not beyond her domain.) A flood of knitting books in the United Kingdom followed, written by Miss Watts, Frances Lambert, Cornelia Mee, and Mrs. Banks, meeting the growing demand for fancy knitting patterns, by certain fancy ladies.

Directions in pattern books were eventually greatly simplified although not yet standardized; they then began appearing in magazines. The result of all this printed activity? Says Rutt, "Fancy Knitting was now becoming a possibility for the working classes as well as the middle classes."

Sanquhar

What the original knitting of Sanquhar, a royal borough in southwest Scotland, may have looked liked is anyone's guess. The Future Museum ruminates, "It is unlikely that the vast numbers of stockings made in the 1770s and 1780s were patterned." But by the early 1800s, knitting in the town had already taken on its highly distinctive allover two-colored motifs, described in one account as an "overlay of boxes," the pattern recognizable to us now as Sanquhar.

Then, almost as quickly as it arrived, it was gone.

The stocking trade was established in Sanquhar as part of a government initiative to regenerate

❋ A mid-nineteenth-century book of knitting samples constructed by Elizabeth Hume. Most of the samples are of fine lace, but there are some of undyed Shetland wool and colored knitting as well. Many of the patterns seem to have been taken from Jane Gaugain's *Lady's Assistant in Knitting, Netting, and Crochet. Victoria & Albert Museum Textiles and Fashion Collection, #2006AC7689*

The Tulip Wreath Flower-Vase Mat

MATERIALS

12 shades of amber, 7 shades of lilac, 4 shades of green. 4 Skeins of each colour. 5 Steel Needles, No. 14. Cardboard foundation, covered with white or amber cambric, 8 inches in diameter.

FOR THE MAT

Knit 4 rounds of each shade of amber, beginning with the lightest. Cast on 2 stitches on each of 4 needles; bring the wool forward, knit half the stitches on the first needle; t. f. and k. [Footnote: k. means knit; k. 2+ knit two together; p. purl; t. f. thread forward.] the other half; repeat the same on each of the other 3 needles; k. the next round plain; repeat these two rounds until there are 48 stitches on each needle; then cast off, and sew this on the covered cardboard foundation.

FOR THE TULIPS

5 tulips to be knitted in 7 shades of amber, and 5 in 7 shades of lilac; 4 rounds to be knitted of each shade; 4 needles. Cast on 2 stitches on each of 3 needles; t.f. at the commencement of each needle; k. 1 plain round; purl a round, increasing at commencement of each needle. Repeat these two rounds till there are 22 stitches on each of the three needles; then first k. 3, k. 2+, k. 1, k. 2+, k. 3; turn the work back, and purl the stitches.

3rd: K. 2, k. 2+, k. 1, k. 2+, k. 2.

4th: Turn back and purl.

5th: K. 2, k. 2+, k. 1, k. 2+, k 2.

6th: Turn back and purl.

7th: K. 1, k. 3+, k. 1.

8th: Purl.

9th: K. 3+.

20 tulips will be required.

THE LEAVES

(10 of which will be necessary).—4 shades of green, 12 rows of each; 2 needles.

   Cast on 3 stitches; k. plain, till before the centre stitch; t.f. and k. the centre stitch; t.f., k. the remainder plain; p. the next row; repeat these 2 rows, till there are 12 open stitches up the vein of the leaf; then k. 1, k. 2+, k. plain, till 2 from the centre stitch; then k. 2+, t.f., k. 1, t.f., k. 2+, k. plain, till 3 from the end; then k. 2+, k. 1; p. the next row; repeat till there are 8 more open stitches, that is, 20 from the beginning; then k. 2+ at the beginning and end of every other row, till the last ends in a point. Now sew the leaves round the mat by the part where the stem should be; then sew the tulips on as in engraving, sewing the leaf about 6 rows from the point on the stem of the tulip.

—From *The Ladies Work-Book*, Unknown, John Cassell, La Bell Sauvage Yard, London, (Project Gutenberg)

the Scottish economy. The wool trade had been important to the region since medieval times, and in the 1700s, Sanquhar, by virtue of its location on the River Nith and the excellent quality of its sheep, was established as a market center. It was the site of an annual wool fair that, according to the Dumfries Museum, regulated prices for the whole south of Scotland. The majority of local residents were variously involved in knitting by this time. The craft offered a bit of financial cushioning in the event of crop failure, and in more prosperous times, gave enough supplemental income for such "luxuries" as medicine and books.

How the stereotypical Sanquhar patterns emerged throughout the few brief years of its development and popularity is a matter of some debate. They share certain characteristics in common with patterns from Aberdeen and North Yorkshire, as well as from farther afield—say, Scandinavia. They also bear similarities to local hand-loom weaving patterns, another important industry in Sanquhar; this, speculates the Future Museum, "may account for the two colour changes which resemble plaids and checks."

Not to be overlooked is the matter of necessity, and its hand in the machinations of invention: Markets for hand knitting were rapidly declining by the early 1800s, even as the distinctive Sanquhar style was beginning to emerge—the war with America, for example, rendered unavailable the single greatest importer of stockings from Sanquhar (the state of Virginia). In such a climate, remarks the Future Museum, "a highly distinctive and well made garment would still find a buyer. Its special quality could compete with machine made goods and was difficult to imitate." And so, the knitters of Sanquhar developed unique, difficult-to-copy patterns as a means of survival. Nevertheless, by the 1830s, Sanquhar knitting had virtually disappeared as a viable business.

Still, the tradition quietly persevered. Families continued to pass down their skills through the ranks, and the occasional lover of craft placed an

order. A judge named Mr. Hedley was reported to have "accidentally discovered that Sanquhar gloves were ideal for riding and driving and hence, it seems, created a popular demand for them." (These older gloves were not knit strictly of wool, but of a fiber known as drugget, a mixture of wool and cotton, or wool and flax, that was more durable than wool alone.) Then, in the 1960s, the Scottish Women's Rural Institute came out with a series of leaflets that detailed the surviving traditional patterns. These include the following:

The Duke—a reference to the Duke of Queensbury (whose castle resides in Sanquhar), this is called the "showiest" of all Sanquhar patterns, with its squares filled with other patterns

Pheasant's Eye—a small dot-in-a-circle pattern that is also found in Yorkshire knitting, this pattern derives from a traditional local weaving pattern

Fleur de Lis or *Prince of Wales*—also taken from weaving patterns, with a dark check meant to represent the three feathers decorating the emblem of the Prince of Wales. The Future

✳ A pair of gloves knitted by Mrs. Aitken for Mrs. Marjorie MacDonald, to wear while curling. In the 1950s, Mrs. Aitken could command five shillings a pair for such gloves, in contrast to the Wilsons' less profitable practice. *Sanquhar Tollbooth Museum, DUMFM: 1992.13.1=2*

Museum has this to report about the name of this pattern: "Sanquhar stockings 'were so fine as to be drawn through a ring for the finger, and so much admired, that they have been worn by the present heir apparent to the crown.' This being the future George IV, the 'dandy.' It is more likely, however, that the Prince of Wales commemorated by the pattern was the future Edward VII, who visited Sanquhar in 1871. In the autumn of that year the Prince of Wales visited the Duke of Buccleuch at Drumlanrig for a shooting holiday. There was anxiety as to the reception the Prince might receive when driving through the town, as the townspeople

were regarded as 'dangerous Radicals.' Sanquhar, however, welcomed the Prince with three floral arches across the High Street and every home decorated with flags and greenery."

Glendyne—to honor both a place and a person; Robert Nivison, Lord of Glendyne.

Midge and Flea—one of the oldest Sanquhar patterns, it most closely resembles other traditional eighteenth-century knitting.

Shepherd's Plaid—yet another pattern from weaving, to produce a checked effect. According to the Future Museum, "A large woolen shawl or plaid was part of every shepherd's goods and gear,

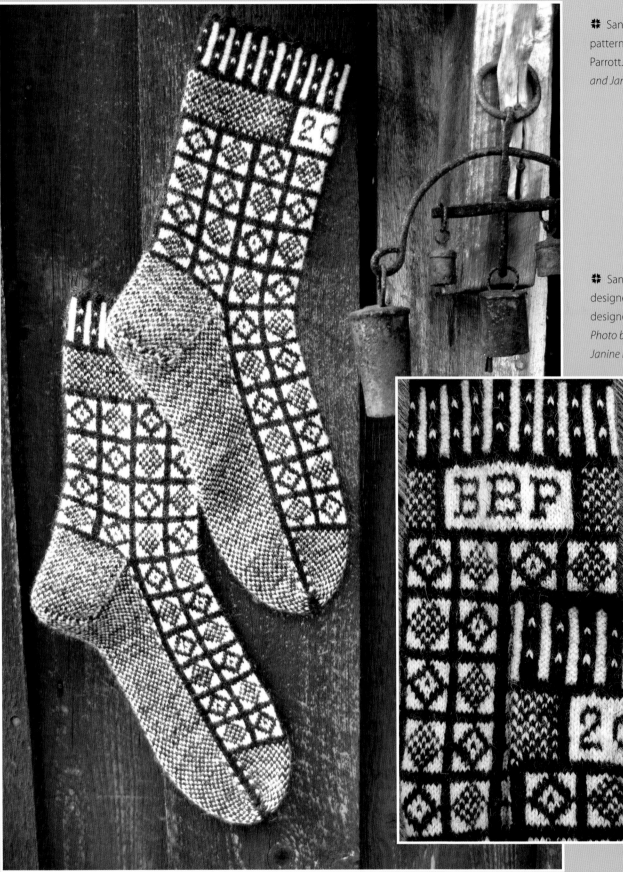

❋ Sanquhar socks in Duke pattern, designed by Beth Parrott. *Photo by Sue Flanders and Janine Kosel*

❋ Sanquhar socks with designers initials and date, designed by Beth Parrott. *Photo by Sue Flanders and Janine Kosel*

Scottish kilt hose, designed by Anne Carol Gilmour. *Photo by Sue Flanders and Janine Kosel*

used as protection against the weather and for wrapping and carrying lambs."

Rose, *Trellis*, *Drum*, *Coronet*—all may stand alone as patterns in their own right, or further embellish the Duke.

Initials of the wearer were also worked into the cuff, or for gloves meant for market, commonly, the word *Sanquhar*.

Gloves and stockings in Sanquhar were worked in the round on four, five, or six double-pointed needles from 2.25 to 1.5 mm thick, and as short as 75 mm, for rapid knitting of the fingers. Gloves featured a unique, three-sided finger construction, with gussets between in a tiny salt-and-pepper pattern, and two-color ribbing at the cuff. As patterns cannot be altered for size, needle size was the variable in knitting smaller or larger gloves or stockings. Patterns were typically knit with three-ply yarn that has become challenging to find lately, in color combinations of black and white or navy and natural. Brown and yellow was apparently a popular combination in the 1920s, and red and green has been seen from time to time.

Kilt Hose

Nestled into the history of Scottish sock knitting is the tale of kilt hose—socks worn by Scottish men along with their now-iconic tartan "skirts." Originally, these socks were made of cloth (often the same cloth used for the kilt itself), and were bound at the knee with garters. But to backtrack a moment to the kilt itself: "From some time after the advent of weaving in Scotland, certainly as early as the thirteenth century," writes Galer Britton Barnes in *Piecework*, "[highland] clansmen wrapped themselves in plaids: woven blankets of dyed and natural wools in varying hues, often in stripes."

Eventually, this mode of dress was altered to a garment wrapped around the waist that hung to mid-knee—what we know today as the kilt. It was worn by clansmen and members of military regiments, and although some accompanying

socks were eventually knitted in corresponding tartan patterns, Barnes says these are rare "probably because of the interior bulk and the tendency to snag created by carrying many colors of yarn, not to mention the complexity of the pattern. When they are knitted, such stockings are knitted flat and seamed."

Most kilt hose, then, was single color and composed of knit-purl patterns with names often the same as those of patterns that turn up in Aran knitting: Marriage Lines, Ridge and Furrow, Ropes, Anchors, Thistle, Midge, and Fly. Cables, honeycomb, and moss designs are also popular. The hose are knitted from the top down, although the top pattern, "because it is folded over when

Portrait of seated gentleman in highland dress. Note his knitted argyle-patterned kilt hose. *scotlandsimages.com/Crown Copyright 2008 The National Archives of Scotland*

worn, must be knitted with the right side facing in," writes Barnes.

Stuart Reid, whose concern in his book *Wellington's Highlanders* is particularly with military regiments, places the advent of knitted kilt hose to the early 1800s, although he admits "some illustrations show them worn much earlier. Knitted hose can be easily identified in portraits and other contemporary illustrations by all-pink feet . . . [and] a turned-over top."

The Shetland Islands

The Shetlands are a group of more than one hundred islands, only fourteen of which are inhabited, situated two hundred miles off the coast of Norway. Hand knitting on the islands has been documented since the very early sixteenth century, just a few years after Norway handed the islands over to Scotland in order, writes designer Sheila McGregor in *The Complete Book of Traditional Fair Isles Knitting*, to "provide the balance of the dowry of Margaret of Denmark on her marriage to King James III of Scotland." Indeed, the islands' peripatetic politics mirror the great host of influences at play, as trade routes from southern Europe, the Baltics, Scandinavia, the Faroe Islands, and Iceland all converged there. What this has meant to knitting is, possibly, everything.

✳ Wedding Ring Fine Shetland lace shawl. According to the Shetland Museum and Archives, "Throughout the nineteenth century most Shetland families lived in overcrowded, smoke-filled, inadequately lit houses, that didn't even have proper washing facilities. The women constantly laboured on the crofts, and knitted whenever their hands were free. They would usually have had two pieces of knitting on the go—coarse stockings, and something in fine Shetland lace." *Shetland Museum and Archives Photo Library, #01399*

Sharon Miller

Sharon Miller is the author of the be-all, end-all book on Shetland lace knitting, Heirloom Knits. In the early 1980s, following her own nascent interest in this knitterly art form, Miller began to research the old, classic patterns. What resulted was a comprehensive guide to all the main Shetland lace patterns, which she charted herself, plus valuable tips and information on how to combine patterns to create singular, highly personalized stoles and shawls.

"My mum bought my son, Jon, a lace hap done in what I thought then was very fine wool (a UK two-ply). It was really lovely, and it was that piece that sparked my first interest—the sheer delicate beauty of it from what I had considered a rather pedestrian craft till then, when compared to Irish crochet and the early samplers I was then interested in. I knitted Jon a layette in fine wool. Like many money-pressed new mums, I was keen to knit jumpers for him, and he was well kitted out in homemades. I did not like baby designs of the 1980s, which were often in thick acrylics, as they were too bulky for a baby in my opinion—out of scale. I saw a christening shawl picture done by Gladys Amedro in about 1988 for Princess Beatrice, which I cut out of the newspaper and kept—still have it! This led me to ring up Jamieson & Smith to buy their fine Cobweb wool; that was the first time I was aware there was still such a product.

"My mother had collected and passed on to me old *Weldon's Needlecraft* magazines from the 1900s. These are full of old knitting patterns as well as crochet and embroidery, which initially caught my attention. I started collecting mostly Paton & Baldwin's silver baby patterns from the 1950s, which were done in fine wool discontinued by the late 1980s. I had been making traditional Shetland lace haps from the patterns since about 1988 for family and friends using Cobweb yarn. This led me to get a brochure of theirs which had the 1950s Bestway Shetland Lace pamphlet in it, which I then bought and devoured! It is classic of Shetland lace and was fully written out. I could not follow the tiny directions readily and so started writing them as I had learnt from Barbara Abbey in my own system:

TO.OT = 'knit 2 tog, make 1, knit 1, make 1, knit 2 tog.'

"This showed up the underlying pattern a little and made it easier to predict, as the pattern symmetry became apparent from even this shorthand. What I found incredible at that time were the references to seemingly unbelievable fineness of thread and the sheer intricacy of the patterns.

"I discussed with my ultra-clever computer-literate knitter friend Susan the difficulty of all this (e.g., getting the row information to align correctly), and she suggested charting and explained the basics. I had tried it on graph paper, but it was very messy. She recommended a PC cross-stitch program, and with a bit of tweaking from Mike, my husband, we were able to get it to make stitch charts. From then on it was easy, as I made charts from the *Weldon's* et al, and gained insight into patterning. I started to knit them up and saw that a 'recipe book' of charted centers, borders, and edgings could be done. I had also learned how to read existing knitted pieces by this time.

The Wedding Ring Shawl, knit in finest Gossamer Class Yarn—so fine it can be drawn through a ring. *Image copyright Sharon Miller of* Heirloom Knitting

"I said to the literary agent that I contacted that my intended book would either go like a rocket or bomb like a stone. She encouraged me to try to get it published, but the bigger houses weren't interested, so I took it to the *Shetland Times*. Jamieson & Smith put me in touch with helpful Shetlanders and were very helpful in supplying photos and additional information. The Shetland Museum sent lots of images for me to digest, and Margaret Stuart of the then-Weisdale Mill Textile Museum also helped a lot, as did the Shetland Guild of Spinners, Weavers and Dyers, who oversaw the technical side of *Heirloom Knits* for accuracy of the wool-processing information. Mary Thomas's and Richard Rutt's knitting histories, Paton's *History of Knitting*, Rae Compton's and James Norbury's books were all ransacked for information, as were the Shetland titles of Sarah Don, Gladys Amedro, Linda Fryer, Tessa Lorant, Hazel Carter, and others. Coming from a historian-trained background, I know the importance of research—we all have to learn from, then build on each other's work to further knowledge.

"Primarily I want to document the Shetland lace tradition as accurately as I can at this moment. It was a lovely surprise to find there were many keenly interested knitters worldwide as enthralled with the beauty of this fine lace as I was. I don't see preservation (other than of actual knitted pieces and artifacts) as very important, as the essence of Shetland lace is pattern invention in certain broad parameters: That's a posh way of saying I 'identify' Shetland lace by general characteristics or norms of patterning (e.g., no nupps; I've never yet seen them in old Shetland work), very geometric yet complex motifs freely combined, normally done in exquisitely fine wool, with usually pieced-up construction.

"All craftspeople get satisfaction and stress release from what they do, or they wouldn't do it. I also love gardening; there will be a moment when, after years of work, the planting will be just right, and till then you keep striving against the weather and the weeds. With the lace, the reward or truest pleasure comes from seeing the dressed piece, and more particularly for me from 'cracking' a hard, unrecorded pattern or preserving an antique shawl in danger from decay. It's nothing but satisfying that an everyday pastime can produce a unique work of undisputed art. Challenge in this situation is what you set yourself: It should be achievable with effort but not stupid amounts of stress. Life does that at times, I find! In Shetland lace, the main 'challenge' is to exercise patience and attention, and to develop the ability to handle ultra-thin yarns. For me, the working out of patterns is like a knitting Sudoku, and I love that a comparatively few number of stitches (usually under fifty at most) are capable of what is to me an infinity of explorable combination.

"Knitting lace gets addictive; each time you 'see' a design, the deconstruct-flip-stagger-invert process is evoked automatically in my head. I do not have a favorite pattern. All are special, it's like being asked to pick a favorite snowflake!

"In pursuing and writing about Shetland lace, I am continuing to inform myself, and helping others to understand, love, and enjoy it, too, is the icing on the cake."

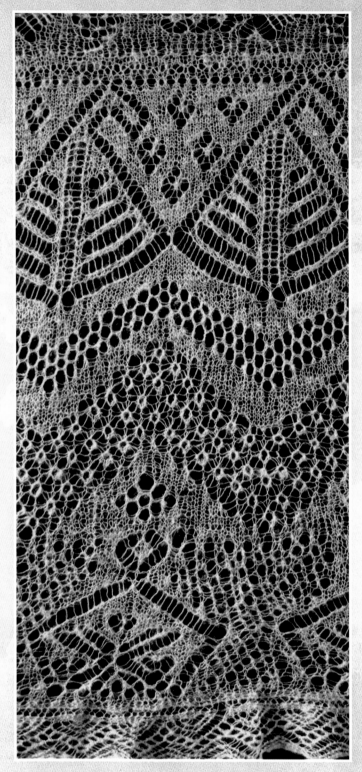

The Wedding Ring Shawl, detail. *Image copyright Sharon Miller of Heirloom Knitting*

PATTERN

Beautiful Shetland Shawl

The centre is done with fine white Shetland wool and large ivory or wood pins. Cast on for the centre 180 or 190 stitches; the pattern does for any number that will divide by 10.

First row:—Knit 1, make 1, slip 1, knit 1, pass the slipped stitch over, make 1, slip 1, knit 1, pass the slipped stitch over, make 1, slip 1, knit 1, pass the slipped stitch over the knitted one, knit 3, and repeat.

Second row:—Seamed.

Third row:—Knit 2 (make 1, slip 1, knit 1, and pass the slipped stitch over 3 times), knit 2.

Fourth row:—Seamed.

Fifth row:—Knit 3 (make 1, slip 1, knit 1, and pass the slipped stitch over 3 times), knit 1.

Sixth row:—Seamed.

Seventh row:—Knit 4 (make 1, slip 1, knit 1, pass the slipped stitch over 3 times).

Eighth row:—Seamed.

Ninth row:—Knit 2 (knit 2 together, and make 1 three times), knit 2.

Tenth row:—Seamed.

Eleventh row:—Knit 1 (knit 2 together, and make 1 three times), knit 3.

—From *Exercises in Knitting*, Cornelia Mee, David Bogue, London, 1868 (Project Gutenberg)

✳ An unidentified woman, about twenty-five years of age, wearing a fine lace shawl c. 1844, by Mathew B. Brady. *Library of Congress Prints and Photographs Division, Daguerreotype Collection, #LC-USZ62-109946*

In the Shetlands, as elsewhere in Scotland, hosiery knitting was a viable cottage industry helped along, no doubt, by the preponderance of island sheep (*see page* 80). But the advent and development of two very particular sorts of knitting—influenced by any one, or even all, of the sources mentioned above—were to put Shetland on the knitting map: Unst lace and Fair Isle stranded color knitting.

Shetland Lace

Shetland lace, especially lace from the island of Unst, is the kind of knitting that makes people's jaws drop open. "Fine as a cobweb" (James Norbury's description), "this fragile flower" (Alice Starmore's description) is traditionally knitted in two-ply, cream-colored neck wool so thin that it must be spun by hand, and few hands these days are capable of "spinning a woolen thread two or four hairs thick and then plying two of the threads together" (knitting designer Alice Korach's description; lace yarn from the island of Mainland is slightly thicker, according to designer Elizabeth Lovick, about the same as modern lace-weight yarn). However, glancing through photos of the intricate, elaborate designs that typify Shetland lace certainly makes a knitter want to try.

There are still significant obstacles to knitting Unst lace, and having to spin your own hair-thin yarn, originally derived from hand-plucked fleece, is only the beginning. Korach mentions that although the classic fancy shawl was knit only in white, some were knit in the Victorian mourning colors of black or purple, and some were striped or bordered with red for celebrations. In either of the two latter examples, you'd also have to dye your own yarn, in addition to spinning it. For the former, you'd have bleached the shawl white once it was knitted, in what Starmore and Matheson in *Knitting from the British Isles* call a "painstaking process, involving the pouring of rock sulphur over a peat fire, and then suspending the work over it." There's also the matter of needles, or "pins" as the Shetlanders dubbed the size 0 to 00000 needles they used to stitch shawls and stoles and wedding veils. Last anyone checked, they had to be special-ordered from Scotland.

And still again, there are compelling reasons to give this lace a whirl. First of all, there's the history. To sum it up: Once the Shetland Isles' hand-knit hosiery trade fizzled out in the early nineteenth century, an English merchant named Edward Standen suggested that the locals try their hands at something a little more . . . willowy. A goodly amount of success ensued ("success" being a relative term here, given that the knitters operated under the oppressive Truck System, in which they received goods as payment rather than actual money). Shawls, veils, gloves, and stockings were all exported in droves to the upper and middle classes of Britain.

Even more success was had once a woman named Margaret Currie stepped in as a go-between for the knitters, offering their boggling shawls for sale to the likes of Queen Victoria no less, and effectively ending the Truck System. Some of the Shetland patterns may have derived from Spanish patterns that reached the islands via trade routes, theorizes traditional knitting enthusiast Madeline Weston, pointing out that lace knitting was already well established in Spain in the fourteenth century. Lovick mentions that the first documented bit of lace from Shetland was a baby's bonnet from 1832 so complexly shaped and patterned it must prove that lace knitting had been practiced on the islands for quite some time.

There's more to recommend this sort of knitting. Although Shetland patterns look complicated, they are actually based quite simply on knit, slip, yarnover, and a decrease or three. Garter stitch is the norm, in order to facilitate patterning on every row.

The classic fancy shawl is square and begins with an elastic cast-on such as the open-loop or picot-chain cast-on. (Bear in mind that the fancy shawl was for selling; everyday "hap" shawls were the only ones worn by the working women of Shetland until World War II, and they feature a garter stitch center and a border of Old Shale pattern with a peaked edging.) No edges are bound off. Rather, one edge is knit lengthwise, then the inside edge is picked up, and from it one border and the center of the shawl are knit all in one piece. The other three border pieces are knit separately, then grafted to the central panel. Intriguingly, Shetland lace does not open up—literally—till after it's been blocked. Korach writes, in an article for *Knitting Around the World from Threads*, of the "extreme blocking" necessary at a project's end: "When a lace shawl is correctly stretched, it becomes almost one-third larger, and all the holes created by the yarnover/decrease combinations open to reveal the patterns."

Though Mary Thomas asserted that there were only ten authentic Shetland lace patterns, Korach is skeptical, pointing to the vast wealth of lace patterns to be found in, say, Barbara Walker's pattern books. All seem to agree that Print o' the Wave, Ears o' Grain, Razor Shell, Bird's Eye, Horseshoe, Fern, Old Shale, Acre, Cat's Paw, and Fir Cone are absolutely authentic. Starmore, in an article for *Threads* magazine, gives directions for others: a single eyelet, Turkish Faggoting, Lace Trellis, Arrowhead, Gull's Wings, and Lace Ladders, and assuredly there are more.

And lest we forget: the finest traditional Shetland lace shawl from the island of Unst should be able to pass easily through a wedding ring—this in spite of its breadth of six feet square.

V-neck Shetland patterned sweater marketed in the 1990s as the Prince of Wales Jumper, after the one he wore when golfing at St. Andrews in 1922. *Photo by Shetland Museum, #01351; Shetland Museum and Archives Photo Library*

Fair Isle

In the minds of many, Fair Isle knitting has become synonymous with any kind of stranded color knitting. But in truth, it is a technique, hailing from the small Shetland island of the same name, possibly as early as the 1850s, which follows rigid and particular rules. According to Alice Starmore, in her comprehensive *Book of Fair Isle Knitting*:

- Fair Isle often takes as its main pattern starting point an OXO motif (a series of alternating octagons and crosses), which was commonly found on Finnish and Estonian gloves of the early nineteenth century.
- It's worked in the round, on four needles, of soft, firm Shetland wool in pattern bands over seventeen or nineteen rows, with rows of patterns either stacked directly above each other or staggered, like bricks.

- The pattern, which is usually symmetrical and consists of an odd number of rows, must contain diagonal lines in order to evenly distribute the tension of stitches and ensure a fabric that is elastic.
- Only two colors are used per row, and those colors must change frequently within that row (at least every seven stitches, if not fewer)—as Starmore points out, this keeps the strands short and the resulting fabric even. James Norbury elaborates on the use of color thusly, although these are not hard and fast rules: "In the 1st row a light shade is used for ground shade. In the 2nd row the same ground shade is used and the 1st contrast color introduced for pattern. In the 3rd row the medium is used for ground shade, but the 1st contrast still used for the pattern. In the 4th row medium is still used for the ground shade and the 2nd contrast for the pattern."

風工房の
フェアアイルニット

Fair
Isle
Knitting

❄ Shetland knitting,
Japanese style: Kazekobo's
take on the Scottish classic.
*Photo by Yuji Ito, from Hata's
Fair Isle book published by*
Nihon Vogue Publishing
Company

And yet, within these rigid strictures, a wealth of richness and variety is possible. There are only two colors per row, but as many as the knitter wants throughout the garment. Traditionally, yellow (from onion skins), red (from madder), and indigo (from indigo) were juxtaposed against natural black, gray, fawn, brown, or green. OXO seems a pretty inflexible pattern until you consider all the variability one can muster when smaller patterning is added to these elements—various cross, diamond, seeding, and random shapes within the Os, for example—or the additional patterns that can be worked in around the OXO: Peeries, Waves and Peaks, Norwegian stars, borders, more seeding, tessellated patterns—the combinations are limitless.

Shetland Wool

Like Icelandic sheep, Finnsheep, and Norwegian Saelsans, the Shetland sheep is an old, short-tailed landrace breed, meaning that it is "primitive" and "unimproved." These can be good things when it comes to sheep and their fleeces. The sheep themselves are small, fine-wooled, and hardy, and they may share genes with ancient Soay sheep that Neolithic farmers are thought to have raised on the Northern Isles some 4,500 years ago. These sheep were possibly bred with sheep brought over by Norse settlers, then bred again with Roman sheep that were milling about the island a few centuries later. There is some speculation that Shetlanders may have been selecting sheep for their soft, fine wool way back in sheep-breeding days.

Traditionally, Shetland wool comes in eleven colors and thirty different coat patterns, some of which still bear old Norse and Shetland dialect names. The designated colors are light gray, gray, white (the most popular color since the turn to the twentieth century, unfortunately rendering some others colors quite rare), *emsket* (dusky bluish-gray), musket (light grayish-brown), *staela* (silvery gray), fawn, *mioget* (honey-colored), *moorit* (reddish brown), and dark brown. Coat patterns include the amusingly named *mirkface* (white face with black spots) and *sponget* (dark colored with small white spots, or vice-versa).

As for the wool, it is a great favorite among hand spinners, especially for spinning from the locks (spinning fiber that hasn't been combed or carded). It is soft, durable, light, and fine, officially short stapled (about 3.5 inches), and crimpy—although some wool is as long as eight inches and wavy rather than crimpy. According to traditional knitter Madeline Weston, Shetland spinners could produce six thousand yards of yarn from two ounces of fleece for lace knitting. Some sheep have a double coat of coarse outer and fine inner fibers, which can be spun separately; some have a single coat. Regardless, so popular is and

Loading sheep onto the "Good Shepherd." *scotlandsimages.com/National Trust for Scotland*

has been Shetland wool that it prompted Scottish baron and agricultural writer John Sinclair to write this in 1790 in his *Statistical Accounts of Scotland*: "Shetland Wool, taking all its properties together, is perhaps the completest article of its kind in the universe, possessing at the same time the gloss and softness of silk, the strength of cotton, the whiteness of linen and the warmth of wool." High praise indeed, but certainly not too high for a fiber that would allow hand knitters to create both the vibrantly colored and durable Fair Isle sweater and the delicate Unst lace shawl.

Starmore postulates that both the OXO pattern and stranded color knitting came to Fair Isle at the same moment, with travelers, sailors, and fishermen who were possibly from the Baltic Circle (in fact, the OXO motif is found in all the Scandinavian and Baltic countries). She absolutely dismisses the fanciful theory espoused by Norbury and others that the pattern arrived on the island with sailors washed ashore after the wreck of an Armada ship in the sixteenth century.

The island's knitters, who had once knit plain socks to trade for food, tobacco, and clothing, found with stranded color knitting another means of creating barter-worthy—and eventually, cash-worthy—garments for the overseas and tourist markets.

The first Fair Isle garments were gloves, stockings, caps, and tam o' shanters. Knitters moved on to ganseys in the early 1900s, patterning the fishermen's sweaters with bands of Os and Xs from the hem to the shoulder. By the 1920s, when Shetland lace (see pg 76) had declined in popularity, mainland knitters picked up the Fair Isle stranded knitting practice as well, and the technique virtually exploded. Starmore writes, "Allover patterns appeared; some of them developed from the transposed OXO bands, and a few vertical allover patterns developed from OXOs that were set one above the other. Another major development was the introduction of hundreds of border patterns . . . and peerie patterns . . . Many were taken directly from cross-stitch sampler booklets, which were available in great quantities. Large stars were added to the repertoire in the 1940s, coinciding with an influx of Norwegian refugees during World War II." Chemical dyes brought a further brightening of available yarns.

In this manner Fair Isle knitting greatly evolved and yet remained the same, its initial governing rules still firmly entrenched. A recent article in the *New Statesman* reports that the Fair Isle Crafts co-op still produces traditional Fair Isle garments, but on a hand-frame rather than strictly by hand.

Ireland

What everyone knows of knitting in Ireland is this: Aran sweaters. Although how it is that Aran sweaters should end up in this chapter, rather than the one on fisherman's sweaters, is probably not lost on most knitters by now. It's become common-enough knowledge that Aran sweaters as we know them today were not, as once proclaimed, ancient sweaters knit for fishermen on these three islands drifting about in Galway Bay, displaying the romantic symbolism of rugged, religion-drenched lives (which is not to say that fishermen of Ireland did not wear sweaters to keep out the cold and wet while they were at sea; they just weren't necessarily the fancy, cream-colored variety associated today with the Aran Islands). Rather, they were a construct (no pun intended) of hardworking fisherwives who sought to supplement their meager income with a little hand knitting for the tourist trade sometime after the potato famine in the late nineteenth century. Previously, they'd mostly knit stockings—according to Rutt, in navy blue with white diamond bands around the tops and toes—as well as caps, shawls, and yes, even sweaters.

The true story of the Aran sweater seems to be, at least in part, this: In 1891, the Irish government set up the Congested Districts Board to help families to survive the potato famine. The board encouraged locals to weave and knit garments to sell, and in the early twentieth century taught them how to knit stitches such as Honeycomb, Figure Eight, and Double Diamond. Some years later, a Dublin craft shop owner named Murial Gahan, who had a special interest in preserving local crafts, visited the islands and took some samples of knitting home to sell. Apparently, these were early examples of "Aran" knitting—a simpler style of knit-purl patterning that some people have speculated came to the island knitters via the Scottish herring lasses (*see page* 63).

The first known patterned Aran sweater, which resides in the National Museum in Dublin, dates

⧉ Oyster dredging off Clarinbridge and the Keave, County Galway, pictured here is one of the brothers, Martin or John Burke, Tonroe, Oranmore, County Galway 1967.

Courtesy of the National Museum of Ireland, #DF 4327

from about 1930. By 1946, Aran sweaters as we know them today began to appear, although on a relatively small scale. In the 1950s, Irish fishermen began wearing the sweaters themselves, and a full-throttle push to commercialize hand knitting on the islands was encouraged.

Meanwhile, a torrent of myth had begun to swirl around the sweaters. In 1967, German textile historian Heinz Edgar Kiewe published *The Sacred*

History of Knitting. In it, using some sweaters he had purchased in Gahan's craft shop in 1936 as a jumping-off point, he fabricated an elaborate and compelling tale: The sweaters were part of a centuries-old tradition on the islands, with each pattern steeped in symbolism straight from the pages of the *Book of Kells*. The trellis pattern was meant to suggest the "bond of man with God and religion;" the braided stitch patterns, "the holy

three strands of hair ribbon or straw, the plaited holy bread of the Old Testament." And so on. He further surmised that the distinct patterning of the sweaters symbolized individual families, in much the same ways Scottish clans have their individually patterned tartans. Taking a passage from J. M. Synge's book *The Aran Islands*, Kiewe also speculated that a drowned sailor could be identified by the patterns on his sweater when he washed up on shore.

This was all nonsense as it turned out, but great fun to contemplate nevertheless. What was not nonsense was the extreme popularity that the sweaters enjoyed, helped along, no doubt, by Kiewe's assertions.

Still, there's no denying that Aran sweaters are a part of the Irish knitting tradition—they're just relative latecomers to the story. They were knit up of cream-colored, five-ply wool a little thicker than worsted weight, known as *bainin*. It is knit flat, on two needles, and the pieces are sewn together. It can incorporate as many patterns as the knitter chooses, and there's a wealth to choose from, in any combination the mind can conjure. Even though Kiewe is said to have named many

of the patterns himself, and also imbued the names with religious significance, there are also "secular" names for the stitches. To name some of the most common is worthwhile, if only to show their range: Moss, Wishbone, Chain Cable, Long Cable, Lobster Claw Cable, Hourglass Cable, Aran Diamond with Rope pattern, Simple Aran Braid, Wide Plait Cable, Five-Fold Aran Braid, Blackberry Stitch, Simple Plait Cable, Little Twist Plait, Wide Twist Plait, Cluster Pattern Braid, Fancy Welt Rib, Irish Wave and Knot, Bobble Pattern Braid, Bobble-and-Wave, Bobble Chevron, Allover Bobble, Waving Rib, Aran Honeycomb, Broken Lattice, Mock Cable Chevron, Tree of Life, Single Leaf Twist Rib Diamond, Crossover Chevron and Moss, Twist Stitch Diamonds, Wheatsheaves, Figure Eight Diamond, Wave Welt Rib. It's enough to keep a knitter occupied for years, if not decades.

Even without the fancies of Kiewe, Aran knitting has its own true, fascinating stories. For example, the Irish Culture and Customs website mentions a knitter from Inishmaan, the middle-sized island, who learned to knit on goose quills because there weren't enough knitting needles to go around the island.

A Welsh knitter—probably of a sweater sleeve, from the looks of it—shown here in regional costume of, in the words of Dr. Iorweth C. Peate, "high hat, petticoat, bedgown, apron, and shawl . . .the bedgown was a sort of long coat, forming a waist, and closing over the bust, and a long tail which folded behind over the petticoat, with the apron hiding the petticoat front." *National Library of Wales*

Wales

The history of Welsh knitting is somewhat sparsely recorded. Supposedly, there has never been a knitting style that could be construed as wholly Welsh. Perhaps as early as the sixteenth century, many in this region of the United Kingdom, as elsewhere, undertook sock knitting as a means of earning money. Later there was some amount of knitting of ganseys for fishermen. Really, the only indication of regional variety are the Monmouth caps Rutt makes so much of in his *History of Hand Knitting*. It is thought that they originated in the fifteenth century in the Welsh border town of, naturally, Monmouth, and were largely sold to seamen and soldiers, the latter of whom apparently wore them under their helmets. Curiously enough, they were also purchased from makers outside Monmouth, as their manufacture transferred to other realms by the seventeenth century.

An extant cap that seems to fit the written description of a Monmouth cap was stockinette knit in the round on four needles of dark, two-ply wool, then felted. Its structure, according to Rutt, would have been accomplished like this: "First a hem or brim of double fabric was shaped . . . Above the hem the cap was shaped by decreasing three times in every tenth round, at the end of the needle in the tenth and thirtieth round, the middle of each needle in the twentieth round. After the thirtieth row the remaining fifty stitches were decreased . . . till eight stitches remained. These were drawn together and topped with a button . . . The resulting cap is a close-fitting deep skull-cap, hard wearing and warm."

Historians have noted that so ubiquitous was the Monmouth cap, and so integral to the lives of Englishmen, that few writers ever thought to describe it in any sort of detail. It was listed by Captain John Smith of Jamestown as among the most essential components of an English colonist's kit when traveling to the New World.

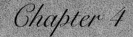

Chapter 4

SCANDINAVIA AND ICELAND

A Norwegian girl in national costume;
knitting among the mountain cow pastures, 1937.
Photo by Anders Beer Wilse, Courtesy of Norsk Folkemuseum, #NF7907

*T*HE COUNTRIES OF SCANDINAVIA have a long and especially rich hand-knitting tradition, including intricate color patterns that are possibly even more popular today—in and out of Scandinavia—than they were at the time of their origins.

Which Nordic country was the first to start knitting? James Norbury claims that people have been knitting in Norway since as early as the ninth century, and that the Norwegian tradition helped to develop traditions in Sweden as well as Denmark, which he thought could boast no such craft prior to the fifteenth century. Richard Rutt, on the other hand, asserts that Denmark was knitting before Norway and Sweden. In her book, *Folk Mittens: Techniques and Patterns for Handknitted Mittens*, author Marcia Lewandowski dates Scandinavian knitting generally to the early 1600s. Susanne Pagoldh, author of *Nordic Knitting: Thirty-One Patterns in the Scandinavian Tradition*, theorizes that knitting came to the Nordic countries in the sixteenth and seventeenth centuries, but only as a means of clothing the wealthy in knitted silk "sweaters" and stockings. Two hundred years later, she finds that these original patterns had been adapted to the masses, and to wool, and to very small, individual regions, where they are now considered traditional folk dress. Designer Sheila McGregor cites the two sides in the debate as being between Denmark and Sweden, which only shows that the true origins of knitting are as befuddled in Scandinavia as they are throughout the world generally.

There is plenty to mull over, but also plenty that is known. According to McGregor in *Traditional Scandinavian Knitting*, "The earliest knitting in Scandinavia was probably knitted entirely in stocking stitch from white wool, and colored, if at all, by boiling up in a dye vat once it was completed." When was that, exactly? Let's not quibble. This style, argues McGregor, was the only style till the mid-nineteenth century, when men and women, through their clothing, began to identify themselves as hailing from a particular place. Folk costumes began to incorporate jackets, stockings, caps, and so forth, knitted with full patterns or patterned borders that varied from town to town or region to region. This, maintains McGregor, "is the main reason why this part of the world is so rich in inspiration."

Pagoldh points to various sources in most if not all the Scandinavian knitting traditions: pattern books from Germany and Italy, which became available to Scandinavian knitters by the sixteenth century; patterns that were adapted from weaving; and religious motifs in various materials—tile, ceramic, wood—from around the world.

Denmark

According to author Marcia Lewandowski in *Folk Mittens*, knitting came to Denmark in the early 1600s with a group of Dutch knitters, called into service by the Danish court to produce royal stockings. Susanne Pagoldh and Sheila McGregor both cite a piece of evidence that Danish stocking knitting was somewhat older: a Danish knitting peg, used to hold and extend stocking needles, dating to the late sixteenth century. Regardless, stockings were being knitted for export by the mid-seventeenth century, and hand knitting proved an essential source of income, particularly in the region of Jutland.

Men, women, and children there all knitted, spun, carded wool from homegrown sheep, and separated spring wool from summer wool, which had more luster. Both dog and human hair were commonly added to strengthen wool and, in the case of the former, to protect against gout (as folk wisdom maintained). Garments knit for home use were "simple, one-color woolen stockings, mittens, sweaters, and underclothing," writes Pagoldh in *Nordic Knitting*. "The men wore knitted underpants, and the women wore knitted underskirts. The quality of these garments was often poor, the stitches were still large and loose even after fulling in warm, soapy water or fish broth." McGregor adds that these underskirts were "extremely thick and heavy objects, which are said to have been able to stand up on their own and which were dyed red for winter wear."

Despite very little regional patterning of note, Pagoldh makes mention of some curious details. For example, in order for a Jutlander to knit while she ate, thereby maximizing her moneymaking time, "The yarn ball would be fastened onto a hook hanging from the knitter's shoulder or set in a bowl and then pulled from the inside of the ball so that it wouldn't roll around." Jutlanders, who knit countless socks for export, were nevertheless in 1636 forbidden by King Christian IV from *wearing* stockings—they were "still considered at that time to be part of the dress of the higher class," Pagoldh remarks. For this reason, knitted footless stockings were common in the region all the way up to World War II.

In Denmark, caps and nightshirts were part of the national costume, as they were in other Scandinavian countries. *Nikulorshue* caps, patterned with five colors, were knit so long they could be doubled for warmth. Often they were knit with yarn dyed using a traditional method called *ikat*, or flame coloring. In this Scandinavian version of tie-dyeing, a skein of yarn was knotted in sections, then placed in a dye bath. "With careful planning," writes Pagoldh, "you can space the knots for a desired pattern (zig-zag, for example) which will be revealed as the yarn is knitted . . . Another decorative possibility is to knot the skein in so many places that the yarn becomes totally variegated. In stockinette stitch, this yarn gives an irregular salt-and-pepper pattern which was used for indigo blue stockings." Ikat also was used to pattern knitted sleeves on woven vests for a result that Pagoldh calls "striking." McGregor makes no mention of ikat directly, but writes of the oddly named *nikolorhuen*, or "cap of nine colors," on which she can count only five colors and on which "the yarn for the pattern stripes has been tied-and-dyed, hence all the shades and the rather irregular occurrence of the small color motifs in the pattern."

Though *nattrøjer* (*see below*) are considered the quintessential Danish knitted garment, men in Denmark did not begin to wear patterned sweaters until the nineteenth century and previously had worn "undershirts" that were white only, or perhaps, on rare occasion, striped. McGregor makes one mention of a rare, stranded sweater called a *skatroje* from the region of Sejro, with dark blue geometric patterning on a background of white.

Nattrøjer

(With special thanks to Vivian Høxbro)

The oldest example of Danish knitting is a seventeenth-century fragment of indigo-dyed wool knitted in a damask pattern with eight-pointed

stars—at least, if you believe Richard Rutt. Some scholars, says knitting librarian and amateur historian Susette Newberry, trace the roots of so-called damask knitting in the country to Dutch families who settled on the island of Amager. They favored simple knit-purl patterning in their knitting, which harks to the "damask" knitting in seventeenth-century Denmark in which a single-color textured fabric was created to resemble intricate woven damask. Sheila McGregor points out that while damask knitting was especially popular in Denmark, similar patterning has been in evidence on garments from Norway, Sweden, Finland, and Estonia and culminated in the nineteenth century with Norwegian Setesdal knitters turning to cabled stockings.

Regardless, it is the *nattrøje*, the tight-fitting women's "nightshirt" worn under a bodice with most of the sleeves showing, that is most commonly associated with damask knitting in Denmark. In

fact, it's part of the national costume. So long was it popular that styles vary greatly, from long and tight to quite short, about thirty centimeters in total. It would have been knitted on small, circular needles in fine, natural-colored yarns that were then dyed green, red, blue, and black, depending on the season. Pagoldh mentions that eight-pointed stars inside diagonal squares were especially popular motifs.

The somewhat erroneously titled *nattrøje*, which translates to "nightshirt," was actually worn not only for sleeping but also during waking hours. It is perhaps the most stereotypical example of Danish knitting, worn first, according to Sheila McGregor, by both men and women but eventually becoming

⁜ A contemporary *nattrøje* utilizing a classic motif, knit by Beth Brown-Reinsel, who has researched the sweaters at various museums throughout Denmark. "The high gauge and variety of patterning within the prescribed construction of these pieces is so inspiring," she says. "Each knitter expressed her creativity and individuality through her garment." Brown-Reinsel's *nattrøje* is knitted at a gauge of seven stitches per inch in traditional Guernsey yarn, "because the knit/purl designs require a high-twist worsted-spun yarn for clarity and definition," she explains. It first appeared in *Interweave Knits* (Winter 2004). You can purchase the pattern at patternfish.com/patterns/4310. Nattrøje *knit by Beth Brown-Reinsel; photo by Coni Richards* a garment exclusively for women. McGregor calls the *nattrøje* the "direct descendant" of the textured silk shirts favored by the gentry in the seventeenth century, as well as a probable influence on British gansies.

Susanne Pagoldh mentions that *nattrøjer* would have been difficult to knit, requiring careful counting, as well as the use of thin yarn worked on fine needles, to most effectively exhibit the detailed knit-purl patterning. She therefore hypothesizes in *Nordic Knitting* that "each parish was supplied by its own knitter, perhaps a childless widow or spinster who supported herself with knitting. These skilled knitters would have confirmed the old traditional styles while occasionally adding small improvements or changes of their own which in turn would be copied by the less talented." During the day, the sweaters would have been worn (by women) under cloth bodices. "[L]arge and elaborate patterns were placed where they would be seen and smaller all-over patterns, particularly two-by-two checks in purl and plain, used where they would be out of sight or covered by silk trimmings," writes Pagoldh. McGregor indicates that some color choices represented regional preferences: in Nordfalster, red was worn for feast days and green for regular days; in Rosnaes, red was for summer, green for spring, and blue for winter. Probably, they were knit first in white and dyed later.

With a few notable exceptions, *nattrøjer* employ the use of only purl stitches on a plain background. These patterns include welts and checks, birds, stars, and squares; the unusual and exquisite patterning on Dutch Amager sweaters (accomplished by Swedish maids) included peacocks, crowns, and angels—"not like anything else seen in Denmark, nor in Sweden for that matter," marvels McGregor. Pagoldh makes mention of checkerboard squares and diagonal lines at the lower edges of *nattrøjer* to "counteract the tendency of the edge to roll up." Two-end knitting (*see page* 110) was sometimes used at the borders.

Faroe Islands

The Faroe Islands represent a fascinating hodgepodge of cultures and influences. Originally settled by early Gaels in perhaps the late seventh/early eighth century (in the form of monks, who are credited by some with introducing sheep to the islands), then by Norse settlers (by some accounts around the late ninth century), in 1380 the islands were governed both by Norway and Denmark, who once shared consolidated power. Although techinically the islands remained in the possession of Norway, they are now exclusively a Danish territory.

Sheep were an essential commodity on the islands, which have no timber and few other natural resources. Their fleece was regarded as "gold." Raw wool and a coarse woolen fabric known as wadmal were traded for other goods in medieval times. Then, in the sixteenth century, when knitting is said to have reached the islands, knitted socks became a hot commodity. Why stockings or other crafted goods were exported before that time is an interesting point of speculation. Historians Osva Olsen and Ingvar Svanberg postulate that *nålbinding*, which preceded knitting on the islands by a possible period of centuries, was too labor intensive to make it a viable technique for mass production. To enhance its meager effects, everyone got involved: men carded and spun, women stitched.

In the year 1765, though, one hundred thousand pairs of knitted stockings were exported, mainly to Norway. Sweaters, particularly fishermen's sweaters, were also eventually knit for export, although plenty were needed to clothe local fishermen. Marcia Lewandowski reports in *Folk Mittens* that for the two-month journey to Iceland, four changes of clothes were needed by a Faroese fisherman; and for the four-month trip to Greenland, seven changes. According to Susanne Pagoldh, no knitting for the local fishermen was done between Christmas and New Year, for fear that the men would never return. "But it was all right to knit garments to sell," she says.

Vivian Høxbro

Vivian Høxbro is the famed doyenne of contemporary domino and shadow knitting. Her first book, the aptly titled Domino Knitting, was published in 2000; Shadow Knitting in 2004; Advanced Domino Knitting in 2008; and Knit to Be Square in 2008. She is a much-beloved teacher of techniques in both her homeland of Denmark as well as abroad.

Neither domino nor shadow knitting is native to Denmark, but both have been significantly influenced by various other Danish techniques, thanks to Vivian Høxbro's interpretations. For the uninitiated, here is her description of shadow knitting, from her book of the same name (for a full description of domino knitting, see page 239):

[Shadow knitting] uses just two stitch patterns, garter stitch and stockinette stitch, and the patterning is minimalistic . . . [W]hen the person wearing the garment moves, the pattern becomes visible. It almost seems like magic. In shadow knitting, the right side of the work always begins with a knit row. The patterning is worked on the wrong side, alternating two rows worked in a dark color and two rows worked in a light color (or vice versa . . .). The pattern itself is formed on the right side by the purl ridges . . . An American knitter once told me she saw it as 'uphill' (ridges) and 'down-dale' (smooth). This is an excellent way to describe the shadow-producing texture.

"I met domino knitting in Germany in 1993 at a sales show in Germany, where Horst Schulz (the creator of 'patchwork' knitting) showed what he was doing. I got interested, and he gave me a handout.

Abstract stole. "I call this 'lazy domino knitting,'" says Høxbro, "as you begin a domino square but stop before it is finished; then you go on to the next square. When finished, you 'damage' [i.e., felt] it in the washing machine." Photo by Vivian Høxbro

I asked him if I could design in this way of knitting, and he, as generous as he is, said yes! That was the beginning of a lifelong passion.

"Several years later, my knitting guild traveled to Berlin and took a class from him. But I fainted and did not even get one single square done. In a way, it was good, as I had to find my own kind of domino knitting. It is just lots of fun, and I will enjoy working with it for the rest of my life. I teach it for even beginners, and it is just a special way of thinking about knitting. It is a joy. Domino knitting is the love of my life, except for my husband and my grandchildren.

"I once got a letter from Meg Swansen telling me that there were domino knitting shawls in a book on traditional Faroese shawls. I got the book and, yes, there are two shawls, but they are not traditional; the editor just liked them so much that they were included in the book. Later I got a fax from Marilyn Murphy at Interweave Press. She had found an article by Virginia Woods Bellamy from 1947. Actually, she is the first inventor of domino knitting. But I am sure that the Faroese designer

Masai vest, inspired by Masai wedding necklaces. *Photo by Vivian Høxbro*

also invented this technique, and Horst Schulz too. I have not invented anything. I just 'stole' it and made it my own and added a Nordic spirit to it. My domino designs are very different from what I have seen so far.

"The name domino knitting was the result of a competition in the Danish Knitting Guild. The winner said, 'You join different figures where they fit, exactly as in the game dominos.'" Obvious, isn't it?

"Shadow knitting I saw for the first time in the weekly magazine I worked for, in an article called something like 'The Finer Points of Japanese Knitting' by a woman named Mieko Yano. Later I saw it in Sweden in the work of Maria Gustafsson, who called it 'optical knitting.' It happened that shadow knitting was brought to Sweden by a Japanese craft teacher who married a Swede. In Japan it is called 'The Hidden [or Secret] Pattern.' Shadow knitting is not difficult—it is a little hard to get started, but then it is piece of cake—and so different. For me, domino knitting is all about the process, and shadow knitting is all about the result.

"I truly love the Danish nightshirts (*nattrøjer, see page* 89) from my area, and of course they are my history. But I am working completely differently from what they did so many years ago. I am, however, very grateful to be a part of the Danish (and worldwide) history of knitting, and I truly hope that I have added my little bit to it. I am sure Americans will see my designs as very Scandinavian-like; but I am also sure that the Danish knitters find my designs very different from the Danish way, which is much more subtle. You could call it 'my way.' If I would be asked what is my specialty—my signature—it is colors. I just love to work with colors.

"My goal is to design garments that are fun to make from the beginning to the end; nobody knits today because they need clothes, they knit to enjoy. I also want the finished garment to be something to be proud of and a garment that you can wear proudly for many, many years."

Navajo jacket, inspired by Navajo weavings Høxbro saw at the Denver Art Museum in Denver, Colorado. *Courtesy of Vivian Høxbro, Photo by Lars Dalby*

Typical Faroese knitting patterns incorporate stranded horizontal bands in round motifs, both small and large. The main color is usually held by the right index finger while the pattern colors are held by fingers of the left hand. Up to three colors per row are used, and sweaters have no clearly defined front or back, "which means the elbows wear evenly," says designer Madelynn Fatelewitz in an article for *Threads*. Typical of the selection are patterns taken from Hans M. Debes's collection of more than one hundred classic designs, which he gathered at the behest of Danish Queen Alexandrina and published in the 1932 book *Foroysk Bindingarmynstur*. Among these designs are Wheels, Kittens, Ring of Dancers, Sheeptracks, Goose Footprints, Fleas, Lice (*see page xx*), Sea Waves, Hammers, Day and Night, and Hills and Dales. Sheila McGregor in *Traditional Scandinavian Knitting* additionally mentions Faroese inventions such as Hammers and Shears, as well as large Zigzags she remarks "may have come from a type of semi-ornamental, semi-functional type of needlework known as decorative darning." Writes Susanne Pagoldh in *Nordic Knitting*, "The old patterns were often named after the knitter who first created the pattern. One pattern which has been preserved is the eight-pointed star in a diagonal box."

Natural-colored wool is favored, although the Faroes do have a strong tradition of vegetable dyeing. The islands are known for a purplish hue called *korki*, obtained from the same lichen that gives litmus paper its particular tinge.

Sheila McGregor reports that in the old days, "people wore wool from head to foot." Garments

Hand-knit slipper socks, in a variety of colors, from the Faroe Islands. *Spectrum Photofile*

typically knit in the Faroe Islands include caps, underclothes, jumpers, trousers, mittens, *leggold* (footless leggings worn by the women), *skoleistur* (felted footlets worn like slippers), *skolingar* (felted outer shoes worn for extra warmth and to prevent slipping when walking on wet cliffs in traditional skin shoes), and items of the national costume, including *knappatroyggja* (jackets) and *frynsamuffur* (wrist warmers) for men and short-sleeved, patterned bodices for women, knit in red, blue, green, and white.

Bundnaturriklaesis (Triangular Shawl)

By far the garment the Faroes are most famed for is the *bundnaturriklaesis*, or triangular shawl. With a tradition reaching back only about one hundred years, the shawls were knitted by working women for working women—simply, for themselves. They

are unique in their construction, even among the general oeuvre of Nordic shawls, in this way: they feature an extra central gore. Each shawl is made of two triangular panels, joined in the middle by a trapezoidal back gusset, and they are described as having the shape of butterfly wings. This is also partly due to their shoulder shaping, which allows the shawls to remain in place once they are draped around the wearer's shoulders, without any pinning. However, they are also extremely long at their ends, which allow them to be tied around the waist. Additionally, they are "large enough to draw over the head during bad weather," says Pagoldh.

The shawls are begun with a cast-on of hundreds of stitches, the bottom edge of the shawl. Decreases as the work progresses shape the garment as knitting continues toward the neck. The shawls are reversible,

❋ Sandi Wiseheart's Summer Shawlette, her interpretation of the Faroese triangular shawl, knitted by and worn here by Carrie Coker Bishop on her wedding day. You can download the pattern for free at Knitting Daily: http://www.knittingdaily.com/media/p/14016.aspx. *Photo by Shawn Fowler, courtesy of Carrie Coker Bishop*

❇ *Tajarutit* in many colors. These wrist warmers are part of the Greenlandic woman's national costume; red wrist warmers decorated with white beads, such as the oak leaf patterned ones at the right of the photo, are traditional. *Knit* tajarutit—*Greenlandic wrist warmers by Lis Stender; photo by Lis Stender, inukdesign@greennet.gl*

Greenland

Granted home rule by Denmark in 1979, Greenland, for all its associations with Scandinavia, has a very brief, very new tradition of knitting. Susanne Pagoldh, citing a source at the National Museum in Nuuk, traces knitting—of mittens in particular—to the 1850s, when it was brought back to the island by maids who had worked in Danish households. Sheep breeding in Greenland only began around 1906. The first pattern book appeared in 1983, and that was translated from an Icelandic booklet. Until World War II, all knitting in Greenland was accomplished on straight needles, as circulars (and apparently double-pointed needles as well) were unknown till then.

One item thought by many to be essentially Greenlandish are beaded wrist warmers (*tajarutit*). While it's true that beading itself—and in particular, beading of elaborate collars that some credit with influencing Norwegian and Icelandic yoked sweaters—is a phenomenon distinct to Greenland, knitted wrist warmers for men (*frynsamuffur*) do appear in the knitting vernacular of the Faroes and elsewhere. Carol Huebscher Rhoades' 2006 article for *Piecework* expounds on the late-nineteenth century, Northern European craze for beaded wristwarmers, which, she says, followed an already longstanding tradition of general bead knitting. In Greenland, says Pagoldh, beaded wrist warmers were knitted only for women; plain ones were often given as gifts to hunters. Lis Stender, who wrote and self-published a book on the subject, says that red wrist warmers decorated with white beads (and on some occasions, white wrist warmers with red beads) are traditional to the formal costume of women in the western part of the country. They are knitted in thin wool. Wrist warmers made of extremely warm musk ox wool, for daily wear, are usually knit without beads. The unbeaded variety was presumably the first to appear on the shores of Greenland, arriving with Norwegian whale hunters in the early years of the nineteenth century.

❇ Close up of the bead work on the edge of a scarf, inspired by Greenland's wrist warmers, designed by Donna Druchunas. *Photo by Sue Flanders and Janine Kosel*

as traditionally only garter stitch is used, and they are frequently bordered with lace.

Pagoldh mentions two possibilities for the origins of the shawl's name, bundnaturriklaesis: the word for "knit" (*binda*), or "from the fact that the shawl is worn bound at the back."

Norway

Famed for the lice-patterned sweaters of the Setesdal region, Norway has a tradition of knitting that is old enough to predate stranded color knitting by a period of well over a century. Suzanne Pagoldh makes mention of an old example of a knitted relic: a fragment, found in Bergen, dating to about 1500. Nancy Bush, in an article for *Piecework*, claims that this is the oldest knitting discovered in Norway.

(But was it knit in Norway, by a Norwegian? Neither woman will hazard a guess.)

Pagoldh is clearer about the status of knitters of yore: "It should be noted," she writes in *Nordic Knitting*, "that knitting was most closely associated with society's lowest levels: thieves and the poor." No glamour to knitting here. It was utilitarian, workaday stuff. Pagoldh's assertion probably relates to the mandate given by King Christian of Denmark in 1639 that all poorhouse women and girls be taught to knit stockings. (Between 1536 and 1814, both Denmark and Norway were ruled by the Danish monarch.) Norwegian knitting authority Annemor Sundbø writes in *Everyday Knitting*, one of her several excellent books covering the history of Scandinavian knitting: "Most organized knitting instruction seems to have taken place in poorhouses and penitentiaries." Sundbø writes elsewhere that the first Norwegian knitter to be mentioned by name was a stocking knitter named Lisbet Persdotter, who "appears in court records accused of witchcraft in 1634."

Single-color, damask-patterned knitting was prevalent in Norway too, adorning woolen so-called "nightshirts." Norwegians don't seem to have knit many of their own until the nineteenth century; prior to that time, great numbers were imported into the country, largely from England.

Like their more luxurious counterparts—Sheila McGregor mentions a collection of intricate silk jackets held by the Bergen Museum—these garments were knitted in one color with knit-purl eight-pointed stars at their fronts, then embroidered. This arrangement, writes McGregor in her *Traditional Scandinavian Knitting*, that is "seen in Denmark and, indeed, knitted most everywhere in Scandinavia in one version or another." As many other histories of knitting have noted, the eight-pointed star, or "rose" as it's known in Norway, is one of the oldest motifs in textiles generally, found far beyond the confines of Scandinavia in thirteenth-century Spain and perhaps, predating that, Arabia. But still, somehow it has come to be associated with knitting in Norway most of all.

Textured knitting was also common on various regional stockings, perhaps most notably on the *krotasokkar* of the Setesdal region. As McGregor describes them:

> The [twisted] patterns covered the entire leg, with a large "ankle" pattern reaching almost to the top of the calf. The patterns are in fact much simpler than they appear, being made up mainly of twisted plain stitches (*vridd moske*), a popular stitch in textured knitting in Scandinavia, alternating with purl stitches. There are small cables (known as *holekrok*—whole twist; *flete*—pleat; *vre*—twist; every household seems to have had its own names), but these involve only three or four stitches and a single traveling stitch.

As in all cold climates, coverings for hands as well as for feet were paramount. Nineteenth-century Norwegian knitters could be found working on the usual mittens and gloves, but also *rosesaum* mittens, a fingerless variety originating in Hallingdal that were brightly and intricately embroidered with stylized flowers; intricate single-color openwork wedding gloves for both bride and groom; and bead-knitted wrist warmers, worn for special church occasions to add a festive touch and also, writes Carol Huebscher Rhoades in a much-welcomed article on the underreported

✳ An eight-pointed star motif, such as this one featured on the knapsack designed by Sue Flanders and Janine Kosel for their book *Norwegian Handknits*, is found in the knitting of many countries around the world, and yet it has come to be associated with Norway most of all.
Photo by Sue Flanders and Janine Kosel

subject for *Piecework*, to hide "too-short or dirty shirtsleeve cuffs."

Sundbø (*see page* 103), sifting through the knitted rags that, beginning in the early 1980s, came through her shoddy factory, where discarded garments were recycled into new goods such as mattress filler, found herself in a unique position to comment on Norwegian knitting trends throughout the years. "Norwegian culture has always struggled with the conflict between exotic impulses from foreign countries and the desire to keep the Norwegian traditions alive," she concludes in *Everyday Knitting*. Independence from Denmark occurred in 1814, at which point it became necessary to "show Norwegian identity." A knitted display of patriotism was assuredly helped along by the fact that, after the advent of the Napoleonic wars in 1816, blockades prevented the import of foreign knitted goods. Norwegians, who had previously relied on inexpensive machine-knitted goods brought in by Danish and Swedish stocking merchants, were forced to knit for themselves.

Sundbø again: "Today we talk about knitwear with Norwegian patterns. Simple patterns have been given local names, although the motifs originally were universal and had other associations." By way of example, in her book *Invisible Threads in Knitting* she compiles a comprehensive list: crosses (including the Andrew's cross, which appears as both the *kross and kringle* Setesdal design and the Fair Isle OXO), hourglasses and crowns, lines and stars, knots, cables, hearts, anchors, rosettes, and all manner of wildlife. In short, the list encompasses all the designs and motifs that, accurately or not, have come to be associated with the knitting craft of this small, chilly country, even though, as Sundbø is quick to point out, knitting in Norway was not an "everyday" activity until the early nineteenth century, and stranded color knitting did not appear until about 1840.

The latter reached even as far as Lapland. Writes Pagoldh in *Nordic Knitting*: "After the nomadic Laplanders encountered trading shops and knitting, they replaced the hay inside their fur mittens with knitted mittens." Examples of these show largely red, blue, green, and white patterning and often (no big surprise) eight-pointed star motifs. Textile scholar Ruta Saliklis finds influence in the regions of Telemark and Hallingdal for design in the decorative farm painting known as *rosemaling*. "Vividly colored acanthus leaves, foliage, and tendrils could be seen on a range of objects, including house walls and ceilings, furniture, carriages and carts, and farm equipment," she writes. "The knitters naturally decorated their knitting with similar designs."

By 1891, enough interest in preserving what tradition there was in Norway had been generated among the populace at large that the Norwegian Home Art and Craft Association was established. "Traditional craft objects," including articles of regional dress, "became popular souvenirs for city people and tourists," states Annemor Sundbø in *Everyday Knitting*. In 1927, Annichen Sibbern began the arduous process of collecting traditional Norwegian knitting patterns. Sundbø calls Sibbern's resulting book, *Norske Strikkemonstre*, the first pattern book published in Norway, a "knitting bible." A number of years of utter disinterest in knitting were to follow. A resurgence of enthusiasm is credited by American knitting historian and designer Donna Druchunas to Dale of Norway, which began designing sweaters for the Norwegian winter Olympics teams in 1956; by Sundbø to the designer Per Spook and his "modern" Norwegian sweater designs in 1981; and by Sundbø again to the "'genuine' Norwegian products" that flooded the market when Norway was awarded the Winter Olympic Games in 1994. And so the cycle of tradition began anew.

An example of richly patterned mittens (c. 1950) from Norway's vast trove of decorative knitting.
Credits: Photos courtesy of Norsk Folkemuseum

Lusekofte

The lice pattern is the smallest pattern that can be created in stranded two-color knitting. It is, quite simply, a single contrasting stitch of white on a vast sea of black—the colors traditionally used in Setesdal, the region with which the lice pattern has become virtually synonymous. It spawned a whole breed of sweater in a tiny, inland valley in Norway, which in turn would go on to become the defining garment of Norwegian identity: the *lusekofte*.

Strangely (except in the context of knitting history, where plenty of "fact" is a border-hopping mishmash), the lice pattern probably didn't originate in Norway, or even in the valley of Setesdal, where in the mid-nineteenth century it managed to wriggle into the regional costume. Annemor Sundbø, who wrote a definitive if highly personal and quirky book on the subject of *lusekofte*, finds evidence of the louse in a variety of places: in the English spotted frocks written about in the early nineteenth century; in the Faroese sweaters known as I*slender*, worn by fishermen and trappers; and in coastal sweaters from the Finnish islands. It may have been knit right into the fabric; it may have been sewn or otherwise napped in to create a warm inner pile. But who knit it first, and where? It's just another of the great mysteries of knitting.

As to how the sweater, if not the pattern speckling it, entered the Norwegian knitting vernacular, that is a lot more certain and well documented. Around 1840, the residents of the southern valley of Setesdal—a notoriously dandy-ish bunch, if accounts are to be believed—decided the time had come to update their folk costume. The men

✳ Selbu run amok! An ensemble of selbuvotter patterned garments by the Norwegian fashion designer Per Spook. *Photo by Anne Hansteen Jarre; Copyright Nasjonalmuseet for kunst, arkitektur og design/The National Museum of Art, Architecture and Design*

swapped their short, baggy trousers for long ones, and their all-white sweaters for a strange-looking cropped jacket. A bit later, an additional change was adopted: the dappled variety of sweater that is currently under discussion here. In Sundbø's account, though, two-color stranded patterns had been creeping toward the valley from all sides for a couple of decades. She makes mention of blue, black, and red *toridalstroya* from regions around Setesdal as early as 1936.

The *lusekofte* patterns of Setesdal were allover designs, in black and white to "provide a foil for the brilliance of embroidered and bound cuffs, neckband and front facing, all finished with silver or pewter buttons," writes Sheila McGregor in *Traditional Scandinavian Knitting*. The lice distinguished the sweaters "from common working jackets called *grautekupta*," says Sundbø. The embroidered trim

(according to Sundbø, a "purely Setesdal folk art tradition" called *loyesaum*) was simply transferred from woven jackets. "Worsted cloth was embroidered free-hand in red, green, blue, yellow, lilac, rose, brown and/or white from soft, four-ply yarn, then stitched to the cuffs and collar," Sundbø explains. According to Pagoldh, the earlier the example of the sweater, the plainer its embroidery.

Originally, the bottom-most part of the sweater was knit in plain white wool; this was because it was customarily tucked into the tops of men's trousers and was not seen in public. Why waste wool and patterning on the ostensibly invisible? Showing the white was therefore considered akin to showing your knickers—scandalous!

The variety of patterning possible with the humble louse is as varied as the knitters' imagination—which is to say, pretty near infinite.

✢ Treasures from Sundbø's ragpile: cast off, hand-knit sweaters from all over Norway and Scandinavia. Top right: The *lusekofte* of Setesdal prominently and exuberantly features the lice pattern on the body of the sweater and rich *loyesaum* embroidery at the neck and cuffs. Bottom right, a Selbu-patterned cardigan; top left, the iconic Norwegian Fana Kufter. *Photo by Annemor Sundbø*

edge, but never decorated the edge itself. "It was normal to have quite different patterns at the yoke, top of sleeve and cuff. All the patterns . . . are in very much the same style and combine without effort," she writes. "A unity of design comes from this."

And a certain unity of a nation. Even today, the lowly louse, and the *lusekofte* it adorns, is the abiding symbol of Norwegian heritage, worn by common folk, royalty, and celebrities alike.

Selbuvotter

By now, the story is famous: how a teenaged milkmaid named Marit Guldsetbrua Emstad knit a pair of black-and-white mittens and started a trend that would persist, and indeed blossom, for decades. This is the sort of stuff that legends are made of, but in the case of Emstad, it was the basis for an entire, factual industry.

Until the mid-nineteenth century, citizens of the isolated northern Norwegian town of Selbu wore mittens fashioned of *nålbinding* to church on Sundays. Sheila McGregor reports in *Traditional Scandinavian Knitting* that these mittens were sturdy but plain and shapeless. In stark contrast to other local crafts, according to Annemor Sundbø, *tela tagliata*, an Italian textile technique for making linen lace, was what Selbu was renowned for, which she posits must have been a source of inspiration for Emstad. Lying at a major crossroads for trade between the Norwegian district of Trondheim and Sweden—a route that also linked to other trade routes into Russia, Armenia, and Turkey—the tiny town of Selbu had numerous sources for pattern inspiration. "Patterns typically associated with Selbu today can be seen in some of the earliest pattern books from Italy, France, Switzerland, and Germany from the sixteenth and eighteenth centuries," writes Sundbø.

One day, one of Emstad's fellow milkmaids knit a pair of black-and-white patterned stockings for their employer. He was so pleased with them he asked Emstad if she was able to knit something similar. "She took up this challenge and by the

Sundbø points to the fashioning of characteristic motifs like the St. Andrew's Cross; the *kringla*, or wheel of life; eight-pointed roses; eyes; zigzags; and waves. But almost any pattern can be constructed with such a basic element, and the *lusekofte* provided an ample platform on which to experiment with one of them, or five, or ten.

McGregor identifies certain styles by region. In Valle, each pattern was offset by double lines and a diamond-and-cross pattern mid-yoke. In Bykle, patterns may have reached up to the sweater's

Annemor Sundbø

A nnemor Sundbø is a true historian of Norwegian knitting. In 1983, quite to even her own surprise, she became the owner of Norway's last "shoddy factory," a mill where woolen rags are recycled into fill for quilts, mattresses, and sleeping bags. Among the rags she discovered a veritable treasure trove of Norwegian and Scandinavian knitting history: fishermen's ganseys; rose-patterned sweaters and Icelandic sweaters; lusekofte and Selbu mittens; socks and underwear; slippers and red-tasseled caps. Her resulting book, Everyday Knitting, is an absolutely essential reference for anyone interested in Norwegian or world knitting, and her follow-up, Setesdal Sweaters, is an impressively comprehensive study of the Norwegian lice pattern. Not surprisingly, she is also a knitter in the Norwegian tradition, as well as a teacher of knitting design.

Sundbø herself, sorting through the never-ending mound of textiles at her shoddy factory. *Credits: Photo of Sundbø, Ånund T. Flateland: Leonard Jansen collection; "treasures" photographed by Annemor Sundbø*

"Lice pattern has become an identity mark and a concept of a Norwegian hand-knitted sweater. The Setesdal sweater has been a source for thousands of new variations and modernized design. In Setesdal, the sweater belongs to the men's folk costume. For all Norwegians the sweater is a folk garment, which can be worn for all purposes, as much as for an audience with the Royal King, as for everyday use and for skiing. For me, personally, I have had a chance to study my rag pile and gotten know how much inspiration the patterns have given knitters through the last one hundred years, and I have studied many thousands of photos from before 1900, and I know more or less all the family and farm styles.

"My book *Setesdal Sweaters* gives samples from authentic sweaters from the past, and some samples from the rag pile. I find a great importance in keeping traditional designs alive. They belong to a universal symbol language. Most knitters regard a design as something to please the eye, but motifs and ornament are communication without spoken language, without borders or taboos. Traditional knitting is handed over from a time when the knitted items were gifts, amulets, and protection not only against weather and wind, but also against the dark and evil. In Setesdal it is important to copy old sweaters so they can be accepted in the Setesdal men's folk costume, but also this tradition has changed over time with different styles and wool quality. The costume sweater always has hand-stitch|ed| embroidery, an individual expression, a freehand outline with strict rules but repeating like a poem with rhythm.

"I love Lisa Anne Auerbach's lice-patterned 'graffitti' sweaters. She is using tradition perfectly connected with her personality and individual expression. I am proud that she has used motifs I have rescued from my rag pile. I also love the red lice-patterned Agnus Dei, God's Lamb in a knitted masterpiece from 1748. In this gap it is a red thread, a connection, a communication, and protection.

"When design becomes a language for you after studying symbol, it is more and more exciting to 'read' the message. I am very interested in recreating and copying as close|ly| as possible to get to the original; I myself am not so keen to modernize and create new styles, but I don't

mind other knitters doing it—as long as they are not copying other knitters' ideas for commercial use. When I knit something for myself, I am more concerned that the wool quality fit the purpose rather than copying a traditional pattern.

"When I started knitting and was knitting under the desk in school, and spent hours in knitting shops, I knitted what was fashionable at that time, and it was a fashion wave with lice-patterned sweaters, but every year the national ski team represented Norway in new-style sweaters. Most of them were inspired from traditional knitting. But now knitting is getting fashionable among the young, even boys. Young people meet itting at cafés, there are blogs and retro art and trash art, third-hand creations, street art, and so on. Things our grandmothers didn't do."

⊞ Selbu socks, whose variety of patterning is nigh on endless. All these were found by Annemor Sundbø at her shoddy factory, Torridal Tweed. *Photos by Annemor Sundbø*

following summer had managed to knit a pair of mittens with white as the main color, covered all over with black stars copied from bridal embroidery," writes McGregor. When Emstad and her sister turned up for church one Sunday wearing such mittens, "every woman in the parish went home with only one idea in her head: to knit herself a pair of black and white mittens with an even better pattern . . . and a new item was added to the local folk costume."

Pagoldh in *Nordic Knitting* describes the copious mitten stitchery that played a part in every wedding in Selbu: "All of the male wedding guests expected to take home mittens, but the bride didn't have to knit them all—the women guests helped. A few days before the wedding, the women guests would show up with mittens for the bride. The mittens were hung up in a particular order in the bride's loft. For large weddings, there could be a hundred or so pairs of mittens. It was the bride's duty to see that each pair of the mittens went to the right man. A woman who had knitted a pair of mittens got to take them home again with her husband. It was exciting for the young and unmarried women to see who got their mittens." This on top of the fancy stockings the bride herself was expected to knit for the bridegroom, his father, brothers, and his in-laws.

Sundbø writes that the mitten patterns were highly personal affairs, containing motifs "closely associated with the wearer." These included the now omnipresent Norwegian star, and "crosses, anchors, hearts, wreaths, flowers, the tree of life, hourglass, dogs, lions, men, women, ring dancers, letters, numbers, initials with crowns, and family crests with hearts," Sundbø records. The list also included clovers, lilies, rosettes, spiders, reindeer, stags, moose, and on and on and on. Many of the motifs were copied from other crafts such as embroidery or wood carving, where others were taken straight from nature.

Knitting in Selbu might have remained a quaint local custom if it hadn't been for the decline of the millstone industry that had previously formed the base of the little town's economy. By this point (1900), townspeople had managed to set up a small cottage industry for themselves, knitting and selling their mittens. It sputtered along until just after World War I, when the Selbu style of two-color knitting became phenomenally popular in Oslo and beyond. Demand and a strong need for income led to a steady and unfortunate decline in quality until 1934, when the Selbu Handiwork Cooperative was founded. Says Pagoldh, "The center procured yarn, standardized patterns, and bought and sold garments. Another responsibility was to control and preserve the well-known Selbu quality. Garments were graded into various classes, and quality was guaranteed."

Even men took up the needles in the cause for cash. From here, Selbu patterning moved from mittens and gloves to socks and sweaters, and the rest, as they say, is knitting history.

Fanakufter

Perhaps only slightly less famous than sweaters from Setesdal or Selbu, the cardigans named for the Fana district near Bergen, where they were part of the traditional man's costume (although

Sundbø says they originated on Norway's western coast) still share several of their characteristics. They feature lice patterning like the former, and a star pattern like the latter. They're knitted in two colors, like both of them. And like both of them, they are knit in the round in three sections (body and sleeves) from the bottom up, with the right side facing in order to keep track of the pattern. Here is Annemor Sundbø's description of the garment, an iconic Norwegian design in its own right: "The classic Fana sweater is striped with a lice pattern. The stripes are all the same width and the lice are knitted in a contrasting color. The lower border on the body and arms is made up of checkered pattern, while a star pattern is knitted across the shoulders. The next opening is square and usually faced with hand-woven ribbon." Such strictures may help explain why the Fana sweater enjoyed a bit less worldwide renown than its cousins, which allowed for more creativity and whimsy in the design process (although parents of daughters of a certain age will recognize the tell-tale patterning on the cardigan of the now-retired American Girl doll Kirsten, who, despite this traditional Norwegian garb, was meant to hail from Sweden).

The sweater started out as a pullover, worn under a vest and tucked into trousers, and therefore was knitted to be formfitting. Around 1900, according to Pagoldh, it became a cardigan, stitched up of fine, two-ply yarn in white and either black or brown on double-pointed needles. "The front opening was cut and edged with woven bands," she adds. Pagoldh identifies the blue-and-white colored sweaters as being predominantly for children.

The ever-tireless historian Annemor Sundbø speculates on the origins of the striped sweater and its entry into the Norwegian knitting vernacular. She cites a Faroese pattern book containing seven blue-and-white striped undershirts ("but I have no evidence documenting that these pre-date the Fana sweater" she writes in *Everyday Knitting*) and

TECHNIQUE

The Selbu Star

It is believed that the Selbu star, or snowflake pattern, was the first two-color work to appear in Norway. As the story goes, Marit, a young farm girl from Selbu, Norway, created the first pair of two-color mittens featuring the Selbu star pattern. She wore these warm mittens to church and caused great enthusiasm among the parishioners. Since that fateful day in church, the Selbu star has become one of the most popular motifs used in Norwegian knitting. Here's a basic pattern for a Selbu star.

MATERIALS

Dale of Norway Heilo (100% wool; 109yds/50g per ball); 3 balls Black #0090 (MC) and Option 1: 2 balls Red #4018 (CC). Option 2: 2 balls White #0017 (CC).
Size 5 (3.74mm) circular needle – 24"
stitch markers

GAUGE

24 sts and 30 rows = 4" [10 cm] in two-color St st. Adjust needle size as necessary to obtain correct gauge.

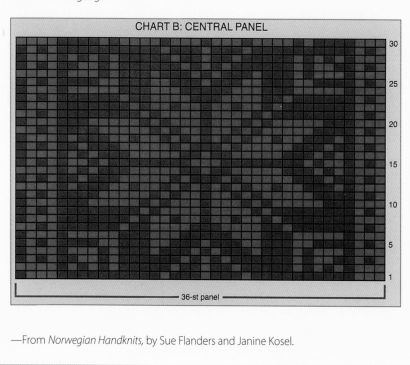

—From *Norwegian Handknits,* by Sue Flanders and Janine Kosel.

Norwegian inheritance records dating to 1837, although she finds no evidence of lice patterning in the sweaters listed there. She contemplates the blue-and-white striped sweaters worn by French and Belgian sailors, the uniforms of professional rowers mentioned by Charles Dickens, machine-knitted Danish undershirts from the 1750s, and

❄ Two varieties of the classic Fana sweater (a little worse for wear after their sojourns in Annemor Sundbø's ragpile). *Photos by Annemor Sundbø*

the striped sweaters found in paintings by Adolph Tideman. Still unsatisfied with her discoveries, Sundbø speculates that the "Fana" designation originally referred to the *Fana-trøye* (which is how Pagoldh classifies this entire genre). Sundbø claims the *Fana-trøye* was an all-white dress sweater with a ruffled appearance and plain/purl-stitch checkerboarding on the bottoms of the sleeves and hem and across the shoulders. (In fact, many

quintessential two-color Fana sweaters show such checkerboarding, translated to two-color knitting.)

Sundbø feels confident, at least, in one fact about Fana: The sweaters were a typical engagement gift, only to be given once the intended had actually proposed, so as not to risk the relationship coming to an end. Which of course begs the question: is Fana where the old boyfriend sweater legend originated?

Stocking Caps

"Hardly any garment is more 'Norwegian' than the red tasseled caps," Sundbø writes in *Everyday Knitting*. Red caps were symbols of protest against the Nazis in World War II; in fact, they were outlawed for a time by the police in Trondhjem for this reason, according to Susanne Pagoldh. But the caps had a much more longstanding tradition throughout the country, dating back to at least the early eighteenth century. As Sue Flanders and Janine Kosel report in *Norwegian Handknits*, folk elves known as *Nisse* are depicted wearing red stocking caps. "Bachelors wore red caps as symbols of their 'freedom,'" says Sundbø; married men wore (coincidentally?) grimmer dark brown or black caps. By the late eighteenth century, so popular were red caps that they were being mass-produced on knitting machines.

But caps of all sorts seem to have been ubiquitous throughout Norway for centuries. Men wore them, awake and asleep, and removed them

This red stocking cap, designed by Sue Flanders and Janine Kosel, was inspired by the *Nisse*-style hats worn by Norwegians in an act of defiance against the Nazi occupation during World War II. *Photo by Sue Flanders and Janine Kosel*

only "in church on Sundays," reports Pagoldh. Redundantly, they could also be worn under hats. At one time, nightcaps were given by new brides to their husbands the morning after their wedding night.

In Telemark, caps were close-fitting, peaked, and tasseled, knitted up in two colors with randomly repeating patterns. In Nordhorland, they featured bands of red stars highlighted with yellow, green, and blue accents. In Hordaland, they were dark blue with patterns of stars. In Rogaland, they were edged with pile and topped with a colorful tassel. And Sundbø remembers from her own childhood in the 1960s: "Every sport had cap fashions. Ski jumpers used blue caps with a white stripe on the brim and a little white tassel . . . Cross country skiers . . . used a kind of cap which was reminiscent of a helmet, buttoned under the chin. The 'Kleiva' cap with patterns from Fana sweaters had a large tassel . . . Skaters and all skating enthusiasts all used caps like the one worn by the famous Norwegian skater, World Champion, 'Hjallis,' in the 1950s."

Solveig Hisdal

A sweater from the Fall/Winter 2009 collection, inspired by Hisdal's trip to Beijing. *Photo and design by Solveig Hisdal for Oleana*

Solveig Hisdal is an acclaimed Norwegian textile designer and recipient in 2000 of her country's most coveted design honor, the Jacob Prize. Since 1992, Hisdal has been the primary designer for Oleana, a company founded that same year to create new textile industry jobs in Norway, at a time when so much industry work was being outsourced to countries where labor was cheap.

Although Hisdal's collaboration with Oleana focuses on design and the making of machine-knitted garments, in 1997 she authored the book *Poetry in Stitches*, for which she wrote patterns for twenty hand-knit sweaters. The book became an instant sensation, featuring as it did not only sweater patterns exhibiting her bright, intricate design trademarks, but also the Nordic artifacts that inspired them. Intimations of Setesdal, Selbu, and *nattrøjer* are all present in both her Oleana designs and her book, once tragically out of print and commanding used prices in the $500 range (and happily, recently re-released by Unicorn Books). Intricate, repeating motifs of leaves, flowers, and stars pervade; a cardigan may be reminiscent of knitted Dalarna sweater sleeves. All of this goes to prove that Hisdal is that most exciting of paradoxes: a forward-thinking visionary historian who fashions things that are new and unique from things that have come before.

"I learned to knit in grade school, but I must admit that I never became a very clever hand knitter. In *Poetry in Stitches* I have written about my first try. So I would probably not have made a hand-knitting book if I was not asked by a publisher and then decided to give it a try. The design process has always been the most important part for me. I have not made any hand-knitting designs since I made *Poetry in Stitches* and two designs for the book *Norsk Strikkedesign*.

"I have always been interested in designing clothes in general. To me, tradition has meant a lot, both the knitting tradition and what I find as inspiration in our folk costumes. My first hand-knitting design in the early 1990s was inspired by both these things. The colors, the patterns, the structures, the details, and the embellishments (I used glass beads on some of the patterns) were all easily recognizable as part of the Norwegian tradition.

"It was a great joy for me to look into our museums to find so many beautiful garments, both knitted and woven. I found lots of pieces with beautiful embroidery, hand-printed wool and cotton, damask and brocade in materials like wool, silk, cotton, and linen. This gave me an important look into our textile history. I have used my knitting patterns for Oleana in both blankets and woven silk textiles used for skirts.

"When I start with a new design, I may have decided on a theme—with the Oleana collections, I have used impressions from Istanbul, Alhambra, and Beijing (China) in addition to Norway. I start by looking through my photos, books, and magazines to find something that can start the design process—a detail or a color combination that appeals to me. I sketch several patterns, and when I have decided what to go for I draw the pattern in the size that I think will be right (scaling it up and down before I find the right size). I draw it on paper, I copy it, and then I may mix several patterns and work with it until I feel it is how I want

Also from the Spring 2010 collection, an alpaca sweater inspired by the breastcloths that are part of the folk costume of Hardanger, Norway. *Photo and design by Solveig Hisdal for Oleana*

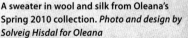

A sweater in wool and silk from Oleana's Spring 2010 collection. *Photo and design by Solveig Hisdal for Oleana*

it. I then draw the pattern on a computer and finally knit it on one of our twenty Shima Seiki knitting machines. Then I have to decide on the color combinations and how many colors to use.

"I like the idea that you can affect (influence) the whole garment—the colors, pattern, and shape.

"For the hand-knitting designs, I made the first samples on my hand-knitting machine. I may go back in time to find inspiration for my work, but it is equally important for me to know what is going on in fashion and design right now."

Sweden

Both men and women began knitting in Sweden sometime in the seventeenth century, although a century earlier, King Erik XIV was the first man in all of Scandinavia, says Susanne Pagoldh, to wear imported knitted silk stockings. Knitted silk "sweaters" were also imported by the wealthy throughout the 1600s. The Swedes, perhaps, learned knitting from exposure to these luxury items. But were they the first in Scandinavia to knit? Or was it the Danes? The debate still rages, according to Sheila McGregor in *Traditional Scandinavian Knitting*, although she opines that the traditions are so similar that it almost doesn't matter. And Marcia Lewandowksi reports in *Folk Mittens* that Gotland Island, to the southeast of the Swedish mainland in the Baltic Sea, is purported to be the home of the oldest knitting tradition not just in Sweden, but in all Scandinavia.

Inger and Ingrid Gottfridsson in their excellent *Swedish Mitten Book* credit the early appearance of knitting to Gotland's role as a major northern European trade center during the late Middle Ages. Natural motifs, of flowers and vines and other foliage, were especially prevalent. The island had a long history of sheep farming and wool gathering, as well as attendant art forms such as dyeing. Juniper and oak bark were used for gray; chamomile and thinmoss (lichens harvested from fences) for yellow; thinmoss and iron vitriol for brown; stonemoss (lichens collected from rocks) for ruddy brown; indigo and woad for blue; cochineal, aniline, and madder for red; and for green, yarn "was first dyed yellow with angsskara, a daisy-like flower, then dipped in indigo. An aqua color was obtained by dipping the yellow yarn into a bath made of vinegar and salt which had been stored in a copper pot."

By the 1650s, tenants living on the governor's estate in the region of Halland had been taught to knit stockings for sale, and possibly also sweaters, by their Dutch mistress (or her servants), and the idea spread quickly from town to town, so the story goes. In Halland, knitters had to import a lot of their wool, as the barren land could not support ample sheep, and additionally, knitting fast became such a popular resource that demand for wool was high. Halland knitters favored monochromatic sweaters with star designs in purl relief, but multicolored patterned sweaters were not unheard of.

To the north of the country, McGregor notes that a love of bright colors was in evidence in the local knitting. In the south, people knit a "vigorous combination of old design patterns with a modern design flair." All across the country, according to Pagoldh, Swedes knit dates and monograms onto a sweater's chest. In some districts, three initials were common; in others, such as Hälsingland, four were used "so that there were the same number of initials as numbers in the date." In Gotland, mittens might be knitted with double-thick collared cuffs that extended as far as the elbow. Mitten patterning here—and stockings, caps, suspenders, and sweaters often followed suit—was typically a repeat; patterning extended on all sides of the thumb, breaking off only to allow the incorporation of a contrast pattern, often ivy, according to the Gottfridssons, at the wrist.

James Norbury in *Traditional Knitting Patterns* postulates that Sweden had no native color knitting tradition of its own, but rather developed it from the craft of Danish knitters. Garments were often fulled for extra warmth, and Lewandowski notes that wool was often spun with dog hair, for additional water resistance, and with rabbit fur, to give extra softness. On Gotland, wool for work clothes was sometimes strengthened with cow hair. From the seventeenth century onward, both wool and knitted garments were used as a medium of exchange in Gotland, especially with tradesmen from the mainland. And the island's sweater hags collected as many as eight hundred sweaters and

These gloves, which turned up in Annemor Sundbø's ragpile in Norway, show patterning, she says, that is similar to that found on some mittens from Gotland. *Photo by Annemor Sundbø*

other knitted garments apiece (some they knitted themselves) and brought them annually by sea to Stockholm; thus were Gotland knitted goods introduced to a wider audience and wearer-ship.

Lewandowski, perhaps citing the Gottfridssons, makes a few further interesting remarks about the development of the craft. "Over the years," she writes in *Folk Mittens*, "superstitions grew around Swedish knitting. It was believed that garments with patterns winding counterclockwise would bring bad luck and prevent the wearer from entering heaven. It was also considered bad luck to knot together loose yarns. Garments knit by young maidens endowed the wearer with good luck and long life." The Gottfridssons mention that spinning was forbidden during the period between Christmas and Twelfth Night: sheep would languish if anyone dared to drop a spindle.

Knitting continues to thrive in Sweden. Writes McGregor in *Traditional Scandinavian Knitting*, "Many older Scandinavian knitting traditions may be known mainly from museum specimens but in Sweden the craft is alive and well and can teach us a great deal." Knitting historian and designer Elsebeth Lavold, creator of the fascinating Viking Knits project reports: "A lot of younger people knit. They blog and they are active on the Internet. There is a lively Knitting Society with over twelve hundred members, over thirty local committees, and lots of activities. Knitting cafés are reasonably frequent and there are people knitting art rather than garments. A knitting guerilla [called Masquerade, who] deposits knitted pieces on lampposts and other suitable places, is active."

Two-Strand (Two-Ended) Knitting (*Tvåändstickning*)

Tvåändstickning is a unique, labor-intensive, dense, and almost wholly forgotten method of knitting with, naturally, uncertain origins. The oldest known intact example of it is a (possibly) mid-seventeenth-century glove found under a slag heap in the Swedish province of Dalarna, according to one of two *tvåändstickning* articles published by Linda Sokalski in *Threads* magazine. Susanne Pagoldh writes in *Nordic Knitting* that the technique has been used for decoration in Nordic countries since at least the 1600s. Though the technique may have originated in Germany, and plenty of evidence of it has been found in Norwegian border towns (and a bit in Denmark and Finland), most knitters these days associate *tvåändstickning* with Sweden—a country where, in some provinces, it seems to have been the only method of knitting practiced. McGregor says that in some small outposts, it has never gone out of fashion.

Tvåändstickning is durable, stiff, and extra warm. It looks like no other kind of knitting. When knitted plain—and traditionally, it was knit pretty much exclusively in fine, all-white wool, linen, or cotton, sometimes made extra white with the addition of rabbit hair—its stitches look extra closely packed. When knitted in pattern, the (geometric) pattern

---

TECHNIQUE

Tvåändstickning/Twined Knitting

A center pull ball is necessary for twined knitting. Hold both strands of the working yarn (one from the ball center and one from the outside of the ball) in your working hand (left or right depending on your knitting style) and separate the strands with your index finger. Knit the first stitch with one of the strands. To knit the next stitch, pick up the other strand and wrap it clockwise over the first strand and knit the stitch. Then pick up the first strand you knit and wrap that clockwise around the strand just used for the second stitch and knit with that. Keep knitting by alternating strands in this manner. If you are knitting correctly, your working strands will become twisted around each other and you will need to stop at the end of each needle row and untwist your yarns. Also, the back side of your work will have an even "twining" of stitches that run in the same direction.

Purled twined stitches are worked in the same manner by wrapping them clockwise around each other but are held to the front of the work, as in a normal purl stitch.

—From Wendy J. Johnson, Saga Hill Designs

This *tvåändstickning* man's church mitten from late nineteenth-century Dalarna is fashioned from double-spun white one-ply wool. The fringe is attached with a row of crochet, and embroidery decorates the thumb and the back of the mitten. *Courtesy of Nordiskamuseet*

stitches (called *krokmaskor*) are raised from the surface of the fabric to give a surprising depth and subtle three-dimensionality. When knit in multiple colors, its difference from some simple Fair Isle patterning is not immediately apparent—not until you turn the work inside out, that is, and notice, as Sokalski notes, a distinct absence of floats. And herein lies the secret to *tvåändstickning*: there are no floats because the yarn—and as the name clearly indicates, it is used two strands at a time, one from each end of the ball, and in the case of multicolor *tvåändstickning*, one strand from each ball of color—is twisted before each stitch is knit so that the strands are continuously alternating. *Tvåändstickning* features a stitch that exists only within its peculiar domain: the crook stitch, which is made by alternating knit and purl stitches, from first the yarn in front, and then the yarn behind the needles.

Tvåändstickning is nothing if not painstaking. Here's how Sokalski describes it in *Threads*: "[H]old the yarn in your right hand, one strand in front (or below) your index finger and the other between your middle fingers. Pick up the strand below your index finger by tilting your index finger into position, and use it to knit the next stitch, which results in a half-twist of the two strands. Then insert your index finger between the strands, followed by your middle finger, to return to the starting position." You can purl too, twisting in what seems to be the opposite direction.

Small wonder, then, that *tvåändstickning* was less commonly used to construct sweaters, but was reserved for decidedly more diminutive projects like stockings, socks, gloves, and, above all, mittens (Pagoldh points out that the durability of *tvåändstickning* was especially appropriate for stocking heels and work mittens). However, McGregor mentions in *Traditional Scandinavian Knitting* a white *tvåändstickning* sweater variety knitted with "small seeding patterns in alternating blue and red bands" that was favored by fishermen and seal hunters and may have had its origins in Iceland or the Faroes.

In the province of Dalarna, *tvåändstickning* was also used to knit the sleeves of men's and women's

Elsebeth Lavold

Swedish knitwear designer,
Elsebeth Lavold

Elsebeth Lavold is a Scandinavian (her designation) knitter and textile designer. In the mid-1980s, she took the first steps toward what would become her Viking Knits Project—translating Viking and Iron Age interlace patterns into knitting. It's no exaggeration to say that knitting enthusiasts have gone absolutely bananas for this project in which, she says, she coupled her "passion" for braided patterns with her "long-term interest in archaeology."

In 1997, the exhibition "Knitting along the Viking Trail" opened at the Textile Museum in Borås, Sweden, the beginning of an international tour which, to date, has included twenty museums and exhibition halls and is currently ongoing. In 1998, Lavold's book, Vikingamönster i stickat (Viking Patterns for Knitting) was published in Sweden, followed by translations into Norwegian, Danish, Finnish, German, and English. It hasn't stopped there. Lavold is currently at work on a fourth book of Viking Knits and has begun marketing her own line of natural yarns, all of which are suitable for Viking-ly undertakings.

"I usually introduce myself as a Norwegian, born in Denmark, but nowadays functionally Swedish. Let me explain: I was born in Denmark, I learned to speak, read, and write in Danish, and I still speak Danish fluently. My Danish heritage is very much alive and up to date. I am a Norwegian citizen, although I wasn't born there and I have never lived there. I speak a kind of 'vacation Norwegian;' not perfect, but with enough of the correct sounds for people to identify which part of the country my family comes from. I have, by now, lived in Sweden the longest part of my life, over forty-five years, and still I don't feel Swedish. And I guess I never will. I feel at home here, it is a society with which I am thoroughly familiar, and which I understand. In short, I consider myself Scandinavian. I don't know to what extent it shows in my design.

"I'm sort of a square peg in a round hole. I have never fit into the different textile groupings in Sweden. I'm not a 'crafts' kind of designer, since I don't work in a textile tradition. I'm not a 'design' kind of person—to me, the process is as important as the result. And I'm not a 'fashion' kind of person, since I want my designs to be long-lasting, or at least, not just part of the latest fad. I enjoy working in a tradition, but I had to invent the tradition myself, which happened in the course of living my life and following my interests and inclination.

"Just designing garments was never a driving force for me. Technical challenges are a necessary part of my design. Another aspect is the joy of knitting, the repetitive movements of the hands, the conscious mind being just slightly occupied, leaving the deeper layers in peace to do their thing. Flow and effortless attention are other words for the same thing. That is truly among the things that make life worth living and which deepen the understanding of the self and the world.

"When I started to explore whether it was possible to knit Viking Age cable patterns, it was partly because I had always found Viking Age artifacts so beautiful and somehow modern. But without the technical challenge of finding an easy and beautiful way of reproducing those cable patterns, it might never have become more than a couple of pretty designs. For me, it is the combination of the technical challenge and working in a traditional context that touches me on a deep level, and has helped me develop my own style. My biggest problem is the white sheet of paper, too many choices, anything is possible—here the Viking Knits help me focus on what is integral to me.

"Among the first artifacts to catch my attention was a bronze buckle, five inches long with a border consisting of several different patterns (p. 50 in Viking Patterns for Knitting). It has been the inspiration for several designs. Anything can trigger a new design. Sometimes it's a yarn or a color, or I need a soothing trance knitting project (the kind where the hands do the work and the mind can take time off). Sometimes it's a new garment type or shape, sometimes an ornament or the placement of an ornament (I once made a man's sweater inspired by an Italian bathroom tile) that starts the design process. Many of my garments have a story connected to them, about the origin, the trials and tribulations involved in producing them:

"'Vebjörg' from Viking Patterns for Knitting has a yoke at the back made with mitered corners. This was when I had just discovered that it was possible to miter corners in patterns. After working it out in a basic lattice cable pattern, this was my first tryout in an irregular cable pattern—and quite nice if I may say so.

"'Menja' from The First Viking Knits Collection started with the collar, shaped with short rows. Getting the shape and the pattern to work together took some knitting and reknitting, and echoing the garter stitch by knitting on a garter strip at the hem is a neat detail that enhances the garment.

"'Hjördis' from The Second Viking Knits Collection started with the swagger shape and the pattern panels, balanced by the shawl collar

For Lavold, inspiration for the Nanna sweater came from a buckle from Norway.

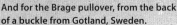
And for the Brage pullover, from the back of a buckle from Gotland, Sweden.

Lavold's Viking design for Menja

and the possible/probable contacts between peoples.

"I don't have a favorite technique, but I am drawn to any pattern or technique that doesn't require a lot of attention, so I can get into 'Zen mode' quickly. I don't have a favorite garment, but I have noticed that I make a lot of garments with mock turtle collars (which are staples in my own wardrobe). I also love simple shells/tank tops and big chunky cardigans. I tend to favor yarns in the U.S. 4–11 range. I'm a loose knitter, so I can't hold on to really thin needles, and I hate knitting with broom handles (I once knitted a fur vest on 20 mm needles—I'll never do that again).

"I hope the Viking Knits project has empowered knitters, given them courage to attempt to create their own knitted pieces. I also hope that it has shown that knitting is a craft with an unlimited potential for expression, both on a personal and on a technical level. And I hope that it has shown that tradition and innovation can go hand in hand."

and the plain sleeves. The hat was an early trial of the pattern, where, after a repeat, I realized it would be too small for anything. Waste not, want not, and I turned it into a hat. The shape of the hat derives from the fact that there are six panels in the pattern part.

"'Inggun' from *The Third Viking Knits Collection* started with an idea of a moss stitch vest with seams and fake seams dividing the garment into sections. The 'seam' lines could then continue and become armhole edgings. The collar is a style I had already tried in a jacket for *Vogue Knitting*, but here used with a different cable panel.

"'Brage' (from the exhibition) has quite a complex story with many levels to it. I started off wanting to make a sweater containing the three key elements of Viking Age art, which are also the three key elements of this project: a cable pattern, runes, and animal ornamentation. I chose the most complex cable panel—the Lillbjärs panel—the only one that doesn't conform to the standard (in this panel the increases and decreases are made on the wrong side as opposed to the right side, which is usually the case, and the decreases are purled—not knitted), but it was well worth the trouble. It was placed on one side so I had to calculate how many extra stitches were needed to make up for how much the cables pulled the fabric together and how to make the ribbing flow seamlessly into the cable pattern. Then there was the question on what to write with runes. I made the sweater for my husband. His name is Anders, which is a Christian name and thus not suitable for Norse. When we were married, my cousin, who teaches religion, named my husband and myself Idun and Brage, the Norse Goddess in charge of the apples of youth, and the God of mead and poetry. Since my husband used to be a singer/songwriter and spices his own schnapps, Brage was a given, and with him being born in the year of the dragon according to Chinese astrology, making a dragon appliqué was an easy choice. And I found the perfect dragon motif on the back of a brooch from Gotland.

"I am not an archaeologist or an historian, but I have an insatiable curiosity and an analytical mind. I love trying to put pieces together to see if I can create a larger picture. With the Viking Knits project, I got caught up in creating a typology and finding (and creating) patterns that fit into the categories. I am working on a sequel, where I have scoured the whole world for patterns of the same type. The working title is *Vikings, Celts and Others*. Now I'm trying to trace the origins of the patterns—ha!—

Lavold's Viking design for Inggun.

Lavold's Viking design for Vebjörg.
*Credits: Photos: Anders Rydell;
photo/drawing composites:
photos—Anders Rydell, drawings—
Elsebeth Lavold*

sweater jackets that are part of the folk costume of several parishes, according to Pagoldh. The sweaters, dating back to the early 1800s, had sewn, button-front bodies. The sleeves were knitted of white and black yarn that was then dyed—most often red, says Pagoldh—and fulled to make what must have been a virtually impenetrable tube of fabric.

All *Tvåändstickning* was knitted in the round on five double-pointed needles; wedding and Sunday-best mittens were often elaborately embroidered with flower, star, and snowflake motifs and decorated with colored pile.

Bohus Stickning

The story of the Bohus Knitting Cooperative is legendary. Deep in the midst of war and economic depression, unemployed stonecutters and their families in the southern province of Bohuslän found themselves in dire need of income. A group

of women hit upon the idea of petitioning the wife of the governor, Emma Jacobsson, to set up a cottage industry in the province. Jacobsson in turn hit upon the idea of a knitting cooperative, although there was, apparently, no surviving tradition of knitting in Bohuslän. And in 1939, the Bohus Stickning Cooperative was founded.

At first, according to Margaret Bruzelius in her article on Bohus for *Threads* magazine, the women knit socks and mittens. Soon after, Jacobsson began to design sweaters with patterned yokes, which were eagerly snapped up by shops. Jacobsson hired other designers until there were six in all—a pantheon familiar by now to all worshipers of Bohus: Jacobsson herself; Vera Bjurström, famed for her embroidered designs, in particular her Feather-Stitch and Slanting Square; Anna-Lisa Mannheimer Lunn, who invented the most popular Bohus design of all time, the Blue Shimmer, and who, says Bohus expert and author of *Poems of Color* Wendy Keele, "introduced the yoke and inset yoke styles to Bohus Stickning;" Annika Malström-Bladini, a talented colorworker; Karin Ivarsson, a latecomer to the co-op, who worked largely in monochrome; and Kerstin Olsson, who worked with shading and geometric patterns.

The designers used, says Bruzelius, "folk motifs from other southerly Swedish sources, avoiding patterns that were in any way reminiscent of other Scandinavian knitting traditions." In all, in its thirty years of existence, Bohus produced more than four hundred original designs, the patterns for which were held as a closely guarded secret until relatively recently. It is held in far greater esteem than Binge—the Halland Knitting Cooperative that preceded it by thirty-one years—whose mission was to resuscitate that region's hand-knitting cottage industry and also, less successfully, according to Sheila McGregor, collect its traditional patterns.

The Bohus knitters were organized into groups by region, and a "leader" selected. Each leader would see to it that yarn and patterns were distributed, collect finished goods, and host a monthly tea where new patterns were sometimes taught. Wool was collected from various national sources and meticulously sorted. (McGregor credits Bohus with saving the native sheep breed, which was then on the verge of extinction.) At first, the collective's yarn was spun in Finland; according to Keele, Finnish mills could produce a finer-weight yarn than Swedish ones. When that possibility dried up with the war, wool was sent to the Swedish Wahlman mill, where it was spun together with angora for a softer product; this is one strong component in the particular hazy effect of Bohus. Keele reports that Bohus would go on to produce four types of yarn in all: Angora (50–60 percent angora, 40–50 percent wool); EJA (the initials stand for Emma Jacobsson Angora) (25–30 percent angora, 70–75 percent wool); Finewool (100 percent finger-weight wool); and Rya (100 percent worsted-weight wool). Colors were selected by Jacobsson herself and worked up by master dyer Gösta Juhlin.

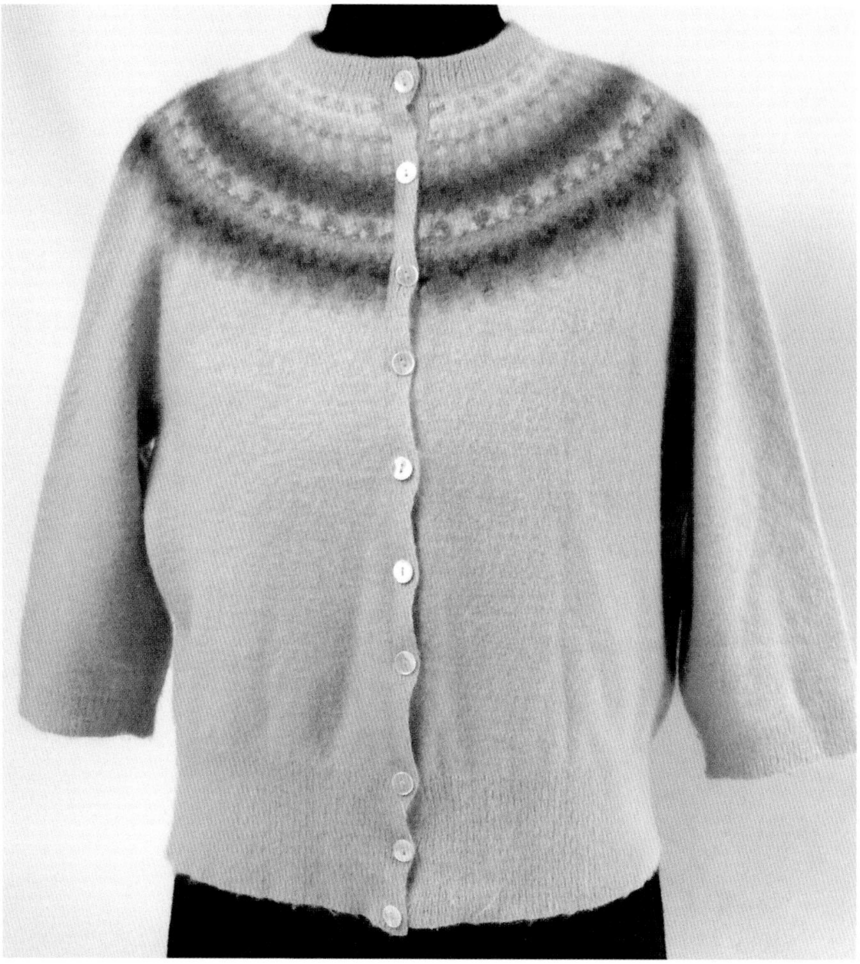

The Dallas cardigan, whose design and colors were chosen by Kerstin Olsson specifically for the American market.

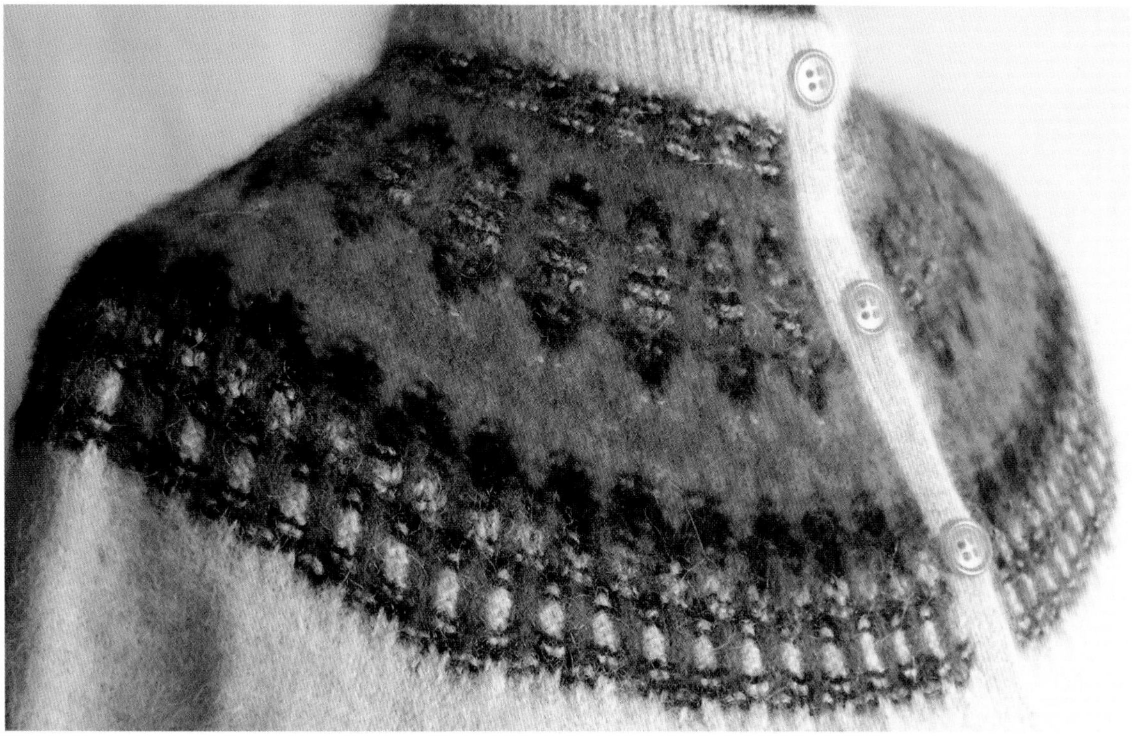

Detail of the Humlan (Bumblebee) yoke, designed by Anna-Lisa Mannheimer Lunn. *Credits: From the collection of Susanna Hansson, originally appearing in the book* Bohus Stickning—Radiant Knits: An Enchanting Obsession *by Susanna Hansson and Wendy J. Johnson, Saga Hill Designs*

The sweaters came to be knit at an exacting nine stitches to the inch on 2.5 mm needles. They featured many color changes—up to thirteen in one yoke alone. The stitch patterns seem simple enough but follow a very specific formula. According to Bruzelius: "Purl stitches on the face of the fabric create two parallel, broken lines of color and increase the intricacy of the color patterning. The color variations are accentuated by the depth and shadow in the fabric's bumpy surface. Slipped stitches distort the knit rows, increasing the fabric's textural interest . . . Stitches are either worked or slipped, and worked stitches are either knit or purled."

The Bohus sweaters were sported by fashionistas and movie stars the world over. And then, the era of Bohus came to an end. By the 1960s, according to the Bohusläns Museum, "The knitting patterns had become so intricate and the wool so delicate that many knitters found the work too difficult" and quit the cooperative. War had

❉ A woman's *spedetröja* from the Skytt district of Skåne, early nineteenth century, which was part of the regional folk costume. This snug-fitting red sweater was knit of fine red wool on circular needles and was meant to be worn peeking out from under the bodice. The bottom is edged with knit-purl checkerboard squares, and most of the body of the sweater is patterned with cables and small diamonds. Green, blue, and red sweaters were traditional to Skytt. *Credits: Courtesy of Nordiskamuseet*

long ended, times were more prosperous, and, in 1969, Jacobsson retired. But the legend has lived on. In 1999, the Bohusläns Museum orchestrated an exhibit that set off a new craze for Bohus, which was echoed in a 2009 Bohus exhibit at the American Swedish Institute in Minneapolis. For this latter event, Bohus knitting instructor and collector Susanna Hansson and textile artist Wendy J. Johnson of Saga Hill Designs developed the book *Bohus Stickning—Radiant Knits: An Enchanting Obsession.* Kits composed of yarn dyed by an original Bohus master dyer, Solveig Gustafsson, are still on offer from the Bohusläns Museum, as well as from Gustafsson's own website.

Regional Sweaters: Ullared Jerseys, *Spedetröja,* and Delsbo Jackets

"From the heavily forested Halland area of Sweden comes the Ullared jersey worn by loggers in the nineteenth century," writes Marcia Lewandowski.

And as would be expected of garments made for outdoorsmen working in frigid temperatures, these sweaters are highly wind resistant and dense, knit in thick black and white wool, then dyed red once the garment has been fulled. Most extant examples seem to date from the 1890s, a period when, according to Sheila McGregor, single-colored jerseys had come to be viewed as "old-fashioned." Cuffs were sometimes crocheted for extra durability, and a central panel bearing the wearer's initials and date of manufacture was once *de rigeur.* The patterning is similar to the Norwegian lice pattern (*lusekofte, see page* 100), except on the Ullared jersey, the lice lie within a grid of squares or diamonds for added visual interest. McGregor describes it further in *Traditional Scandinavian Knitting:* "The all-over diagonal pattern is set within a definite frame made up of a border pattern knitted at the lower edge, up either side of the seam line and across the yoke."

A Delsbo jacket from the Hälsingland region. The white patterns are knit with cotton for a brighter effect, and the whole is trimmed with woven pile. This would have been worn by an unmarried girl on a Sunday afternoon, after church (never in church), when young people gathered to socialize. *Credits: Courtesy of Nordiskamuseet*

In the Skåne region, to the south of Halland, *spedetröja* (deriving from the Swedish word for knitting needle, *speda*, according to Suzanne Pagoldh) entered the folk costume as early as the eighteenth century. They were meant to be close-fitting so as to be worn with ease under a vest, with only their relief-patterned sleeves showing. According to Gail Ann Lambert's thesis project on sweaters, they were similar to Danish damask sweaters in their juxtaposing of purl and knit stitches, and they commonly used twisted-stitch patterns as well. Knit in the round with fine wool in one color, they often sported eight-pointed stars and were frequently fulled so that individual stitches "became unrecognizable," according to Frances Lambert and her *My Knitting Book*. A bit of fancy occasionally prevailed, in the form of silk bands sewn to the neck opening and sleeve hems. The cuffs were sometimes embroidered as well.

Finally, from the east-central region of Hälsing-land come the stranded-knitted Delsbo jackets worn by the region's well-to-do farmers. Black and red and green all over (with a little white cotton thrown in for good measure), these colors typified the "showy" (Pagoldh's word), nineteenth-century garments. Like Ullared jerseys, surviving examples of Delsbo jackets bear dates as well as initials, and as Sheila McGregor points out in *Traditional Scandinavian Knitting*, all that came before such colorwork was plain, textured knitting, usually pullovers for men, cardigans for women. The sweaters in both instances were boxy in structure and replete with patterning. McGregor calls them an "outstanding example" of regional jackets, of which there were myriad variations: "The differing styles of folk costume show very clearly how localized an affair it was," she writes. Her chart for one such jacket has "enough pattern material for half a dozen more!" In fact, it features twelve patterns in all, a large heart occupying a portion of the front, four initials tucked right under the squared neckline, and the date occupying an otherwise (rare) plain band just below.

Finland

Annemor Sundbø posits that nuns in the city of Naantali were knitting stockings as early as the sixteenth century. Susanne Pagoldh is less inclined to date the knitting so early; the nuns' craft may have been *nålbinding*, she thinks. Other authors have speculated that this comparatively late introduction was due first to the prevalence of *nålbinding* in Finland, and second to the vibrancy of its economy, which did not send desperate housewives (or husbands, for that matter) scrambling for a means to supplement meager incomes.

Nevertheless, by the early seventeenth century, knitters in the small city of Naantali were certainly making stockings to export. In fact, stockings were enormously important to life in Naantali—and Finland generally, with men, women, and children all participating in their manufacture, both for sale and for home use. In some regions, stockings were an integral part of a girl's wedding dowry. Pagoldh makes some mention of the knitted stockings of Aland, a group of self-governing islands in the Baltic Sea. She shows examples of wave- or peacock-patterned stockings and writes *Nordic Knitting*: "The tradition of giving stockings as wedding gifts lasted until the nineteenth century . . . [T]he bride . . . lovingly knitted intricate patterns. Otherwise, thick, usually striped, stockings and socks were knitted in red and gray yarn spun from blended wool and linen."

Because of the, shall we say, delicate nature of some knitted garments, which were considered along the lines of underwear, knitting in public in Naantali in the eighteenth century was outlawed, due to what authorities deemed its "shameful" nature. Knitting in public may have also been banned because the authorities thought it took up too much time and encouraged gossiping.

Footless leggings were popular in Finland even as footed socks were common among the populace during the eighteenth century. Pagoldh points out that Finnish women had long had a tradition of wearing different types of coverings on the feet and different parts of the leg. Short socks in winter were worn on the feet, wool leggings on the lower legs, and linen protectors on the knees, the latter two of which were tied into place with cloth bands. Leggings, known as *säärystimet* in Finnish (from *sääri* for "leg") and *benholkar* in Swedish, were also a means to protect the legs in summer while working on the farm. Often enough, they began life as stockings, and when part of the foot had worn away, they were cut off and the remaining portion of knitting was, *toute de suite*, transformed into leggings. In the nineteenth century, Finland was also hit with the Europe-wide cotton craze, and stockings, once knit of wool and felted for extra warmth and durability, were knit from white cotton yarn—at least, special-occasion socks were. At some point, notes Pagoldh, red-and-white striped stockings became all the rage for a time.

As in any cold climate (and more than one-third of Finland lies within the Arctic Circle), hand-knit sweaters were immensely important to the well-being of the local populace. Interestingly, though, sweaters were luxury items, worn only by the well-to-do, all the way up to the nineteenth century, when average country folk began to make and wear them (although it has been suggested that the technique of knitting pullovers had arrived in Finland by the eighteenth century). Some patterns are reminiscent of patterns from other counties— for example, Österbotten's lice-patterned sweaters greatly resemble Setesdal lice-patterned sweaters (*see page* 100), only, as Sundbø writes in her *Setesdal Sweaters*, the patterning travels further up the sleeve. Another difference: The lice are usually made of contrast color on a white background (as opposed to the other way around). Some are made of a unique combination of knitting and crochet (see the description of Korsnäs sweaters on page 122). Some are simple, undyed affairs; some are striped or more intricately patterned, and these were commonly made as gifts from women and girls for men and boys. The richest

❋ Kainuu Flower Mittens have a distinct Eastern influence and may have been a bride's gift to her new mother-in-law or other important family member. Says Finnish knitting designer Tuulia Salmela, "It was common to give handknit stockings as gifts when one married, and the color and patterning are so rich 'they seem to have been made to show off a talent in knitting.' *Photo by Tuulia Salmela*

❋ "My mother-in-law dug these mittens out of her late mother's stash of mittens," says Salmela of this fingering-weight wool pair. They feature a modest striped cuff common to everyday Finnish mittens. *Photo by Tuulia Salmela*

Footless leggings with a simple repeating tree motif. *Photo by Gunnar Bäckman, courtesy of the Ostrobothnian Museum*

patterns in Finnish knitting seem to have been reserved for mittens and gloves, often given as holiday or wedding gifts, and decorated with all manner of flowers, stars, and diamonds, as well as *tvåädnsstickning* (see pg. 110) tassels, and the strong, "luminous" (Pagoldh's word) patterning that so typifies knitting from this chilly country.

After World War I, Finland's Swedish-speaking Martha Collective, seeking to document and preserve the country's textile heritage, sent a woman named Hjördis Dahl on a pattern-gathering expedition around the country. She collected examples from far-flung farms, and just in time. World War II witnessed the destruction of a large part of Finland's knitting heritage, as old sweaters—the surest document of the hand-craft tradition—were recycled into other materials as resources grew scarce.

Nålbinding

It's not knitting, but the almost-lost, arduous needle art of *nålbinding* has a story that unfurls in many regions during certain eras right alongside that of knitting and, indeed, often predates it by centuries. It finds its way into this sub-chapter due to the fact that it was so highly regarded, and so persistently used, in Finland, right up to the nineteenth century—a longer-standing tradition by far than is found in most other needlecraft nations (although historian Ruta Saliklis reports that it is still being used in the Middle East to make mittens; and it is still used for making bracelets by women of the Nanti tribe in Peru). Osva Olsen and Ingvar Svanberg in "Nål*binding* in the Faroe Islands" make mention of a Finnish saying that reflects the significance of *nålbinding*: "He who wore knitted mittens had an unskilled wife."

Incredibly, the first evidence of *nålbinding* is possibly from 6500 BC, in the form of a fragment found in Nehal Hemar in modern-day Israel. (Some historians postulate that it even predates continuous spinning by wheel or drop spindle, due to the fact that a continuous length of yarn is not necessary to its construction. More about that later.) Mesolithic and Neolithic specimens have been found in Denmark and Switzerland, Stone Age bits have been found in Egypt, and, from the time of the Vikings—perhaps *nålbinding*'s most famous era—in England, Iceland, Denmark, Sweden, Finland, Norway, Russia, and Central America. *Nålbinding* is ancient, but the word itself (taken from the words *needle* and *binding* in Norwegian) originated in the 1970s. However, it has many other names, among them looping, knotless netting, looped needle netting, needle-looped fabric, single-needle knitting, eyed-needle knitting, and fancy buttonhole filling, and that's just in English.

Archaeologists and knitting historians were flummoxed by the look of *nålbinding* in the past, often mistaking it for knitting. This is because the

❋ A pair of "Fayum Socks" based on a pair found in Antinoe, Egypt, dated to the fourth to sixth century AD. Nålbinding *and photo by Anne Marie Decker (Sigrid Briansdotter)*

A reproduction of a patterned fragment found in Dura-Europas (current-day Syria). The needle points to one of the few stitches where you can see the difference between the crossed knitting and cross-knit looping variants of *nålbinding*. Both the fragment and the socks were knit by Sigrid Briansdottir, who discovered *nålbinding* while she was an exchange student in Sweden. "The parish I lived in was one of the few where nålbinding had survived. However, at the time, they would only teach it to people who were going to stay in the parish. I returned home, and, five years later, while stuck in a hotel due to a snow storm, I found someone to teach me a variant. I went back to the parish 3½ years after I started nålbinding and [finally!] they showed me what variant they did." Nålbinding *and photo by Anne Marie Decker (Sigrid Briansdotter)*

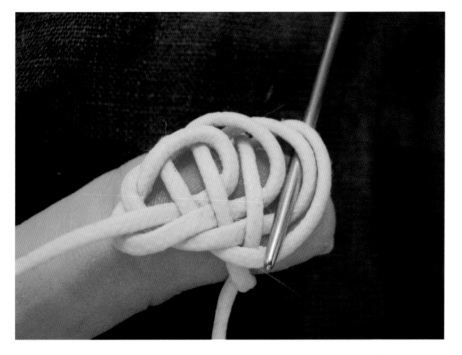

✳ How to *nålbind* #1. Explains Sigrid Briansdotter, *nålbinding* is a single-needle technique that crates "a meshwork of interlocking loops of thread." Nålbinding *and photos by Anne Marie Decker (Sigrid Briansdotter)*

✳ How to *nålbind* #2. The resulting fabric, says Briansdottir, "is generally built spiraling up row by row . . ." Nålbinding *and photos by Anne Marie Decker (Sigrid Briansdotter)*

only way to tell if *nålbinding* is *nålbinding* is to cut a strand from it and see if it unravels—knitting does, *nålbinding* doesn't. Despite its surface similarities, it is a technique that is essentially quite different from knitting. For starters, it is constructed using one large needle, with an eye either at one end or at its center. Into this eye is inserted a *short* length of yarn—in fact, a *long* length would render the technique impossible to carry out. Stitches are made by wrapping loops around a thumb or needle, through each of which the length of yarn is drawn entirely (hence the extreme difficulty in using a long piece of yarn), knotting them and rendering them impervious to the dropped-stitch laddering that plagues knitters. Thus, a chain is formed. The work can be turned at the end of a row, though each new stitch must also be passed through its corresponding stitch on the row beneath it. New yarn is spliced on as the old yarn is used up.

There's actually more than one way to *nålbind*, and the ways have been variously classified. Larry Schmidt in his books on the craft discusses what he calls York stitch, Oslo stitch, and Korgen stitch, which vary, for starters, in the direction of their twist, but at least thirty types of stitches have been identified. The tube of fabric created from this technique is dense, warm, and long-wearing, perfect for mittens, socks and other footwear, hats, bags, nets, and baskets. An early use for *nålbinding* in Scandinavia was for milk strainers, sometimes constructed from human hair.

Korsnäs Sweaters

Korsnäs sweaters (also known as Bosnian crochet, or *smygsmaskvirkning* in Swedish) are a strange and beautiful combination of knitting and tapestry crochet that hail from an almost wholly Swedish-speaking region of western Finland. Weighing as much as two pounds, the sweaters were created beginning in the mid-nineteenth century by young women for their fiancés (although Susanne Pagoldh indicates that they could also be given

❇ Three Korsnas sweaters, showing a variety of shaping, length, and patterning. *Photos by Gunnar Backmän, sweaters courtesy of the Ostrobothnian Museum; from the collection of Karin Rosendahl*

Mittens made entirely of tapestry crochet, the same technique used all around the edges of Korsnas sweaters. *Photo by Gunnar Backmän, courtesy of the Ostrobothnian Museum*

as gifts to especially important members of society, such as midwives and priests) and were meant to indicate the wealth of the wearer. So intricate and labor-intensive were the designs—an admixture of traditional (often traditionally Swedish) designs and the whimsy of the maker—quite frequently the woman making the sweater would require help. Lots of help. If she didn't get it, she might be able to complete a sweater in three weeks time, working nonstop—if she was a master knitter.

Three or four knitters might sit together to work the sweater body in hand-spun three-ply wool, in seed pattern or plain rounds, in four or six colors, each woman working part of a round before turning the work. Writes Pagoldh in *Nordic Knitting*,"The knitted sections of the sweaters had seed patterns in red and blue or red and green on a natural white background. The crocheted parts were always red with figures in blue, green, yellow, light red, orange, or lilac. Both wool and cotton yarns were used. Some dyeing was also done at home." She further notes that the rich coloring may have been the result of the district employing its own dyer.

Donna Druchunas in "Knitting and Crochet: A Marriage Made in History," elaborates further on the technique of creating the Korsnäs sweater: Stockinette stitch knitting was used for the simpler sweater areas and may have shown a patterning of colorwork stripes or a strip of small diamonds at the center of the sweater body. The centers of the sleeves were knitted the same way—in the round, with a small color-on-white pattern. They were crocheted at their bottoms, then knitted, then crocheted again (for cardigans as well as pullovers). Stitches were then sewn where arm openings were to go, and the holes cut. The sleeves followed a similar treatment: crocheted, knitted, crocheted, then sewn onto the sweater. For cardigans, the front of the sweater was cut open and a decorative edging added. A narrow knitted band was attached to all cut-and-sewn seams to hide them.

Everything else on the sweaters was constructed of patterned tapestry crochet, perhaps a successor to *nålbinding*, in which stitches are worked through the back loop only (Druchunas points out that this technique was common in Eastern Europe and Turkey). Crochet, inelastic in nature, keeps the bottoms of the sweaters from stretching out and ensures the garments' durability. Sweaters in museum collections, though clearly worn long and often, are almost all reported to be in excellent condition. Contributing to this may be the fact that necklines on the sweaters are the same front and back; the wearer could alternate front and back, and not create too much wear and tear on one side of his or her beloved sweater.

Hats, mittens, and socks can be made with this combined Korsnäs method as well, although the results, being smaller, are only slightly less stunning.

Entrelac

The technique of knitting entrelac—which literally means "interlaced" in French—is pretty widely evidenced in Scandinavia generally. Diagonally patchworked stockings were common in Norway and Sweden, but many contemporary knitters associate the technique with the designs of American Kathryn Alexander, and with Finland, where it enjoys a rich tradition.

Entrelac is known as *konttineule* in Finnish, and it comes from the word *kontti*, which means a birch-bark backpack or a knapsack that was skillfully woven out of this durable and abundant material. Also known as basket stitch, birch stitch

⁂ A photo of a pair of entrelac socks knitted by designer Tuulia Salmela; here the technique of creating a basket-weave effect is used with only one color, though two, three, or more colors may be employed. *Photo by Tuulia Salmela*

TECHNIQUE

Entrelac Knitting

Entrelac looks a lot more complicated than it is, but the only skills needed are knitting, purling, picking up stitches, and working decreases. You'll also be working short rows for the base triangles, but they're no more than knitting, purling, and turning. Follow the diagram while reading the explanation that follows.

After casting on, you'll start by making a base layer of triangles. The triangles are worked one at a time, back and forth, adding 1 new stitch to each triangle every WS row until the triangle is complete. The triangles "lean" to the right.

Next, you'll pick up and knit stitches along the side of 1 triangle and work a rectangle that "leans" to the left, attaching the top of the rectangle to the side of the adjacent triangle by working an ssk decrease; you'll repeat this until you have created a layer of left-leaning rectangles across the top of the triangles.

For the next layer, you'll work right-leaning rectangles by picking up and purling stitches along one side of a rectangle on the previous layer and attach the top of the rectangle to the side of the adjacent rectangle by working a p2tog decrease; you'll repeat this until you have created a layer of right-leaning rectangles across the top of the first layer of rectangles.

—From Suzyn Jackson, author of *Knit It Together*, published by Voyageur Press

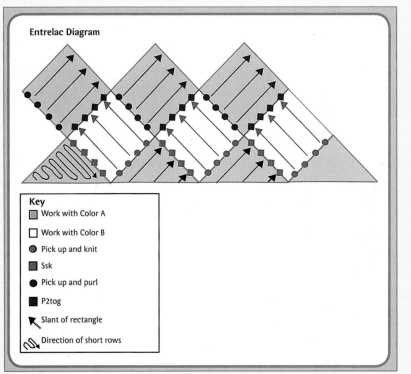

Entrelac Diagram

Key
- ▨ Work with Color A
- ☐ Work with Color B
- ● Pick up and knit
- ▨ Ssk
- ● Pick up and purl
- ■ P2tog
- ↙ Slant of rectangle
- ∿ Direction of short rows

Leena Riihelä and Riihivilla Natural-dyed 100 Percent FinnWool

FinnWool is a fine, soft, lustrous, lanolin-rich wool spun from the fleece of the ancient landrace Finnsheep breed, in Finnish called Suomenlammas. *The breed is native to Finland, although it is being raised in more than forty countries around the world, now, including the United States and Canada. For two hundred years, most of the commercial wool yarns available to knitters and fiber crafters in Finland have been imported, lately from New Zealand. The FinnWool widely available on the international market is actually a blend, mixed in large factory spinneries with wool from other sheep breeds such as merino, Oxford down, Dorset, and Texel.*

Leena Riihelä and her husband, Jouni, former Finnsheep breeders who live outside Helsinki, are among a handful of Finnish artisanal yarn craftspeople who are keeping alive an old and increasingly rare tradition. Using yarns spun to their requirements by Pirtin Kehräämö, a small, nonindustrial mill in Mikkeli, Leena and Jouni natural-dye 100 percent Finnsheep yarns, which they sell both locally and online.

Following another old and vibrant tradition, Leena's mother, Liisa Rajala, works for the Riihivilla webshop designing kits of traditional Finnish mittens in stranded patterns of spruces, tulips, and other natural elements.

"Finnsheep is an old Landrace sheep that has been here for more than a thousand years. It is related to Scandinavian short-tailed sheep breeds, which are genetically close to wild sheep, and it is used to our hard climate.

"Sheep farming has never been a very big industry in Finland. Besides the times of World Wars I and II, most of the wool used in Finland has been imported, even as early as in the 1800s, and sheep have been kept only to get wool for one's own family's use. So traditionally, almost every farm had a few Finnsheep, but not more than that.

"The numbers of Finnsheep have been declining in the past—there are only 5,500 purebreds left in the country—and meat is why sheep are kept now most of the time. Wool is just a byproduct or waste to many farmers. That is really a pity. Many farmers just throw the wool into the compost; they don't know or care to shear the sheep when the wool is at its best and clean, and so if they try to sell wool, which is felted and dirty, no one will buy or want it, of course. So potentially good wool goes to waste because of ignorance. Earlier, when the farms used their own wool, they knew what was good and what wasn't, but now the tradition has been broken, and wool is new to farmers who raise the sheep for meat.

"In recent years, knitting has become more popular again, and many Finnish knitters want to use the wool of Finnsheep to support local farmers and perhaps help save Finnsheep. Even though it might seem economical to raise sheep in warmer countries where sheep can be kept outside all year around, I think it is important for biodiversity that small breeds like Finnsheep are kept alive in their native countries. You never know when their genes, their ability to withstand harsher conditions, or their ability to give birth and feed three lambs instead of the usual one or two of other breeds will be needed in the future.

"There have been projects such as Fine Finnwool and Agrifood Research Finland, for example, that are meant to increase the knowledge of good wool and sheep breeding, and locally they have been successful. Good Finnish wool is available here again.

Japanese indigo—it's ready for the dyebath when bruised spots on the leaves turn blue, according to Riihelä. *Photo by Leena Riihelä*

Velvet pax mushrooms, also used for dyeing, can grow upward of three pounds. *Photo by Leena Riihelä*

"Finnsheep have to be sheared twice a year, in the autumn and in the spring, before the ewes give birth. The wool of Finnsheep is so soft that if it is sheared only once a year, it felts on top of a sheep and is then ruined.

"Finnsheep come in several natural colors, and I love the different natural gray, brown, black, and white shades I get from Finnsheep without dyeing. Besides the colors, the wool is quite soft (not as fine as merino, though) and has very nice luster. I like to use Riihivilla Aarni yarn, [Leena's brand of two-ply sport-weight yarn]. Actually, it is the only yarn I have knitted for the last nineteen years. It is light to knit, and it 'flows' from your needles, yet it is warm, some might even think it is too warm. When I have time, I knit stranded mittens, hats, and sweaters from it (well, I don't have much time for big projects like that anymore, but if I ever had time, that is what I would like to knit). For me, it is difficult to compare it to other wools, because I have so little experience with other wools.

"I have always been interested in nature, sheep, and all kinds of animals, and when I graduated from school, I knew I wanted to work with animals, and that someday I would have sheep. It took ten years before my husband and I got our own farm and Finnsheep, but in the meantime, I had learned about sheep breeding, and also natural dyeing.

"I have never been interested in dyeing yarn just to get colors, which could be gotten much easier from synthetic dyes. It is the history of natural dyeing and the process of getting the color from plants and mushrooms that is my 'thing.' The subtle natural colors pleased my eye ever since I first dyed with natural dyes in 1984; they still do, more than ever. The feeling of doing something the way it was done for centuries, before everything became machine made and industrialized, is important to me, too. I think that must be one reason why other people like to use my yarns—the tradition of it. I think there is a small but growing demand for this kind of yarn.

"I grow some dye plants myself, especially woad and Japanese indigo to get blues, but I also have a friend who grows weld and tansy for me. I use a lot of tree barks and leaves—birch, alder, and oak—and dye with mushrooms that are very common in Finland: red-gilled webcap, other gilled webcaps, and velvet pax. As you know, most of Finland is covered by forests, so there is an abundance of mushrooms in the autumn, and only a very small portion of them gets collected. Historical red dyes, cochineal and madder, I buy from Europe. They don't grow well in Finland, but they are such good sources of red and purple that I use a lot of them. I have heard that some commercial yarns take the natural dyes differently (and not necessarily worse, sometimes even better) because there are

Finnwool Mittens from kits designed by Liisa Rajala.
Photo by Leena Riihelä

chemical treatments like superwash in them that affect the dyes. Our yarn is not treated in any such way.

"I think it gives a different feeling to knit from wool that still smells of sheep (lanolin) and is not industrially processed, even though it is spun in a small mill. This is also connected to why people, wherever they live, want to knit traditional-style patterns; it gives a feeling of continuity. It is the same feeling that I get when I'm dyeing with traditional natural dyes, and I think it all comes down to the continuity, and tradition—wanting something that has roots. Many people want to know where the yarn they knit comes from. They do not want to knit with something that has no past or character."

(or birch basket, which is the direct translation of the Norwegian word *neverkent*), trellis, lattice stitch, woven lattice, and diamond weave, entrelac creates a pattern of textured diamonds that resembles the weave of a basket. It can be knit in a single color or several, on straight needles or in the round, and it begins simply enough with the knitting of a row of triangles. Stitches are then picked up at each triangle's edge, and short rows accomplish the trick of the basket-woven effect. The stitch is particularly useful for creating socks and stockings, due to its stretchy quality.

Susanne Pagoldh notes that entrelac was common across Finland but most especially in the regions of Tavastland and Österbotten, where red, yellow, and green were the colors of choice. Sometimes a piece of entrelac knitting began its life as a sock and went on to become a legging, when the knitted foot wore out and was eventually cut away. Photos of nineteenth-century entrelac stockings—in wool or, more often, in the cotton yarn that was all the rage in that century—show that they were

ornate affairs, often exhibiting an allover entrelac patterning topped with a multipatterned border of waves, letters, and curlicues.

Lapland: Sami Mittens

Almost nothing—nothing at all—has been written about a lovely and intriguing color-mitten knitting tradition from up above the Arctic Circle, in the frigid region known as Lapland. Titled the Rovaniemi technique by Leena Kariniemi-Alve in a 2008 article for *Piecework*, it is a method for achieving a "sawtooth" pattern on the backs of otherwise white mittens, named after the town in which a certain much-talked-about pair originated. The reason for this dearth of information could be this, as reported by Tuulia Salmela:

> The Sami in traditional context do not knit. There are three major groups of Sami in Finland, and although some of the more southern Samis own land and are involved in agriculture, it is incredibly hard to keep sheep in the harsh climate of the north, and reindeer hair cannot be spun.
>
> The Sami are extremely skilled in their crafts (called *duodji* in Sami), which include silverwork, bonework, leatherwork, and embroidery; crochet and knitting are not considered part of their tradition. The materials for their *duodji* come from reindeer skin and bone, but the woolen fabric and colorful ribbons needed for traditional embroidered garments, and the silver for their silverwork, have been imported. The knitting culture among the Sami is distinctly Finnish; no especially Sami knitting tradition exists.
>
> There is even debate about the country-of-origin for the faux-intarsia technique of the *Lapin lapaset* (Lapland mittens). They may have originated in Sweden, just like the Lovikka mittens, which became a huge success in Finland

✳ "A Lapp [Samí] family in Norway," c. 1890.
Library of Congress Prints and Photographs Division, Landscape and marine views of Norway
 # LC-DIG-ppmsc-06257

and are nearly considered Finnish mittens. It is possible to keep sheep in southern Scandinavia, and the Sami in these regions might well have kept sheep and spun and dyed yarn for mittens. Lapland mittens are most likely Finnish or Swedish or Norwegian in origin, rather than Sami, showing an influence of the exquisite use of colors in Sami textiles.

On the other hand, a book titled *Votten i norsk tradisjon* (*Mittens in the Norwegian Tradition*) by Ingebjørg Gravjord, shows a host of mittens in the Sami "tradition"—old, new, or somewhere in between—which were featured in an exhibition

✳ A pair of Sami mittens from the collection of Annemor Sundbø, these typical, she says, of knitting from Kautokeino. *Photo by Annemor Sundbø*

✳ Rovaniemi mittens showing the classic sawtooth patterning, knit in U.S. size 00 needles and Satakieli wool from the Finnish yarn company Vuorelma. *Photo and mittens by Leena Kariniemi*

129

Tuulia Salmela

Tuulia Salmela is a Finnish knitwear designer and amateur historian of Finnish knitting currently living in Helsinki. She developed a top-down sweater method that she teaches to students around her home country, as well as through her book, The Tailored Sweater. "As a historian, I love the past," says Salmela. "I want to adapt the knitting of the past to garments and styles we knit and wear."

"I am interested in the technical side of knitting. Right now, my biggest source of gray hair but also inspiration is knitting sweaters from the top down with seamless set-in sleeves. I like the fact that the fabric grows in my hands, and I can produce garments made for me, not mass-produced items that do not fit. I see myself mostly as a sweater knitter, but I always have a pair of socks on my needles, as I wear only hand-knit socks. Knitting as a source of income is not something I even consider a goal—it is a hobby that pays for itself! My knitting is a way to relax, but also a way to challenge [myself]. I find great pleasure in turning a simple lump of fiber or a strand of yarn into something unique and something that reflects my personal taste like nothing else.

"Socks are simple, fast, and one always needs them. I like the fact that they're more portable than sweater projects, as I knit my sweaters from the top down in one piece. It's also fun to spin four ounces of fiber into sock yarn, as it is a lot faster than spinning for sweaters, but also because in socks one can use crazy and wild color combinations that would be difficult to use in sweaters.

"Finns are continental knitters, holding the yarn in the left hand. There are no exceptions to this, I hadn't even seen an English-style knitter before moving to the States. Everyone learns to knit and crochet in school, even boys. The number of active knitters is surprisingly low considering that everyone knows how to do it. Knitting as a technique still has somewhat of a stigma, the mainstream culture considers it still a grandmother's pastime. Also, it seems that it is still seen as a solitary hobby, with the majority of knitters having little to no contact with other knitters, except for those in their families.

"However, the Finnish online knitting community is tremendously active, albeit relatively small. There are roughly one thousand knitting blogs in Finland, and Finnish knitters are usually very quick to pick up the new trends in the online knitting community. Some Finnish bloggers use English and/or Finnish to blog about their craft, and some are even known outside the country. Online bloggers are active in international swaps and KALs [knitalongs], such as the Project Spectrum, Secret Pal swaps, the Knitting Olympics, et cetera, but they organize their own events too.

"Finland as a country sits in a region of waterways, especially the Baltic Sea, but also rivers and lakes. Cultural exchange happened through these major routes with the traveling tradesmen, and also when people gathered for the fair and major holiday events in bigger towns and villages. Slowly but surely the influences made their way from the big cities of Europe into the rural countryside and changed along the way. For example, Finnish foods are a mixture of Swedish traditions (such as meatballs) and Russian favorites (such as a large number of items made with cabbage and rutabagas). The Finns have added their own twist to the influences they received—they used barley or rye instead of wheat or rutabagas and turnips instead of potatoes. The same goes for knitting; the Finns took what they saw and used the materials they had at hand. The result is a delightful combination of influences and regional, identifiable themes.

"Culturally, even in knitting, Finland sits neatly between the Scandinavian and Baltic (and Russian) cultures and traditions. You can see this in the way Finns knit, in their use of colors and motifs in knitting, especially stranded knitting. A great example of the Scandinavian influence is the red and gray pair of mittens included in one of the pictures. The pair was knitted by my mother-in-law's mother in the fifties, and shows clearly the use of star motifs indicative of Norwegian and Swedish influence. The flower-themed mittens I knit a few years ago are an example of Baltic influence, and the same flower motif can be found in Estonian and Latvian knitting.

"I see myself as a part of Finnish tradition, but not stuck in it. I see myself doing what our grandmothers did before us—altering and adapting the inspiration and influences around me to something new.

"I think the one misconception we have about tradition is that it is somehow fixed or set in time. Tradition changes in time, and it is influenced by fashion, new materials, and so on. What to us is tradition, was new and exciting to the people at another time in history. Our new and fresh ideas now will become the tradition of history in the future. To me, the most dangerous thing to think is that tradition is a set of rules and materials, and I'd love to see tradition being used in a new and fresh way. It is possible to respect the heritage and yet discover something new. There might be a reason why our ancestors did things a certain way, but it may not need to be the only way.

One example of this is knitting sweaters (which, as you can tell, is a pet peeve): Earlier in time, sweater knitting was done either in the round with double-pointed needles or back and forth with single-pointed needles. This was because good-quality circular needles simply did not exist. Nowadays we have wonderful new tools for circular knitting, which is why there is no need to knit in pieces anymore, simply because we have better tools now. Personal preference may still be an inclination to knit in pieces and then seam, but we're no longer stuck with poor tools, and, hence, we can create our new tradition of knitting truly seamlessly.

"It seems that the knitting culture in Finland brings a lot of elements from the international community into the new knitting culture, but there is still a peculiarly small amount of original content rising from Finland and Finnish knitters themselves. You can see this for example in the isolation of Finnish knitting materials. Very few Finnish designers produce materials in other languages, they consider the Finns their audience and publish their materials usually in Finnish.

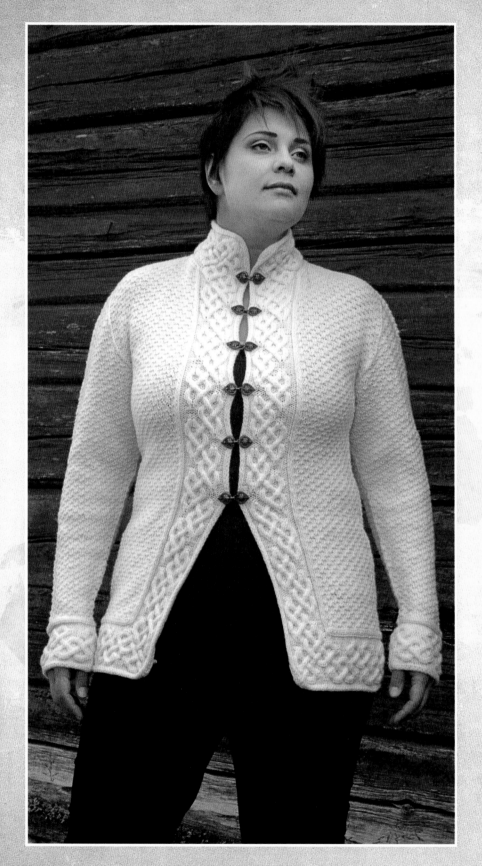

"However, we have several amazing designers working with *Vogue Knitting* and *Twist Collective*, but the Finnish magazines have picked up the online knitting phenomenon relatively slowly. It seems you need to be recognized abroad first, and then they will notice you in Finnish knitting and craft magazines. It has been said the knitting culture in Europe is some five years behind the United States, and it seems to hold true in Finland's case as well. You can see that the development of the knitting culture is in its early stages, which makes it very exciting too.

"I think our biggest names, if you will, are Mari Muinonen (also known as tikru or Made by Myself blog) and Suvi Simola (known in Ravelry as Villapeikko). Both have published designs in *Vogue Knitting* (I think), and are hugely popular in Finland. Both are known for their cabled patterns, but I'd like Finland to be known for all the rich traditions we have, especially in stranded knitting. There are several new designers out there, who are doing wonderful work in this respect, so I'm sure soon we'll have more patterns coming out of Finland for others to enjoy."

Tuulia Salmela wears her Pohjan Neito cardigan, proving yet again that Finnish knitting, even today, is a hodgepodge of influences. "Almost nothing about it is Finnish, except for the simple design and the relatively small cable pattern," she quips. "The cables themselves are from Viking decorations, and the Vikings traveled often to Finland to trade here, so cabling themes are found in Finnish archeological findings." *Photo by Lasse Salmela*

at the Norsk Folkemuseum in 1981–1982. Some of them are reminiscent of a pair in Annemor Sundbø's collection (see photo), with colorful allover patterning. Some have patterned bands at the wrist, or at the wrist and back of the hand. They range in origin from Sør Varnger and Nesseby in Finnmark County in Norway, and Skolte Saami in Finland/Russia/Norway.

As for the Rovaniemi mittens (see photo on page 129), here's how Kariniemi-Alve describes the stitching up of the mittens in her informative *Piecework*, which are lovely no matter where they come from:

> [T]he mittens are worked in the round, but only the main color completes the rounds. The three pattern colors, divided into eleven small balls, are arranged on a long needle . . . to prevent tangling, and each color follows its own narrow path upward. The main color travels over the pattern colors, leaving the inside of the mitten very neat. After completion of one round, the knitting is lifted to allow the long needle holding the pattern colors to turn; the pattern colors are again in the correct order for the next round. All of the stitches in the sawtooth pattern moving to the right are worked by knitting two stitches together through the back loops, then dropping the first stitch from the needle and knitting the second stitch again, and only then dropping the stitch off the needle.

Kariniemi-Alve identifies mittens from Rovaniemi as colored yellow, green, and red on a white background (and notes that these are the colors of the Sami flag); mittens from Inaro are yellow, blue, green, and red on a white background. She notes, too, that the technique for knitting these mittens is written precisely nowhere. To learn, you must go to the Arctic and seek out a mitten teacher of your own.

Iceland

There's been much speculation about how knitting came to Iceland, most of it centered around the theory that it arrived with German, English, or Dutch merchants, or maybe all of them. Regardless, it seems clear that a strong knitting tradition was firmly in place in Iceland by the sixteenth century. Elsa Gudjonsson, in *Notes on Knitting in Iceland*, makes mention of a bishop in northern Iceland who, as early as 1582, was accepting knitted stockings as payment of rent from his tenant farmers.

Men, women, and children all knit, profusely; children learned around age eight and were expected to contribute a pair of stockings a week to the household. By the seventeenth century, knitted stockings and mittens were integral commodities—essential exports to an impoverished region ravaged by volcanic eruptions, famine, extreme cold, and plague. By the eighteenth century, sweaters were also being exported, as was wool woven and felted into a fabric called *wadmal*, which, intriguingly, was accepted as legal international currency.

Hand knitwear was also much needed for use by Icelanders themselves, existing as they did in a bleak, cold, and desolate climate. These goods would have included sweaters, mittens—one-thumbed as well as the two-thumbed variety popular with fishermen in several countries—shoe inserts (*see page* 134), stockings, shawls, wrist warmers like those found in Greenland, men's vests called *brjóstadúkar*, the woman's *peysuföt*—a well-fitting, seamless jacket—and tasseled caps called *skotthúfa* (the latter two of which were eventually sewn, rather than knitted). Pattern books were available in Iceland (and Icelandic) by the early eighteenth century.

"Most Icelandic knitting was strictly utilitarian," writes Louise Heite in an article she wrote on Icelandic knitting for *Knitters* magazine. "Warm socks and mittens, fishermen's sweaters, and snug caps comprised the bulk of the island's export knitting. Icelandic woolens were traded all over the Atlantic basin. Icelandic socks and sweaters were part of the

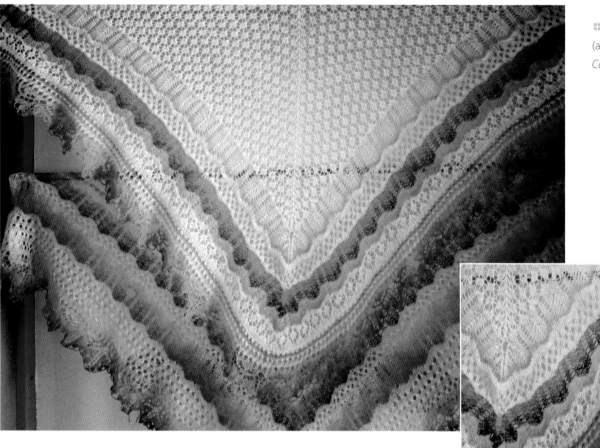

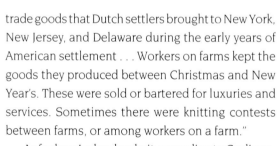

trade goods that Dutch settlers brought to New York, New Jersey, and Delaware during the early years of American settlement . . . Workers on farms kept the goods they produced between Christmas and New Year's. These were sold or bartered for luxuries and services. Sometimes there were knitting contests between farms, or among workers on a farm."

As for how Icelanders knit: according to Gudjonsson, they knitted in the round on four or five needles, with natural-colored yarns, sweaters possibly accomplished with little ornamentation beyond a simple ribbing. However, wealthier Icelanders may have embellished their knitwear with embroidery, or had them stitched from dyed yarns.

Clearly knitting was absolutely integral to the lives of Icelanders. Their gear offers further proof of this; knitting needles were stored in special boxes carved with the owner's name. Often these boxes (*prjónastokkur*) were given by a young man to the object of his affection.

Color knitting in Iceland dates to the seventeenth century, possibly; a fabric scrap from around that time shows a two-color Fair Isle border. Intarsia was common by the nineteenth century, as evidenced by shoe inserts knitted in traditional rose patterns. Such patterns also appear on round knitted tablecloths, wall hangings from the twentieth century, and other home décor items. This sort of insert motif knitting was done on a garter stitch background, rather than stockinette stitch. It may have been unique to Iceland, although rose patterns are common motifs in world knitting generally, from Greece to Scandinavia to Azerbaijan.

In the 1800s, pullover sweaters were knit up in simple two-color stitch patterns, then felted, according to *Knitting in the Nordic Tradition* by Vibeke Lind. Norwegian lice-patterned sweaters were popular until about World War II. They were knit out of unspun roving called *lopi* (*see page* 134) and exhibited wide bands of patterning from the shoulders down to the sleeves. By the 1950s, a new type of color-worked sweater had emerged: the famous Lopi sweater (*see page* 134). Even today, the Handknitting Association of Iceland employs men

⚜ An Icelandic Lopi sweater.

© Hilda DeSanctis/Alamy

the advent of lace knitting they became soft, gossamer affairs, knitted not just in traditional triangle shapes (*prihyrna*) for ease of tying across the chest, but in rectangles (*langsjal*) as well, these worked in one or more colors. Lace-knitted *klukka* dresses, derived from women's slips, are enjoying a resurgence of popularity today among Icelandic knitters.

Lopi Sweaters

The emblematic sweater of Iceland, the Lopi (*lopapeysa*) has a tradition of only about sixty years. When it appeared on the knitting scene in the 1950s, it represented a break in technique from earlier Icelandic sweaters such as pullovers and fishermen's jerseys. The body and sleeves were knitted separately in the round up to the armpits, then all three pieces were put together onto a circular needle. The collar, showing two-color geometric horizontal repeats of snowflakes, chains, and other motifs, was worked with a series of decreases; a similar pattern was usually added to the cuffs and hem.

Some knitting historians have noted a similarity between these yoked sweaters and the beaded yoke collars traditional to Greenland, although there is no evidence that one influenced the other. Similar sweaters had shown up in Swedish, German, and Danish knitting magazines just a few years prior to their arrival on the Icelandic scene, and the sweaters of Bohus (*see page* 114) were certainly a precursor.

Shoe Inserts

Knitted shoe inserts are wholly, resoundingly Icelandic. Dating to times before the advent of the hard-soled shoe, the inserts were meant to provide warmth and comfort to wearers of soft shoes, pretty flimsy affairs made of sheep, seal, or fish skin. In other frigid regions around the globe where shoe inserts were common, they were fashioned of straw, juniper twigs, tree bark, felted wool, and, on very rare occasions, crochet. But knitted inserts appear to have existed nowhere but Iceland. And there, for centuries, hidden

and women to knit these sweaters—no longer just in natural colors, as they were designed originally, but in a wide array of dyed wool.

Lace knitting has a history in Iceland as well, particularly for constructing shawls. Designer Cheryl Oberle writes in *Folk Shawls* of an Icelandic legend that describes how fairy women travel between the earth and their own kingdom: they lay their knitted shawls on the surface of a bog, stand in the center, and sink . . . and sink, till they arrive, clean and dry, in the fairy realm. According to Sigridur Halldórsdottír in *Three Cornered and Lace Shawls*, lace for wrist warmers and mittens arrived in Iceland in the late nineteenth century, thanks to pattern books and magazines from abroad.

Previously, shawls were constructed of coarse yarns stitched up in garter stitch, but with

An assortment of knitted show inserts, plus a pair of the soft-soled shoed they were meant to add comfort to. Photos by Hélène Magnússon, inserts and shoes courtesy of the following collections: Árbær Museum (12, 26, 28), Skógar District Museum (8, 17, 23), Elsa E. Gudjónsson (1, 22), Textile Museum – Halldóra's room, Blönduós (3, 9, 29), Icelandic Craft Society (20, 25), Helga Þórarinsdóttir (nr. 10,15), Akureyri Museum (2, 5, 16, 30) and National Museum of Iceland, Ethnical collections (4, 6, 7, 11, 13, 14, 18, 19, 21, 24, 27).

beneath the feet of men and women old and young, existed a vast wealth of color, technique, and highly individualized style.

As Hélène Magnússon (*see page* 139) points out in her book *Icelandic Knitting: Using Rose Patterns*, shoe inserts, for all their gorgeous variety—they were knitted in striped patterns by children just learning their techniques; in patterns ranging from roses to flowerpots to hourglasses to maces to checkerboards to diamonds; some with plain borders, some

with crocheted, some with borders band-woven with a technique known as finger weaving (*slyngja* in Icelandic), in every color imaginable—were fundamentally utilitarian objects. And yet, they were critical ones. This is evident in the many Icelandic words for all the different types of shoe inserts (note that Icelanders have seventeen different words for varieties of snow and snowfall).

The most basic is *ileppar*, which translates to something like "inserted rag." Then there's

Lopi

Iceland has a long wool tradition, dating all the way back to the time of the Viking arrival in the ninth century. As Louise Heite writes, the Vikings were "as much livestock farmers as they were fishermen" and brought their sheep—descendants of the Norwegian *Spelsau*—along with them when they settled the island. To somewhat drastic ecological consequences, the sheep grazed every last bit of edible plant life they could curl their lips around. "By the end of the Middle Ages," reports Heite, "the birch forests which once had covered the island were virtually gone."

At least the sheep provided compensation, of two varieties (not counting the mutton): *tog*, a long, coarse, curly undercoat that knitters traditionally used for lace shawls, and *thel* (or *pel*), a fine, slightly crimped, extremely soft undercoat that was once used for knitting garments that touched the skin—especially undergarments, which were popular in Iceland right up to World War II. Together, the two coats, which are low in lanolin content and therefore yield a high percentage of yarn per pound of fleece, can be joined together to make the yarn that is now practically synonymous with Iceland: *lopi*.

But let's backtrack for a moment. Wool has been an integral part of the Iceland economy throughout its history. When Iceland was ruled by Norway, it traded hand-spun yarn for much-needed grain. Under the rule of Denmark, in the year 1703 the current city of Reykjavik was designated as a working farm, meant to stimulate industrial development, according to Gunnar Karlsson's book *History of Iceland*. Workshops for spinning wool were set up in an attempt to achieve this mission. (Alas, the project was to prove a failure: Iceland had no internal market for wool, and on the export market, it could not compete with Europe's highly developed wool industry.)

Originally, the word *lopi* referred to carded wool (roving) which was "drawn into a thick strand for spinning on a spindle or wheel," according to Susanne Pagoldh in *Nordic Knitting*. Throughout the ages in Iceland, wool had always been tightly spun for use in knitting; that is, until the early 1920s, when a woman named Elin Gudmundsdótir Snaehólm experimented with knitting the fiber *before* it was spun—she managed a scarf on a hand-knitting machine—then published a booklet about it.

Above: Icelandic sheep are descendants of the Norwegian *Spelsau*; Far right: The famed Alafoss sign. *Photos by Karin Lowe*

Disks and strands of lopi. *Photos by Susette Newberry, unionpurl.blogspot.com*

Of course, unspun wool is delicate indeed, although *lopi*'s combination of both *tog* and *thel* fibers, with their naturally complementary properties, creates an end result that is stable and relatively durable. Another way the yarn is strengthened is by skeining two or three strands, twisting them slightly together. These days, Icelandic sheep are shorn twice a year in winter and spring (which, as some point out, does not allow the hair to grow long enough to easily separate *tog* from *thel*—a major difference from fiber of the past); once upon a time, their wool was merely plucked off their bodies.

Starting in the nineteenth century, a company called Alafoss began producing all Icelandic wool: the unspun *plötulopi*, as well as the three weights of light, lightly twisted yarn now so well known to knitters: Alafoss *lopi*, bulky *lopi*, and Létt *lopi*. In 1991, this task was taken over by another company called Istex. Today, the company purchases the soft, durable, and water-resistant wool directly from Icelandic farmers and subjects it to a thoroughly "green" washing without chemicals or nonrenewable energy sources (thermal power is big in Iceland). The spun yarn is available in seventeen natural colors (were you even aware there were seventeen colors of sheep?) as well as many more dyed ones. The unspun yarn comes in eight natural colors and nine dyed.

Those who knit with unspun *lopi* report that it is delicate to work with but durable in its final form. Breaks and color changes are managed with a unique technique known as the spit join: spit into your palms, twist the yarn strands together, then rub them back and forth between your damp palms.

ÁLAFOSS

1896

Icelandic Shoe Inserts

The inserts are inspired by a pair of inserts decorated with a "stair-rose" pattern that belong to the National Museum of Iceland, Ethnological Collections.

Size: one size to fit shoes 37-39 EU/ US
You can obtain more sizes by changing yarn and/or needle size.
Yarn: Einband-Loðband from Ístex, 70% Icelandic wool, 30% wool, fine lace-weight, 1-ply worsted, 50gr/skein, 50g = ca. 225m/246 yds
- MC: oatmeal #0885, 1 ball
- CC1: bright red #0078, 10g
- CC2: black #0059, 20g
- CC3: bright yellow #9935, 10g
- CC4: green #9823, 10g
- CC5: white #0851, 10g
Needles: 2 mm needles, 2 mm crochet hook
Gauge: 10 x 10 cm = 30 sts and 30 garters (60 rows) in garter stitch

PATTERN NOTES

Mittens are knitted back and forth in three parts using Icelandic intarsia. You will find a helpful tutorial about this technique on Hélène's website (The Icelandic Knitter, icelandicknitter.com under "Support and tutorials")
Special terminology: garter stitch: 1 garter = 2 rows k worked back and forth

ABBREVIATIONS

k: knit
st: stitch, stitches
dec: decrease
k2tog: knit two together
ssk: slip two, one at the time as if to knit, insert left needle through the back loops and knit them together
sc: US single crochet (UK double crochet)

INSTRUCTIONS

Middle section: cast on 46 sts with MC using 2 mm needles. Work pattern A in garter st, then cast off. Always slip first st at the beginning of each row.
Tips: With CC1, pick up 32 sts from the selvedge of the middle section. Knit pattern B. After 6 garters (= 12 rows), dec 1 st from each side in every other row, 14 times, on right side, as follows: ssk, k to last 2 ts before end of row, k2tog. When 4 sts are left on the needles, cast off. Knit another tip the same way, picking up sts from the other selvedge.

FINISHING

With CC5, crochet an edging around the inserts using sc and 2 mm crochet hook. Close the round with 1 slip st. Break yarn. Darn in loose ends.

—From ©Hélène Magnússon, *The Icelandic Knitter*, icelandicknitter.com, helene@helenemagnusson.com

hversdagsleppar for plain, everyday inserts. *Spáríleppar* means fancy Sunday-best inserts. *Randaloddar* means everyday striped inserts (actually, there are five other Icelandic words referring to the same thing). *Langrandaleppar* is for long-striped inserts knitted in three sections—central section first, then stitches picked up for the top and bottom. *Þverröndóttir* is for striped inserts knit in one piece (not a favored method, as inserts knit lengthwise ran a greater risk of stretching out; those knit widthwise were made with increases and decreases at each end to create front and back tapering, as well as decorated with oblong stripes at their centers). *Rósaíleppar* is for special-occasion rose-patterned inserts. *Slyngdir leppar* is for inserts with band-woven edges. And there are many more.

With little exception, the inserts were knitted in garter stitch, which "captures" air to render the inserts extra-warm and resists the tendency to roll. These were knitted "in three stages or in one piece, from heel to toe, and sometimes to fit the shape of the foot," writes Magnússon. The motif-knit inserts were also knit in garter stitch, a technique that is also, potentially, strictly Icelandic. Band-woven inserts were sometimes knitted with Fair Isle patterning: both inserts knitted at once in the round, then cut apart. Patterns were nonexistent and designs were highly subject to whimsy, using as many as eight colors, Christmas trees, plaids. Special-occasion inserts were knit on fine needles from *thel*. Everyday inserts were knitted on larger needles from coarse and/or leftover yarn. From time to time, inserts were knitted from horsehair. Finally, the inserts were felted: The pair was basted together so they would maintain a similar shape and size, then, once felted, they were sat or lain upon overnight in order to press them. Special-occasion inserts were also napped.

Average length of wear for an everyday insert was a few brief months. Special-occasion inserts had a longer life, as they were worn less frequently and also kept tidy and clean in special boxes called *plaggakassar*.

Hélène Magnússon

élène Magnússon is a French-born knitwear designer whose work riffs on, and pays homage to, the Icelandic rose-pattern insert motif. As a student of design at the Iceland Academy of the Arts in the 1990s, she undertook a thesis project that explored the little-known tradition of Icelandic knitted shoe inserts, a project that later developed into her first book, *Icelandic Knitting: Using Rose Patterns*. This book is half scholarship on the unique Icelandic phenomenon of knitting intricate, colorful inserts for soft shoes, and half Magnússon's original designs for clothing, using the shoe inserts as a visual jumping-off point. Sometimes it takes an outsider to reconsider, and reclaim, a previously overlooked heritage.

"I'm educated as a designer in Iceland, in Icelandic, by Icelandic teachers. I didn't know anything about the design world before I came to Iceland. I was very much influenced by the great artist Birgir Andrésson. He was teaching a course about Icelandic identity: what is Icelandic, how do you perceive it, and so on. In another course, where I was supposed to research Icelandic design, I chose to investigate knitting. I was looking for something *really* Icelandic. That is when I started to be interested in the inserts.

"Probably it's my way to search for and build my own roots. I didn't just move to Iceland. I found my roots there. Then I found out that my grandfather's family had settled in Normandy at the time the Vikings invaded. My grandfather certainly looks like an Icelander: very tall, with high cheeks, small nose, light gray eyes. There was an exhibition about French designers in Iceland once, and it just became clear: I'm no less French than Icelandic. I like old things and I respect them. I like things that have a history.

"The thing with the shoe inserts, for example, is that the young generation doesn't know what they are, and the old one thinks they're uninteresting. It had to be a stranger, with fresh eyes and point of view,

Sweaters by Magnússon for both grown-ups and children riff on rose patterns found on traditional Icelandic shoe inserts. *Photos and garments by Helene Magnússon*

Mittens styled after Icelandic shoe inserts, from Magnússon's *Icelandic Knitting: Using Rose Patterns*. Photos and garments by Helene Magnússon

to see these in a new light. People say all the time to me: 'We don't even see what we have. It had to be a foreigner to show it to us.'

"I'm an Icelandic knitter with a French twist. Although, for the inserts, I worked the old tradition very closely, keeping the techniques, the color schemes, the motifs. I'm not sure the result looks really 'Icelandic.' Maybe some garments do, like the Hammer rose vest. I wear it on special occasions with a black skirt and the traditional Icelandic cap (*skothúfa*), and I feel like I'm wearing the national costume. I like to look at things the way a museum curator would, turning around and upside down, taking measurements, looking closely, magnifying, repeating the same gestures over and over, but sometimes not touching at all.

"From the very beginning of my knitting career, I've been improvising, never hesitating to make changes to existing knitting patterns. This freedom is very Icelandic, I think."

Adalbjörg Jónsdóttir

Adalbjörg Jónsdóttir is a ninety-three-year-old Icelandic creator of lace-knitted dresses that are reminiscent of klukkar, although infinitely more elaborate and less structured in their conception. The following profile was compiled by designer Hélène Magnússon, who interviewed Jónsdóttir in 2008.

"As far as I back as I can trace my interest in Icelandic knitting, I've been conscious of Adalbjörg and her lace dresses, probably through the journal *Mind and Matter*, edited by the Handknitting Association of Iceland, which Adalbjörg is a member of and does some work for. Once, in 1977, she was knitting a sweater for the Handcraft Society of Iceland in Icelandic lace. But then she started to make changes, and they liked it so much that they wanted to have it in an exhibition. That's when she had the idea to lace-knit a dress. The idea quickly became an obsession, then an imperious need. She can still remember it, her excitement, and her frenzy. It had to be ready for the exhibition, and she only had a few days.

"From then on, knitted lace dresses were her obsession. She thought of them constantly, and saw them in her mind. "It was insanity," she says. "I was completely mad." For ten years she only knit dresses, always in the same Icelandic wool (*eingirni*). She doesn't know how many, certainly more than one hundred. She participated in many exhibitions, particularly at the Kjarval Museum in Reykjavík, in Chicago, and in Finland.

"She knitted the dresses exclusively *in the round*. The first dress was black. Then a gray one. Then a wedding dress with a headpiece. Dresses were sold, sometimes given, often ordered. Dresses were given,

Jónsdóttir, looking like a butterfly in a dress of her own design. *Photo by Hélène Magnússon*

for example, to the Iceland Craft Society and for conservation in the National Museum. Adalbjörg made a living knitting these dresses. She knitted up to ten hours a day.

"All her dresses are one of a kind. She doesn't like to have precise directions, nor when someone says: 'The same as another.' It's impossible for her to make a new attempt before the preceding dress is finished and being blocked. 'I was lucky the dresses always fit quite well,' she tells me modestly. But she has the talent of an ancient couturière: she understands the body and its proportions.

"She starts with the arms. The panels are knitted separately, larger on the bottom, narrow at the top, attached to the dress with knit two together on three needles. Sleeves are knit in the round. Body and sleeves are joined together for the yoke. The construction is quite similar to that of the Icelandic sweater. Sometimes she crochets the edges.

"She stiches them up just as they come into her head, using exclusively lace weight 100 percent Icelandic wool. This is the only variable she knows for sure when she knits the dresses. E*ingirni* is the only wool that maintains its gauge and can be stretched and blocked as it needs to be. She gives the dresses names: spiral, *Kría* (arctic tern), *perla*, *tvískiptur*.

"The dresses are knitted in natural colors, single color or variegated, or sometimes in colors to which are added a bright thread. She joins yarn together by splitting the ends in two, then rolling them between the thumbs them and felting them slightly with a little saliva. She uses this method a lot with multicolored dresses—sort of an intarsia in lace, in the round, with yarn breaks at each row."

Details of Jónsdóttir's fantastic lacework. *Photos by Begur Olafsson*

Chapter 5

THE BALTICS

A vintage postcard of a knitter in the Baltics.

THE NORTHERLY EUROPEAN REGION surrounding the Baltic Sea—comprising Estonia, Latvia, and Lithuania—has been a hotbed of knitting techniques and patterning over the centuries. Given the bitter-cold winter temperatures in the Baltics, mittens and gloves are the most common handknits, but shawls, stockings, and caps are also part of the Baltic knitting tradition.

Woolen gloves and mittens, probably knitted, dating somewhere from the twelfth to fifteenth centuries, have been found in both Latvia and Estonia. Irena Turnau, in her *History of Knitting Before Mass Production*, dates the first knitting relics in Latvia to the fourteenth century. In another source, she identifies Latvian (as well as Estonian) knitting as "one of the most archaic and with the most varied patterns in Europe."

Handknit mittens are symbolic in all three Baltic countries, and girls learned to knit at a young age, typically around four, when they began to make mittens as part of their dowry. Traditionally, a girl would be judged on the quality and quantity of mittens she had made. It was believed that a young woman who had made many pairs of mittens of fine quality would make a good wife. Favorite handknit mittens and socks were also commonly buried with the deceased.

Mitten designs varied by region. Some featured very little colorwork, while others were covered with ornate or simple two-color patterning. Baltic patterns tend to consist of geometric shapes. In Lithuania, where knitting is relatively new, more organic shapes like flowers, suns, and trees have worked their way into the designs.

Estonia

(With special thanks to Nancy Bush.)

The history of this very recently independent, northerly nation that borders Russia, Latvia, and the Baltic Sea is one of extreme turmoil and hardship. But the history of its *knitting*, at least, is cause for a goodly amount of celebration. Replete with strong, colorful, often-repeat patterning, the knitting reflects close ties to nature, family, and homeland (despite its suffering more than eight hundred years of foreign rule).

It is an old and venerable history. When it begins exactly is anyone's guess. But the first piece of knitting found in Estonia has been dated to the late thirteenth/early fourteenth century; a later seventeenth-century find was knitted in two-color patterning, indicating, according to author Nancy Bush, a high level of early skill among Estonian handcrafters. She postulates that knitting traveled with Crusaders who settled in the Baltics after their return from Palestine. The found fragments were all from mittens, and, in fact, mitten knitting factors so predominantly in the history of Estonian knitting there's no point discussing it separately from the country's overall knitting history.

Why mittens (*labakinnas*) should be obvious—frigid temperatures require a bundling, and sometimes a double-bundling, of all digits. For this reason as well, Estonia has a tradition of knitting gloves (*sormkinnas*), caps, shawls and scarves, socks, and stockings.

Patterning, when there was patterning,

⸙ Women's rose-patterned stockings. South Estonia, Viljandi parish. Mid-nineteenth century. *Estonian National Museum*

would have been similar for all garments (according to Bush, both simple and complex motifs, usually repeating over the entire piece of knitting). "[G]rouped in a stack, or extended, they can be very ornate," she writes in *Folk Knitting in Estonia*. They are highly geometric and feature names like Sieve, Dice, Forked Leg, Butterfly, Blossom, and Piglet. A technique of rose patterning is found in some gloves and stockings from the south-central part of the country. Hundreds of patterns have been collected by Estonia's Ethnographic Museum.

But back to mittens. They feature heavily in marriages and other rites, and a large amount of lore and superstition surrounds them. As in other countries (Norway, Finland, and Latvia among them), a bride traditionally began knitting her dowry chest when she was ten years old; she'd need an average of fifty pairs of mittens (among other garments), all of which would be given away to the groom's family and other important guests and helpers. Godparents of newborns were gifted mittens and sometimes socks; Bush notes that in some regions of Estonia, the dead were buried wearing mittens and, sometimes, socks they had knitted themselves. She further remarks that mittens were thought to offer protection and would be worn when standing trial, when sowing seeds, when cutting hair, when treating sick animals and humans, and also used when choosing a new homestead: "Three mittens were filled, one with grain, one with soil, one with ashes. A child then chose a mitten. If it was one with ashes, a new site was required; if built on the first site, the house would be in danger of burning."

Older gloves and mittens tended to be virtually cuffless; cuffs grew and grew, then finally peaked in gauntlets, toward the end of the nineteenth century. Some cuffs had fringe; others featured a braided cast-on and "contained lateral braids known as *vits*, an Estonian word also used for the hoop on a wooden beer mug." A simple thumb shaping was incorporated into mittens and gloves, with the thumb being worked from held

Mittens, made by Marie Rebane. South Estonia, Suure-Jaani parish. 1860s. *Estonian National Museum*

Needle-netted mittens. Estonia, Saaremaa Island, Sõrve parish. End of the eighteenth century. *Estonian National Museum*

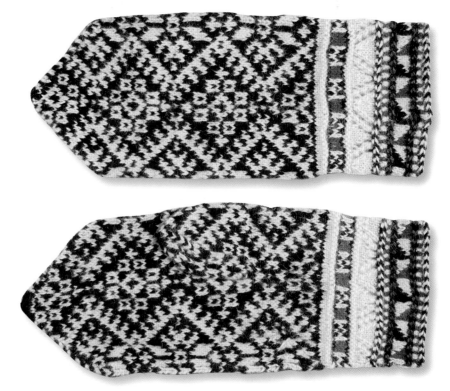

Mittens, made by Riet Köster. Estonia, Kihnu Island. 1910s. *Estonian National Museum*

Maasikaäitsnekiri: Strawberry Blossoms Mittens

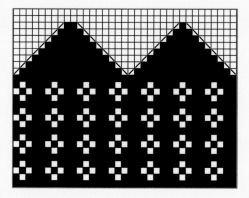

These mittens were inspired by a wonderful mitten pattern from the village of Paistu, in central Estonia. I chose to create a mitten with a very short cuff, to resemble the older mittens found in the collection of the Estonian National Museum.

MATERIALS

Satakieli (350 yds in 100 g). 1 skein each, MC: #003 and CC: #890.
Set of 5 #0 (2mm) double point needles. If you desire a slightly larger mitten, go up a needle size.

GAUGE

21 sts and 20 rows over pattern before blocking.

FINISHED MEASUREMENTS

4 inches wide and 10 inches from cuff to tip—to fit a medium women's hand.

RIGHT HAND

With MC and CC, work a Continental Long Tail Cast On using both colors as follows: make a slip knot of both colors. Place MC around thumb and CC around index finger of left hand. Cast on 80 sts. Remove slip knot when cast on is complete (it does not factor in stitch count). Divide sts onto 4 needles, 20 sts each needle. Join, being careful not to twist. P 1 rnd.

Begin cuff pattern

Rnd 1: K with MC.
Rnd 2: *K1 with MC, k1 with CC, repeat from * to end of rnd.
Rnd 3: *P1 with CC, p1 with MC always bringing the yarn you will use next UNDER the one you just used. These last two rnds create one lateral braid known as Kihnu Vits.
Rnd 4 and 5: K with CC.
Rnd 6: *K1 with CC, k1 with MC, repeat from * to end of rnd.
Rnd 7: *P1 with MC, p1 with CC always bringing the yarn you will use next UNDER the one you just used. These last two rnds create one lateral braid known as Kihnu Vits.
Rnd 8: K with CC.

Begin pattern for hand

Follow chart. Work 3 repeats of pattern. On 4th repeat, place thumb on rnd 39: work in pattern over sts on needles #1 and #2. On needle #3, work 1 st in pattern, place next 17 sts on a holder or waste yarn. Now cast on 17 sts in pattern as established to replace the sts you put on the holder. Work the last 2 sts from needle number 3 in pattern and complete rnd. Continue in pattern until you have worked 81 rnds of pattern and hand measures approx. 7¾ inches from beginning.

Continue following chart to shape top of mitten. Work all decreases with CC. On rnd 82, beginning of needle #1, *sl 1, k1, psso. Work in pattern to first 2 sts on needle #3, sl 1, k1, psso, work to end of rnd. 2 sts decreased.

On rnd 83, *sl 1, k1, psso, work in pattern to last 2 sts on needle #2, k2 tog. Repeat from * on needles #3 and #4. 4 sts decreased. Continue decreasing as for rnd 83 on every rnd until you have 6 sts remaining. Break yarn and thread through the live stitches. Pull up snug.

LEFT HAND

Work as for right mitten until ready to begin rnd 39. Work in pattern over 20 sts on needle #1. On needle #2, work 2 sts in pattern, place next 17 sts on a holder or waste yarn. Now cast on 17 sts in pattern as established to replace the ones you put on the holder. Work the last st from needle number 3 in pattern and complete rnd. Continue in pattern until you have worked 81 rnds of pattern and hand measures approx. 7¾ inches from beginning.

Complete mitten as above.

THUMB

Carefully remove the waste yarn from the thumb hole. Pick up the resulting 17 sts onto two needles. Attach both working yarns at the left edge of thumb hole and pick up and knit 18 sts across back of thumb (where you cast on the 17 sts when you made the thumb hole) as follows: 1 CC, 1MC, 4CC, 1MC, 4CC, 1MC, 4CC, 1MC, 1CC. You will have 35 sts total (17 front sts divided onto 2 needles and 18 sts on another needle for back of thumb. Continue working thumb graph as indicated. When thumb measures 2¼ inches, shape top:

On next rnd, using CC only, decrease as for top of mitten: sl 1, k1, psso, knit to last 2 sts on needle #2, k2 tog. Sl 1, k1, psso at beginning of third needle, knit to last 2 sts on this needle, k2 tog.

Repeat this decrease every round until 7 sts remain, 3 in front and 4 in back. Break yarn and place onto a tapestry needle. Thread yarn through the 7 live sts, pull up snug and fasten off.

FINISHING

Weave in all ends and block mittens on mitten blockers or under a damp towel.

—Pattern from Nancy Bush

stitches on the palm. So finely worked were some of the oldest specimens that, Bush marvels, they featured two hundred stitches around the hand. Those from the southeastern Setu region were often patterned in white and red: white to symbolize light, and red representing the sun, strength, and protection against evil.

Leggings, worn in winter for warmth and summer to protect the legs during field work, predated stockings in Estonian knitting, as they were more practical (they lasted longer, having no feet to wear out). By the eighteenth century, knitting had become so prevalent that women carried a special knitting "pocket" so as to have their mitten- and sock-work readily at hand while they were accomplishing other chores. Knitting largely replaced *nålbinding* as the craft of choice, although the latter continued to be employed

✄ Gloves, made by Ann Mägiste. South-East Estonia, Setumaa. 1880s. *Estonian National Museum*

✄ Women's wedding gloves. Estonia, Saaremaa Island, Mustjala parish. 1870s. *Estonian National Museum*

among certain industrious mitten makers up until the nineteenth century. Patterns were largely adapted from other textile techniques, especially weaving, and they varied greatly from region to region. Stocking patterns often mirrored glove patterns, although it was usually women who wore the most ornately decorated legwear.

Unlike the stockings of, say, Turkey, Estonian stockings were left unadorned at the feet; in hot countries you take off your shoes; in cold countries you leave them on, thereby hiding your (pattern-less) feet from view—or so the theory goes. Nancy Bush identifies stockings with wide belt patterns around the calf and repeat patterns decorating the ankle all the way up to the top. Rare rose-patterned (*roositud*) stockings, with inlay patterns running, says Bush, "from part way down the leg, [to] divide at the ankle as a clock and end near the toe shaping," hail from the regions of Viljandimaa, Pärnumaa, and also islands to the west of the mainland.

⁜ Women's stockings, made by Ann Reinson. West Estonia, Pärnu-Jaagupi parish. 1860s. *Estonian National Museum*

⁜ Men's knitted sweater. Estonia, Kihnu Island. Turn of the nineteenth/twentieth century. *Estonian National Museum*

Lace-knitted shawl. West Estonia, Haapsalu. 1981. *Estonian National Museum*

Between 1880 and 1930, Estonian knitters began to make *vatid*, short knitted jackets whose patterning and shape "contain inspiration from the ideas, patterns, and clothing that Estonian sailors brought home to their wives and daughters," writes Bush. They bear special patterns such as lateral braids, damask stitchery, and small two-color motifs on their sleeve cuffs and bottoms, around the neck, and across the shoulders. They were made for men at first, then appeared as women's wear at the tail end of the nineteenth century.

In keeping with Estonia's infiltrated past, the styles and techniques of many countries—Austria, Finland, Germany, Norway, and Sweden—are found in certain aspects of the country's knitting. The influence worked both ways. Says Sheila McGregor in *Traditional Scandinavian Knitting*, "From Estonia, the stranded technique and many patterns were copied by the Swedish women living on the islands in the Gulf of Riga and from there, or perhaps directly from Estonia, the patterns went to Gotland, on to Sweden and eventually were taken up by most countries around the North Sea. A cap with an Estonian pattern can be found in the Shetland Museum in Lerwick, and Estonian gloves in a Copenhagen collection." Perhaps most significantly, Estonian patterning seems to have had some bearing on the knitting of Fair Isle. "Stranded knitting in bright colors was well developed in the Baltic states long before it reached its heyday in Shetland," writes McGregor. "It may well have predated the Fair Isle innovation as well. Intricate allover jerseys were knitted in Estonia, with patterns very similar to those developed in recent years in Whalsay."

For some knitting enthusiasts, however, the pinnacle of Estonian knitting is the lace of Haapsalu.

Haapsalu Lace Knitting

Dating from the 1800s and peaking in popularity during the 1930s, the lace shawl from the Baltic seaside resort town of Haapsalu was a shawl with aspirations. Inspired by the elegant garments worn by wealthy tourists who came to the town to partake of the famously restorative mud baths,

to Nancy Bush. It is knitted in white lamb's wool (ideally), of hand-spun singles or fine two-ply.

The distinguishing characteristic of the shawls of Haapsalu is the use of *nupps* (*nupp* is the word for "bud" in Estonian, and it rhymes with "soup"). These bobbly bits, writes Russian designer Faina Letouchaia in her article on Estonian lace for the Knitting Beyond the Hebrides Lace Symposium, "are used in combination with yarn overs and decreases, as in Lily-of-the-Valley. [They] may be used to outline some geometric lace design, such as diamond; or nupps might be used to form diamonds in place of yarnovers alternately with lace diamonds . . . [They] are also used to add interest and enhance some organic, wavy lace designs, they are added to leaf and flower lace shapes . . . They give an impression of pearls thrown on the lace." According to Nancy Bush, Haapsalu knitters devised prices for their shawls according to weight, and such *nupps* would have added considerably to the overall number of ounces. They also proved that the shawls were knit by hand.

Openwork diamonds feature heavily too, with nests of diamonds being common. "Star" stitches are created with simple decreases and increases: "three stitches out of three; or five stitches out of five and then purling all stitches on the next row," as Letoutchaia describes it. Square scarves with a center pattern surrounded with a border were made in one piece. A narrow lace edge was knit separately, in two pieces, and sewn onto the completed center. The outer edge of this lace edge is the cast-on edge of the piece; the cast-on was done using a doubled strand of the yarn in order to strengthen the outer edge and keep it from rolling.

Haapsalu patterns are defined as "lace knitting" as opposed to "knitted lace"; the former is accomplished by alternating rows of plain knitting between rows of stitch patterning, the latter by patterning each row. Rectangular shawls (*sall*) were also made, and triangular (*kolmnurk rätik*) shawls became popular in the 1930s, although it is the large, impressive, and completely square *Haapsalu rätik* that is persistently the most mind-boggling.

these shawls were created by local women to fill a need: their own need for cash. Over the course of a productive winter, the average knitting woman would complete twenty to thirty shawls to sell by the time the tourists hit town.

Taking what they already knew of knitting, what they saw of foreign knitting, and what materials they had readily at hand, the women created what is now considered the quintessential Haapsalu shawl: about three to almost five feet square, consisting of a richly patterned center on a stockinette background (which means there is a definite "right" side and "wrong" side to the work), a narrow border, and a lace edging knitted separately in two pieces, then sewn on, according

Latvia

(With special thanks to Lizbeth Upitis.)

As in other countries with strong folk cultures, Latvian motifs are highly representational. In her 1995 article for *Piecework*, Sandra Messinger de Master quotes one Latvian knitter as calling them a "language for personal expression." Thus, "The trees and the sun represent life, happiness, and all that is good . . . The serpent represents a connection with fate and good fortune. Because a rye stalk usually bears a single head, the double rye head is a wish for 'multiplied' prosperity and fertility."

Many of these designs are believed to illustrate pre-Christian mythology, and also to hark back to the country's weaving tradition. Others are familiar to knitters throughout the Baltics and Scandinavia: Cross, Star, Sun, Flowers.

Latvian Mittens

According to Lizbeth Upitis, who wrote the seminal book on the subject in the early 1980s, Latvian mittens strongly reflect the areas in which they were created. Within four distinct regions, and even within townships inside those larger regions, particular designs emerged and were preserved

❋ A plethora of mittens. From the top center: From Zemgale, Wedding mitten: braid and multicolored fringe with Austra's tree, adder, Jumis, and sun; from Kurzeme, Nica: morning star and moon cross symbols; from Kurzeme, Alsunga: morning star, sun, Jumis, and Austra's tree symbols; from Kurzeme, Nica: morning star and moon cross symbols; from Vidzeme: "Stained glass" slip-stitch and braid with sun and morning star symbols; from Zemgale: morning star symbol with scalloped cuff and single-colored braids; from Kurzeme, Nica, wedding mitten: Austra's tree, sun, and cross symbols; from Kurzeme, Barta: sun symbol with scallop; from Latgale: moon cross symbol with three-color braid; also from Latgale: flowers with twisted edge; two from Vidzeme: God and Mara symbols with braid and fringe, and sun and cross symbols with twisted edge and braid. *Photo courtesy of Lizbeth Upitis*

over the years. "The symbols, colors, and designs of mittens were often an indication of group affiliation for Latvians . . . Occasionally, a person could be linked to a specific township because of a unique pattern or technique," she writes. As an example, she cites the scalloped cuffs native to Rucava in the coastal Kurzeme province.

Such clannish identification by means of patterns is familiar by now. What's intriguing in the instance of Latvia, however, is that the importance of identity becomes smaller and smaller, moving from the national, regional, local, and familial to, finally, the individual. "Mittens helped establish a girl's identity," says Upitis simply. Perhaps disturbingly to feminists, though a source of excitement to knitting enthusiasts, this identity was closely linked to marriage: "To a great extent, a young maiden could prove herself worthy of marriage through the quality and quantity of mittens she knit."

A Latvian girl would begin to knit mittens in order to fill her dowry chest soon after she learned the craft at the age of between four and six. When suitors inevitably arrived, they were shown the contents of these chests and, if marriage was eventually deemed amenable, they received the girl's best mittens and socks. Mittens in profusion were also given at the marriage ceremony itself— to the people who prepared the food, to special "patrons" of the bride and groom. Finally, after the ceremony, the contents of the bride's dowry chest were distributed to her new relatives, in order of importance. Hand-knitted mittens were placed by the bride all over her new home: on the threshold, above the fireplace, among the fruit trees, and in the barn. And, according to Upitis and historian Ruta Saliklis, the wearing of mittens was integral to the marriage celebration itself. Says Saliklis, "After the wedding ceremony, the marriage contract was finalized with a meal during which the bride and groom ate with mittened hands. "

M. Catherine Daly identifies the shape of many mittens as "gauntlet," in her essay "Anna Mizens, Latvian Knitter." She further mentions that they were knit large in relation to the actual hand, often extending loosely in order to be worn over sleeves. Coloring and patterning were dictated both by availability (plant dyes) and folk mythology (symbolic motifs). Green, yellow, red, and blue were the most frequent color choices, although combinations varied highly by region. Patterns ranged from zigzags to crossed stalks of grain, trees, moons, and stars.

On the occasion of the Riga Summit in 2006, 4,500 pairs of Latvian mittens were knitted to give to delegates; an article written in conjunction with this project linked patterns to the Latvian deities: "Every deity . . . had its own tasks and mission and it was represented by one or more symbols that characterized it." These were identified as follows:

Jumis—the god of the sky and fertility, with a symbol of two crossed corn or barley stalks
Zalktis—the god of well-being and fertility, represented by a snakelike symbol
Saule—goddess of the sun and fertility, with a complex symbol of central crossed square, eight petals, and several other motifs
Krusts—the cross, represented by an X with four diamonds ornamenting each crease of the X
Meness—god of the moon and war, symbolized by an upside-down crescent
Laima—the personification of luck, symbolized by a repeating arrow motif
Mara—queen of the goddesses, symbolized by a zigzag
Auskelis—the personification of the morning star, symbolized with the common knitting motif of an eight-pointed star

Many Lithuanian knitting motifs, such as this lily pattern, are inspired by nature and have been adapted from older designs used in weaving, shown at the top of the picture and in the photo on the facing page. *Photos by Dominic Cotignola, courtesy of Donna Druchunas*

Usins—god of horses, bees, and light, whose symbol, meant to represent a "sun carriage," looks like a diamond-headed man

Dievs—the supreme god, depicted with an upside-down V topped with a dot

Janis—a deity associated with the Midsummer Night festival, depicted by a bull's-eye atop a two-legged pole

Upitis outlines four regional distinctions:

Latgale—These ancient designs feature bright primary colors on a white background, often fringed at the cuff in white. "Designs from eastern Latgale show influence from neighboring countries . . . Flower designs are often found . . . as well as traditional symbols. These suggest influence from eastern Slavic neighbors," she writes.

Zemgale—Blue, black, brown, and green predominated in this style; mittens were occasionally fringed, and a Polish influence is discerned.

Vidzeme—This region features white mittens with large designs in black, gray, or red.

Kurzeme—Due to foreign sea trade, says Upitis, this region had access to orange, magenta, and "true black" dyes, which locals were quick to incorporate into their textiles. This region also boasts more variety in mittens than the others, and Upitis is able to break down distinctions into even smaller increments. In southern Rucava, the mittens are scalloped at the cuff and have fine palm designs. Further north along the coast, designs are "generally large and ornate. Nica has a rich variety of sun and star designs, while Barta prefers the "firecross" (the same shape as the classic Buddhist and Hindu swastika, in Lithuanian knitting twirling in either direction). Farther north still, deep shades of red, yellow, green, and blue predominate.

In all regions, however, there are certain commonalities. According to Upitis, these include a symmetrical allover design: "Backgrounds are not considered part of the design. Individual elements are expanded or enriched to complete their space. Borders and centers are elaborated until they nearly touch." Traditionally, homespun fingering-weight wool was used, in order to best show off designs.

The Riga website highlighted several interesting Latvian superstitions pertaining to knitting and knitwear:

- Mittens and socks should be knitted in the summer in order to be warm, soft, and strong.
- Mittens washed during an "old" moon will lose their color.
- A person who wipes their nose on a mitten will never become rich.
- A person who gives their hand to another hand wearing a mitten will give away their luck. Watch yourself in winter!

Lithuania

(With special thanks to Donna Druchunas.)

Lithuania, like Estonia, is a "new" nation that was oppressed for centuries by foreign—most recently, Soviet—rule. Regardless, it has a long history of handwork (ceramic and metalware, for example) whose ancient ornament authors Irena Merkien and Marija Banionien, in their *Gloves of Lithuania Minor*, find referenced in the region's glove patterns. Designer Donna Druchunas notes that spindle whorls made of metal, stone, and amber have been found in graves dating from the fifth through twelfth centuries. However, knitting in the region was less popular than weaving until the beginning of the twentieth century,

limited mostly to mittens, wrist warmers, and socks (*zemaitija*, some of which, constructed of white yarn with openwork patterning, bear resemblance to the folk socks of Bavaria). Raglan sweaters became popular during the Soviet era, and were often knit in the round from the top down.

The region's myriad patterns hail from many sources other than other craft traditions. Writes Donna Druchunas in an article on Lithuanina knitting for *Piecework*: "Because national boundaries have moved so frequently in this area, influences have come from all sides. In some parts of Lithuania many of the designs do have a strong Scandinavian influence. In some other areas, designs have similarities to Turkish patterns. In some places

❈ An example of
Lithuanian socks featuring a
geometric motif, designed
by Donna Druchunas.
*Photo by Sue Flanders and
Janine Kosel*

design elements are shared with Latvian and Estonian knitting. And the knitting technique traditionally used in Lithuania, combination knitting, has strong roots in Russia and all of the surrounding areas in Eastern Europe, and is even sometimes found in Scandinavia." Elsewhere, she remarks that distinctly Lithuanian patterns include flowers, trees, clovers, and other plants, motifs that would have made

themselves evident in the surrounding landscape. A book published by the Lithuanian Folk Culture Centre, however, remarks that such naturalistic motifs would have been a later development, following originally geometric patterning.

Traditional clothing was constructed of linen, but also of wool. In fact, says Druchunas, in Lithuania "there are two rare breeds of sheep that

Hand-knit socks and mittens for sale in the Vilnius tourist market. *Photo by Dominic Cotignola, courtesy of Donna Druchunas*

both have coarse wool. This wool was spun into stiff, heavy yarns that were used to make mittens and socks and also for felting to make heavy woolen overcoats . . . It's not nearly as coarse as it sounds, and it can also be blended with some of that imported merino to make softer knitting yarns."

Wool was used for winter wear: the ubiquitous gloves, mittens, and socks with multicolored geometric patterning, frequently felted. It was also used to decorate *čempės* (pronounced "chempes")—heavy linen crocheted shoes worn by women who could not afford leather ones, possibly for church wear rather than everyday farm work, according to Druchunas. Linen was also used for summer socks, ribbed at the top but still held up by bands tied below the knee; "stocking shoes" worn indoors in all weather; and summer gloves, presumably to protect the hands during farm chores.

Although Lithuania boasts two national rare breeds of sheep— Lithuanian Coarse Wool and Lithuanian Black Face (pictured)—linen has always been more important in culture and society, says Druchunas. *Photo by Dominic Cotignola, courtesy of Donna Druchunas*

Chapter 6

EASTERN EUROPE AND THE BALKANS

Five girls knitting, Albania, c. 1923.
Frank and Frances Carpenter Collection, Library of Congress
Prints and Photographs Division# LC-USZ62-106363

*H*AND KNITTING SPREAD INTO Eastern Europe later than the countries of Western Europe. Writes Irena Turnau in *The History of Knitting Before Mass Production*: "One of the reasons . . . was the weakness of the textile production in [Hungary and Slovakia]. The most important reason was a slower demand for stockings, and also the berets and waist-coats worn with the west European costumes. In the sixteenth and seventeenth centuries, men in Hungary and Slovakia wore long national costumes with boots and without stockings. Only those men and women who favored west European fashion, wore knit fabrics."

There was a hand-knitting guild in Bratislava, Slovakia, in the first half of the seventeenth century, with the following masterworks required: a beret, a woolen shirt, socks, and a patterned carpet, all to be completed within thirteen weeks. As for Hungary, Turnau remarks upon the mark of their guilds, which comprised a pair of stockings, a pair of scissors, and a brush of fuller's thistle. "The scissors served for shearing the fulled stockings which were previously napped," she writes. "The mark shows the type of product from the Buda knitters. They made the simplest woolen articles, mainly stockings. They were then fulled in small hand-fulling presses." The knitters of the guilds in Hungary served the needs of the urban middle class. Wealthy Hungarians wore knitted goods imported from Bohemia, Austria, and elsewhere in Western Europe. Silesia (basically, latter-day Poland) was an important hand-knitting center, boasting a guild dating at least to the mid-sixteenth century.

Russia

Irena Turnau calls the history of Russian knitting inadequate and fractured. Still, some small bits can be gleaned from various sources. According to knitting historian Richard Rutt, "Fragments of material said to have a knitted structure and dating from 1100 to 1600 have been found in various places in the USSR." Admittedly, this thread does not lead anywhere useful.

Another source posits that Russian soldiers may have been responsible for some amount of hand knitting. Knitted stockings were a requirement of the army uniform beginning in 1630, and soldiers were supposedly responsible for knitting and darning their own socks. Maybe, maybe not. There is no source that identifies Russian soldiers as knitting, save Central Asia scholar Owen Lattimore, who credits Russian troops with teaching Chinese camel drivers the craft—but not until the 1920s.

Irena Turnau, however, offers a more fleshed-out story: "In the autumn of 1633 . . . a considerable order was placed for long stockings coming above the knee. These were for regiments newly organized and fitted out on West European lines. The small number of [professional] Muscovite knitters could not cope with such a large order in a short time, so the authorities turned to workers in towns from the Vladimir and Galic districts. This . . . proves the existence of a hand-knitting industry, not very developed, but still somewhat organized in many Russian towns." No soldiers knitting here.

"Fat Sheep" on the Golodnaya Steepe in Uzbekistan. *Photo by Sergei Mikailovich Prokudi-Groskii, Library of Congress Prints and Photographs Division, # LC-DIG-prok-01860*

But then, Turnau hardly claims to hold all the pieces of the Russian knitting puzzle.

Rutt, quoting Turnau, dates the first mention of knitted woolen stockings in Russia to the late sixteenth century. He writes: "She is more certain about some of the seventeenth century pieces, especially the veils called *klobuk* . . . In form they are soft domed hoods which extend at the sides to the shoulders and at the back to the nape, and have a broad lappet falling to the breast on either side of the face. Two examples have an embroidered motif over the forehead: a six-winged seraph. Such headdresses are worn by priests who are monks and by bishops, over their brimless hats . . . The silk ones in the Kremlin are said to be knitted in silk on five needles."

"The true history of Russian knitting may never be known," concludes Rutt, "for there appears to be a dearth of written evidence. It seems on the whole unlikely that it really flourished before the eighteenth century, when machine knitting rapidly became important. The immigration of Germans . . . under Catherine the Great probably stimulated the craft."

Author and designer Charlene Schurch has treated the knitting of the Komi, a Finno-Urgic Russian ethnic minority, in her book *Mostly Mittens*, and offers some interesting information. The Komi, she reports, spun flax, hemp, and wool, and they made knitting needles of wood and bone. Like other knitters in cold northern climes, they had a tradition of knitting for important events such as weddings: here, three dozen pairs of socks and three dozen pairs of mittens to present to family and relatives of bridegrooms. Stockings for everyday use were patterned on the leg and plain on the foot so as to save precious yarn resources. The diamond, reports Schurch, was a fundamental design element for fancy socks. Two-color knitting fragments from the sixteenth century have been found within the Komi Republic, in Latvia. Later Komi knitting, from the nineteenth century onward, has been knit with at least two colors. Basic pattern repeats are four stitches wide and four rounds high, using repeating pattern stitches to build the design. The world-ubiquitous star pattern was introduced to Komi in the late nineteenth century through Russian migration.

Orenberg Lace

There are at the very least two stories detailing the origins of Orenburg lace knitting. The first is a legend and is told in Galina Khmeleva's book *Gossamer Webs*: Once upon a time, a Cossack woman knitted an exquisite gossamer shawl and sent it to Catherine the Great. The Empress was so delighted with the gift that she ordered that the woman be given enough rubles to last the rest of her life. The catch: The woman was to be blinded, to prevent

❇ Mittens, made by Anna Kinyeva. Komi ASSR Sysolskii raion Kuratovo selsovet. 1950s. *Estonian National Museum*

her from knitting the same shawl for anyone else. The other, reverse catch: Catherine the Great did not realize that the woman had a daughter, also a skilled knitter, who had learned all her mother's secrets and continued to use them. All the finest "spider-line" Orenburg shawls originate from this woman and her daughter, it is said.

The second story is more concretely rooted in history: At the beginning of the eighteenth century, the city of Orenburg was established as a military outpost in the southerly foothills of the Ural mountains. The Cossacks who settled there soon discovered that even their thickest furs were not enough to keep them warm throughout the brutal winters, but the layered garments of the local Kazakhs and Kalmucks were another

matter: goat skin and felt outerwear over padded jackets and, over all that, warm shawls knit from local goat down. The Cossacks are said to have begun trading tobacco and tea for this down, and their wives either learned to knit the natives' warm, gray openwork kerchiefs, then significantly refined what they learned, having nothing much else to occupy them during the long, lonely winters; or they took the general, local framework of a knitted goat down shawl and imposed their own weblike patterning structure upon it, using their traditional embroidery motifs as a jumping-off point.

The facts about Orenburg lace are something of a hodgepodge, but one thing is certain: they begin with the goat. The down of Orenburg's

✳ A contemporary, everyday shawl from Orenburg, made in the 1980s and measuring
94 cm by 91.5 cm. *Photo courtesy of Textile Museum of Canada, #T94.0047*

dairy goats had been used, perhaps for centuries before the arrival of the Cossacks, to knit warm undergarments, although, according to lace knitter Elizabeth Lovick, the first mention of an Orenburg shawl dates back only to the seventeenth century. In the mid-eighteenth century, Peter Ritchkov, a scientist and historian of the Orenburg region, began breeding the local goats in order to achieve an extremely fine down—he accomplished an amazing fourteen to seventeen microns. Then he and his wife, Elena, set about developing knitting into a cottage industry and elevating the creation of the shawls to an art form. By the late eighteenth century, shawl knitting was the most popular form of needlework in the region, and by the early nineteenth century, it was widely known outside of Russia, first appearing at the International Paris Exhibition of 1857.

In these years, according to Orenburg lace knitting doyenne Olga Federova, several French and British interests attempted to export the raw goat down. When this proved too costly, they attempted to export the actual goats themselves. They met with dismal failure. "Whenever Orenberg goats are relocated," according to the Textile Museum of Canada, "the new climate causes their coats to become coarse after a few seasons, and they lose their fluffy down forever." So the cottage industry was further developed within the region until there was nothing much "cottage-y" about it: More than twenty thousand regional women were employed in the craft by 1910, although most local women could not afford a gossamer shawl of their own. The industry, beginning to tank around this time as a result of poor-quality copies entering the market, was revitalized by Lenin's 1918 decree elevating folk handcrafts to the level of state industry. It was thrown into flux with Perestroika, when state support evaporated. Skilled traditional shawl knitters soon began to emerge, though, driven to revitalize the craft due to economic need and encouraged by St. Petersburg designer Galina Khmeleva. And so

the popularity of Orenburg shawl knitting has come full circle, perhaps more than once.

There are three designations of Orenburg shawls: the Simple Downy Shawls, which are gray, thick, warm kerchiefs and the progeny of the first knitted shawls of the region; dense kerchiefs and *pautinkas* that employ some amount of patterning but are warm and meant to be worn for everyday use; and fancy-dress spider-line *pautinkas* and tippets, unique creations showing a host of geometric patterns—they have been said to resemble frost on a windowpane or animal tracks on snow. All three are knitted with hand-spun yarn made from down that has been combed from the goats at the beginning of winter; one goat averages approximately one pound of down. This is plied with rayon silk thread (for the finest of the shawls) and cotton thread for the more everyday, both of which serve to strengthen the lace and also render it less expensive.

The spider-line shawl is constructed bottom edging first, then the two sides and center, and, finally, the top edging. Typically, a shawl's central designs are Five-Diamond, Medallion, or Allover; and in Five-Diamond, the central diamond may feature other patterns, such as Strawberry, Peas (*pshenka*), or Fisheye (*rybka*). Medallion shawls, says Olga Federova, "display a full-sized diamond centered within a square. The resulting corner triangles may each display a diamond, a motif pattern, or simply remain open. Several interior diamonds echo within the center diamond."

Motifs were handed down orally, although contemporaneously, Federova is responsible for devising a graphing system. Shawls continue to be manufactured by machine, but high-quality handmade shawls are currently very much in demand and can be custom ordered, or knit by the industrious hand knitter. However, Westerners must substitute Cashgora, Shetland cobweb wool, or silk/kid mohair for wool from Orenburg goats—it's not available outside Russia.

✳ A spider-line *pautinka* c. 1880, measuring 113 cm by 95 cm.
Photo courtesy of Textile Museum of Canada, #T92.0233

Olga Alexandrovna Fedorova

Olga Alexandrovna Fedorova is the most esteemed maker of Orenburg shawls, even though she passed away in 2008. In many respects, she was born to that title: her home village of Zhioltoie, just east of the city of Orenburg and north of the border of Kazakhstan, has a "reputation as the center for the finest-quality traditional gossamer shawls and scarves," according to Galina Khmeleva. By Fedorova's own admission in *Gossamer Webs*, "Gossamer knitting runs in my family—my mother knitted, and so did my grandmother and great-grandmother. My uncle, Federov Yermolay Stepanovich . . . planted apple trees and sat under one in his garden and knitted."

Beginning work as a teenager for her local regional cooperative (known as the Kombinat), Fedorova was soon out-knitting the best of the shawl makers. Her knitting, wrote Khmeleva in an article for *Piecework*, "was technically flawless, superior to the already high standards of the Kombinat, while her handspinning prowess set her apart from even the legendary elder spinners of the community." Competitions ensued, not to mention the winning of competitions. Then followed a stint as the Kombinat's chief designer and artistic director, which placed her in the role of teacher extraordinaire, traveling around to various villages to pass on her knowledge of techniques and patterning. Then, she was promoted to "engineer for quality control" within the city of Orenburg itself.

Girls wearing Orenburg shawls, May 1973. ©*RIA Novosti/Alamy*

What made Fedorova's shawls a cut above the rest? Let's start with what makes a superior shawl to begin with. Here's craft book publisher Melanie Falick paraphrasing Fedorova in a 1995 article in *Piecework*: "[A] well-made shawl is soft and light and not at all itchy. It boasts smooth, even stitches (about six to an inch) that are not too tight and a symmetrical, rhythmic design made up of a wide assortment of stitches. The fiber is of even thickness and color, and there are no lingering guard hairs." But assuredly, there is much more to the matter than this—something to account for Fedorova's 1958 second-place winner in an Orenburg competition remaining "eighteen years in the Kombinat safe as a one-of-a-kind sample." Here's Fedorova's own description of that illustrious piece:

I knitted a three-color shawl. The shawl was to be large—180 by 180 cm [70.9 by 70.9 inches], and I graphed it first. I began by making a shawl with one medallion in the middle and three diamonds in each corner. I complicated my edges with a two-row sawtooth design. I knitted one thread of gray down with one of gray silk, one thread of gray down with one of white silk, and one thread of white down with one of white silk. The shawl was worked with forty-seven bobbins. Before I sent it [to the jury in Orenburg], my Zhioltoie neighbors looked at it and praised the work—and they were a tougher jury than the one in Orenburg.

✳ These Bosnian slipper socks, embellished with embroidery and a crochet edging, were designed by Donna Druchunas. *Photo by Sue Flanders and Janine Kosel*

7171—Shepherds and Their Flocks on the Argive Plain. Gree

The Balkans

The Balkans are located in a region of southern Europe practically surrounded by seas: the Adriatic, Ionian, Aegean, and Black, with the European continent directly abutting to the north. It's generally considered to include the countries of Albania, Bosnia and Herzegovina, Bulgaria, Croatia, Greece, Macedonia, Montenegro, and sometimes Turkey, Romania, Moldova, and Slovenia. Richard Rutt describes the knitting across this region as mingling "western and Islamic taste," and although he finds Turkish knitting to be quite differently influenced than general Balkan knitting, he conversely finds that the Balkans were often influenced by Turkey.

Patterning is varied and colorful throughout the region, with bands of flower motifs, stripes, and geometrics common. When knitting began in the Balkans is the subject of conjecture, although Rutt finds it greatly in evidence everywhere in the region by the beginning of the nineteenth century. Of course there were socks, begun at the toe and worked upward. Two pairs were worn together, in fact, by both men and women of what Rutt terms the "peasant and hill tribes:" one thick wooly pair worn for warmth, and another finer, embroidered pair on top of those for decoration.

In Bosnia, Muslim men knit their own white stockings; in the former Yugoslavia (today's Serbia, Croatia, Bosnia, Montenegro, Macedonia, and Slovenia), elaborately floral-patterned stockings were the fashion; in Serbia and Bosnia, men's black or red stockings came to the knees; bridal socks from Macedonia show bands of elaborate horizontal patterning that Rutt claims have "strong affinities with the motifs on Turkish woven rugs;" women's red worsted stockings in Albania feature eight-pointed stars on the cuffs, and several colors used in each row. There were mittens too, of course, and gloves, leggings, and occasionally men's vests.

Mary Thomas in her *Knitting Book* defines knitting in the Balkans as typically using an uncrossed knit stitch that combines the "Western . . . with the Eastern movement . . . in forming an uncrossed Knit Stitch . . . formed by inserting the needle through the *back* of the loop and drawing the needle and yarn through as indicated by the arrow, the yarn being held in the left hand." Conversely, the purl stitch is formed "by inserting the needle through the front of the loop, but taking the yarn *beneath* the point of the needle . . . By this method," Thomas writes, "the yarn makes the shortest possible journey in forming either stitch . . . The resulting fabric is more even and closer in construction, and, since knitted fabrics are also still felted in those districts, it felts more easily." Perhaps the most interesting of the patterns she shows is an Albanian design for a sock top, replete with diamond and checkerboard stripes in

Albanian anklets, designed by Donna Druchunas, made using the Eastern toe-up method. *Photo by Sue Flanders and Janine Kosel*

black, white, and red, with the patterning running vertically rather than horizontally. Irena Turnau, though, finds that knitting came late to Albania, and was not particularly common.

A charming description of knitting in Bulgaria comes from a book titled *Balkan Home Life* by Lucy Mary Jane Garnett: "The whole family, from the old grandparents down to the babies, picnic in the fields from morning till night, and the women work as hard as—or, according to some travelers, harder than—the men till all the corn is bound in golden sheaves. Not even the old women past fieldwork are idle, for while 'minding the babies,' they are still busy with distaff, spindle, or knitting needles."

4192 Greek Peasant Woman Spinning Yarn by Hand.
COPYRIGHT 1901 BY H. C. WHITE CO.

✳ Greek peasant woman spinning yarn by hand, c. 1901. *Stereograph Cards Collection, Library of Congress Prints and Photographs Division # LC-USZ62-65924*

In Greece, it's socks, socks, socks. "The Greek islands were famous for their hand knitting production of stockings," writes Irena Turnau in *The History of Knitting Before Mass Production*. Knitted socks to wear with your *fustanella* (a men's garment like a kilt) were white, black, or patterned with horizontal bands. Red women's socks were banded with geometric OXO designs. Several pairs of socks were worn all at the same time by women, who believed that the thicker their legs, the more attractive they looked.

Then there are gloves. Ruta Saliklis mentions gloves knit by the semi-nomadic Sarakatzanis of northern Greece. They are similar to Arabian stranded gloves, she says, with each finger knit in a different color, and geometric patterning in other colors decorating the body of the gloves.

Turkey

Stretching across the Anatolian peninsula, as well as a swath of the Balkans, Turkey nevertheless shows in its traditional knitting a style very different from its immediate neighbors, according to Richard Rutt. It borders no fewer than eight countries, including Greece, Armenia, Georgia, and Iraq, although its influence seems more to have bypassed its abutters to the south, east, and west, and skipped up in the direction of the Baltics. But let's backtrack for a moment.

Renowned knitter and designer Anna Zilboorg speculates that knitting itself may very well have originated in Turkey. "[I]t is an ancient tradition," she writes in *Simply Socks*; "perhaps as ancient as knitting itself." She speculates, too, that in Turkey it was developed by shepherds, a concept she arrives at for a variety of reasons: the shepherds had ready access to wool; they had a lifestyle otherwise conducive to a pastime that is portable; they were already proficient at the related craft of rug-making and so had at their disposal dyes and, more importantly, patterns. Shepherds also turn up in Mary Thomas' theory about the region, but in an entirely different locale: "At what date the hook and needle was superseded by the smooth pointed needle is not known, but half a finished sock of the twelfth century found in a Turkish tomb reveals that the knitter was then working on five hooked needles, similar in pattern to those yet made by the shepherd of Landes."

"Over the centuries, many independent knitting patterns have developed . . . but the familial likeness to rugs is quite apparent," says Zilboorg. They seem to mirror some Baltic patterning as well. This could be a coincidence, she thinks, except that the pointed shape of the mittens and socks of both regions is also quite similar, leading her to conclude that there must be some connection between the two.

What could it be? Zilboorg points to one ninth-century Byzantine trade route, which would

have taken the Vikings straight east across the Balkan Sea, then sharply south to skirt the divide between present-day Russia to the east; Estonia, Latvia, Lithuania, and Ukraine to the west; then a skip across the Black Sea to Constantinople. She writes, "I like to imagine an ancient Viking bringing home a knitted stocking, which was then carefully taken apart by Norse sheep herders and creatively reinvented." She's right—it's a lovely and compelling notion.

As for the nature of these patterns—which appear on mittens, gloves, vests, and the most quintessential of all Turkish knitting, socks—they feature distinctly Islamic motifs that favor, as Donna Druchunas points out, a preponderance of diagonal lines. "Unlike many European designs that have individual motifs, many Turkish designs are made up

of interlocking patterns," she writes in *Black Purl Magazine* in 2007. "Often, there is no main color and contrasting color in the way many Western knitters are used to thinking about it. The foreground and the background are interchangeable in many designs."

Which is by no means to suggest that Turkish knitting patterns are completely alien to a Western knitter. Many of the motifs are quite the same—stars, diamonds, triangles. Zilboorg attributes the difference in the appearance of overall patterning to what she calls an Eastern principle of design that "results in a balanced pattern, where the eye often switches unconsciously between figure and ground. When a figure is used in a Turkish design, it is placed so that the ground makes another pattern."

Furthermore, she finds that Turkish patterns have more curves to them than Western designs.

❄ A collection of colorful, handknit Turkish stockings, most from the 1980s, and purchased in Istanbul. The Gaziantep stockings on the right come from southeastern Turkey, as do the orange, pink, light green, and purple stockings in the center, which date from the 1960s. *Photo by Susette Newberry, unionpurl. blogspot.com*

Scholar Betsy Harrell in her important *Anatolian Knitting Designs* puts a name to some of the patterns: Apple Slice, Sergeant's Stripes, Watch Chain, Earrings, Beetle, Nightingale, Moth. Harrell further points out that patterns were once extremely distinctive to particular villages, so much so that "even today each village has its own distinctive designs which people from other villages would not wear."

Like knitters in other regions of the world, Turkish knitters knit in the round, on five double-pointed needles, with the pattern facing out, so as to make it easy to follow. But the traditional method of holding the yarn, though rapidly disappearing, would give the average Western knitter pause. Yarn is actually tensioned around the neck, which makes for greater ease in managing multiple yarn strands, and it's a technique that has made appearances in Portugal as well as Peru. Available materials have tended to be mohair, camel hair, goat hair, and wool, both spun and unspun, à la lopi.

Finally, from the *Handbook of Needlework* by Miss F. Lambert, published in 1846, comes this somewhat unexpected tidbit on Turkish knitting:

It is not perhaps generally known that the crimson caps worn by the Turks . . . are knitted. The Fez manufactory of Eyoub, at Constantinople . . . is thus described, from a recent visit by Miss Paradoc.—"As we passed the threshold, a most curious scene presented itself. About five hundred females were collected together in a vast hall, awaiting the delivery of the wool which they were to knit; and a more extraordinary group could not perhaps be found in the world: there was the Turkess with her yashmac folded closely over her face, and her dark feridje falling to the pavement: the Greekwoman, with her large turban and braided hair, covered loosely with a scarf of white muslin . . . : the Armenian, with her dark eyes flashing from under the jealous screen of her carefully arranged veil . . . : the Jewess, muffled in coarse linen cloth . . . : and among the crowd, some of the loveliest girls imaginable."

The wool is spread over a stone-paved room, where it undergoes saturation with oil; it is then weighed out to the carders, and afterwards spun into threads of greater or lesser size, according to the quality of the fez for which it is to be knit. The women then receive it in balls, each containing the quantity necessary for a cap; and these they take home by half a dozen or a dozen at a time, to their own houses, and on restoring them, receive a shilling for each of the coarse and seventeen pence for each of the fine ones. The fez afterwards undergoes various operations, such as felting, blocking, dyeing, etc. when it assumes the appearance of a fine close cloth . . . The last operation is that of sewing on the tassels and packing the caps into parcels containing half a dozen each, stamped with the imperial seal. Fifteen thousand caps a month are produced at the manufactory of Eyoub.

Richard Rutt completely dismisses this account, claiming that its author saw no such knitting and concluding that fezzes were not knitted at all. However, seven fezes in the Cornell Costume and

Turkish Sock Motif

This motif came from a collection of patterns made by Betsy Harrell in an Istanbul shantytown in 1981. There, it was entitled "curtain," with a notation that it is also called "kilim stitch". In a collection of traditional patterns by Kenan Ozbel in 1976, the same pattern appears without the first and last row and is called "apple." This motif appears over and over again in Turkish stockings with many slight differences and many different frames.

There is no doubt that the motif began its existence in rug making. I have a knotted rug from eastern Turkey dated in the 1880s with this motif as the center of the medallion design. It is a Kurdish rug and the motif is typically Kurdish. It probably moved into knitting, however, from its flat-weave rendering because of the shape of diagonal extensions. In rug making, this motif is usually embedded within a hexagonal frame. In knitting, the frame is diamond shaped since this develops easily and naturally on the needles. Extra space at the sides is filled in with the ubiquitous 1-3-1 motif that decorates the center in both rug and stocking designs.

—Designed by Anna Zilboorg

✳ These socks, designed
by Anna Zilboorg, feature
the traditional Turkish "hook"
pattern, developed from
a motif used in rugs. In
this design, simple hooks
change direction in the
center front and center
back of the sock. Both the
figure and the ground are
the same except where they
change direction. *Photo by
Sue Flanders and Janine Kosel*

Textile Collection, hailing from Greece, Egypt, and probably various corners of the Ottoman Empire, including Turkey, are identified as knitted.

Turkish Socks

Thanks to the intense and highly specific interest of several historians, quite a lot has been written over the last thirty years about the knitted socks of Turkey. Kenan Ozbel, with an illustrious career as a professor of art, plunged headlong into his native country's rural villages in the late 1970s in order to produce his exquisite and detailed (if frequently disputed) masterwork, *Knitted Stockings from Turkish Villages*. He also made an extensive collection of the socks he studied. Betsy Harrell, also an academic, followed with *Anatolian Knitting Designs: Sivas Stocking Patterns* in 1981, which documented the complex work of a knitting cooperative in a province in Istanbul (and which may be the main source of Ozbel-related disputation). Several years later, Anna Zilboorg published *Fancy Feet: Traditional Knitting Patterns of Turkey* (reprinted in paperback as *Simply Socks*). All three works have contributed greatly to the general Western knitter's knowledge and appreciation of this sadly swiftly disappearing art.

Ozbel tells us that sock wearing itself has a long history in Turkey, although early socks were made of felt rather than knitted. He makes mention of a pair of felt stockings dating to 500 or 600 BC, found in the Altai Mountains, where Russia, China, Tibet, and Kazakhstan meet—the place thought to be the birthplace of Turkic people. To Ozbel, the significance of these socks is the look of them: They "had patterned upper-leg sections resembling our peasant stockings."

Richard Rutt supposes that the knitting of stockings emerged in the seventeenth century, and, "especially in central Anatolia," says Zilboorg in *Simply Socks*, eventually it "went far beyond practicality. The role it played in village life seems similar in some respects to that of quilt making in America." As in Scandinavia and the Baltics, stockings were given

as gifts to important people and were made in abundance for a girl's trousseau. Wool, of course, was the material of choice and was quite accessible. Ozbel makes some discussion of the breeds of Turkish sheep—Kivircik, Daglic, Karaman—and the use of both short and long fibers. Mohair from Angora goats was common as well, with white, undyed mohair being reserved for a particular type of stocking—so-called white stockings, fashioned of eyelet lace patterns along the leg section, some of which were knitted for bridegrooms.

Ozbel classifies other types of Turkish village stockings: black stockings, worn with short trousers; embroidered stockings, for both men and women; hennaed stockings, for girls and women, knitted of plain white wool then dyed red (often at the toes and heels); fluffy stockings, made of mohair then stuffed inside a warm loaf of bread in order to make them puff up and repel moisture; and finally, the stockings best known to knitters by now, Turkey's fantastical multicolored, stranded Anatolian stockings.

According to Zilboorg, the yarn most frequently used for these stockings is unique. It is, she writes, "strong, hairy, single-ply yarn that is coarse to the touch and knitted as tightly as possible—at ten to twelve stitches per inch. The yarn looks as though is has been spun from the long guard hairs on the fleece and separated from the softer undercoat reserved for rug yarn." The dyes, she finds, are pretty much of the same sort used for coloring rugs, even if they are used somewhat differently: red (from sources Ozbel

Knitted silk socks from West Asia, possibly Turkey, c. early 1900s. *Courtesy of Textile Museum of Canada, #T00.23.1a-b*

identifies as madder, Judas Tree bark, and Turkish pine); yellow (buckthorn, chasteberry, smoke tree, and safflower); khaki (acorns and oak apples); brown (walnut root, shell, and leaf); purple (barberry); violet (elderberry); ocher (juniper cones); pink; and turquoise, common on socks made for children, as the color was thought to protect against the evil eye.

Socks in Turkey are knit from the toe up, although how they are begun is a matter of preference for the individual knitter. "There appears to be no accepted way of beginning," Zilboorg says. The so-called Turkish cast-on may be employed, and

this is defined as an invisible cast-on that forms a closed end. Regardless, socks are generally pointy at their toes, and they are sometimes embellished with tassels; heels are largely an "afterthought," shaped like strange flaps that hang off the backs of the socks. "They may even be cast on with a different color in a manner that leaves a sharp line across the back of the sock," writes Zilboorg. "In the West, knitters have developed many subtle ways of shaping, particularly when the goal is to make the heel fit comfortably; their counterparts in the East have been utterly uninterested in such things."

Kurdish so-called "fluffy stockings." These were purchased in the northeastern province of Erzurum. Knit of two natural colors of hand-spun mohair taken from angora goats, according to Kenan Ozbel, stockings such as these traditionally attained their fluffiness by being placed inside a hot loaf of bread taken straight out of the oven. *Photo by Susette Newberry, unionpurl. blogspot.com*

Much of Ozbel's research points to huge sociological significances in the patterning of Turkish socks, expressing, he writes, everything from the village and family from which the wearer hails to his or her cultural position: married, unmarried, widowed, about to be married. It's a function Harrell, in her own research in Sivas, concluded was largely erroneous, told as she was by the knitters themselves that there was no significance to them whatsoever. This allows Zilboorg to suggest a middle ground: "A man in Ugrup . . . assured me that everything in the socks had meaning. He said that the socks were a way for adolescent boys and girls of the village to talk to each other. Outside their families, they had no social contacts with the opposite sex, and the boys only saw the girls—fully veiled—when they came to get water on Saturdays. That was when their socks would tell stories: The color yellow means 'I am dying of love.' . . . Although I wouldn't take his stories as fact, I can well imagine young boys questioning their sisters about other girls and all manner of games being played between them."

What knitter can't relate to this furtiveness that Ozbel describes? "In some villages, individual knitters keep the new patterns created by themselves secret from the other women. In order to conceal it the knitted part of the stocking is kept in a bag, and when it is completed it is immediately put in the girl's dowry chest. The same secrecy is maintained regarding gifts to be presented to the future groom and his close relations. During the wedding, these stockings . . . are displayed . . . [for] as long as forty days . . . Questions are put to the bride about her patterns, their names, the way they are made, and sometimes she is asked to give a demonstration on the spot."

Both Harrell and Zilboorg have remarked on the rapid decline of traditional sock knitting in Turkey. Quality and variety have diminished, and those socks available on the market—usually purchased by merchants from "gypsies"—do not in any way match their predecessors.

Above left and above: Stockings upon stockings, belonging to Susette Newberry, who spent seven years living in Turkey as a girl. Traditional Turkish stockings are 100 percent wool, although the use of acrylic yarn is common now. The stocking on the right with the black, wool background and brightly colored acrylic designs features a design called zucchini flower, a design popular in a town called Çannakkale, on the Dardanelles (near Troy and Gallipoli). *Photos by Susette Newberry, unionpurl.blogspot.com*

Chapter 7

ASIA

A young Japanese woman in traditional dress with knitting needles in hand.

*I*NFORMATION CONCERNING THE HISTORY of knitting in Asia—at least, history that is written in English—is so scant that a reasearcher must literally comb stacks of documents for the briefest mention of China, Japan, India, or Tibet. In her *Knitting Book*, Mary Thomas has the most to say about knitting in Asia: "[A]s we approach the eighteenth century, it is to find all Europe and western Asia to Tibet, knitting. But while the story of knitting in Europe is difficult enough to follow, it is still more difficult in Asia. The knitting of Bokhara is brilliant in colour and magnificent in design, being similar in pattern to their embroideries. Colour knitting had, and still has, a great vogue in the East. The long thigh-high hose worn by the Tibetans scintillated in colour and pattern. . . . There seems no early trace of knitting in China, and little in India until European influence is felt, for these great countries which gave such magnificent woven textiles and embroideries to the world, seem to have specialised in other forms of work, plaiting, etc., and since, perhaps, as they did not wear hose, never felt the urge to knit."

Luckily, this author has a few research tricks up her sleeve.

Japan

The grouping of more than 6,800 islands known as Japan existed in isolation from the Western world for much of its history. And yet, here too, knitting managed to winnow its way into the culture, despite obstacles the likes of which we've never had to consider much here in the United States or in Europe. For example, with kimonos lingering as the preferred mode of dress throughout Japan until the 1920s, there was very little in the way of garments for a knitting enthusiast to knit.

In her 2002 article "The Story of Knitting in Japan," fiber artist Yoshimi Kihara wrote—as accurately as should could, given the dearth of reliable information, even in Japanese—on the inroads the craft had made into Japanese society. Ancient artifacts unearthed in the Aomori prefecture, postulated by the author of the only definitive history of Japanese knitting, Yoshihiro Matsushita,

❄ Japanese print, created between 1890 and 1900, depicts John Heathcoat, inventor of the knitting machine, showing its first successful result to his wife. *Library of Congress Prints and Photographs Division #LC-USZC4-10405*

to be "knitted," Kihara deems more likely examples of our old friend *nålbinding*. Actual knitting must have arrived with the Europeans, Kihara muses, and the first of those who arrived in 1542 came in the form of a group of Portuguese sailors lost on their way to China. Soon after this occurrence, the Japanese government threw the country back into isolation, although small-scale trade with Dutch and Chinese merchants continued. But by then, the word *meriyasu* had already entered the Japanese language. Derived from the Portuguese for "stitch," in Japanese—then as now—it refers, quite particularly, to knitted stockinette stitch. According to Kihara, the word has even turned up in haiku from the time.

Silk stockings owned by the grandson of the first shogun of Japan are the oldest examples of knitting (dating from the early- to mid-seventeenth century) ever *found* in Japan. But they probably weren't *knit* in Japan. Who were the first Japanese knitters? Possibly Nagasaki prostitutes; possibly, several generations later, samurai. That's right, samurai. And the objects they knitted would have been along the lines you'd expect: items of military usefulness. Toward the end of the Edo period and Japan's enforced isolation, samurai knit sword-hilt bags, sword bags, and decorations for boxes containing their personal affairs; purses; split-toes socks (*tabi*); gloves; and underwear, to wear both in the wintertime and under kimonos. Several strands of cotton yarn held together were used for socks and underwear; sword-related items were knit of silk.

Samurai also knit for the same reason so many other people have taken up the needles over the years: to make money. As Kihara describes it, "The influence of the samurai class, who had helped enforce the rule of the Shoguns, was now waning and the army was being reorganized along Western lines. As a result, there was a demand for knitted gloves and socks, amongst other items of military apparel . . . Many samurai were totally unemployed, and some began to knit full-time for their living." Kihara, citing Matsushita's book, even gives a list of some of the most skilled knitting samurai clans:

the Nanbumatumae-han, the Hitotubashi-ke, the Tayasu-ke, and the Hitachitatugasaki-han. "A samurai knitter called Mr. Terufusa Orihara from Hitotubashi-ke was famed for his skilled knitting of *meriyasu*," she writes.

As familiar as knitting for money is this story: the advent of the knitting machine and the havoc it wreaked on various aspects of hand knitting. The story repeats—again—in Japan, and thanks to it, "the samurai were now completely redundant, obsolete in every way." Factory knitting became the wave of the future. By the very early years of the twentieth century, Kihara estimates that 70 to 80 percent of all knitted goods were produced by industrial knitting companies.

Here is another story familiar to knitting: missionaries. Even as the Japanese government was encouraging the industrialization of textiles, two missionaries were teaching Christian converts to knit with their hands. One of these converts was Izo Matukawa, who was so enamored of the craft he thereafter devoted his life to spreading the word of Knit (at the expense, it can only be inferred, of words of a less secular nature). He went on to become something of a legendary figure in Japanese knitting. Writes Kihara: "To some extent, the beginnings of the Japanese method of making hand-knitting patterns with charts can be traced all the way back to him. It was he who first thought of the idea of adapting knitting patterns along the lines of the markings used on canvas embroidery patterns." Matukawa also taught knitting workshops—possibly the first Japanese ever to do so—and published a handbook titled *Step by Step Knitting Patterns*.

Knowledge of hand knitting spread, taught not just by missionaries, but by "retired teachers and educated widows." By 1890, hand-knitted shawls, mittens, gloves, and socks were appearing in shops, and the Japanese Ministry of Education did its part to encourage the beginnings of a cottage industry by publishing several knitting manuals of its own. Wool, of course, had to be imported—there were and are no sheep in Japan.

Samurai on horseback, wearing armor and horned helmet, carrying bow and arrows, c. 1878. *Library of Congress Prints and Photographs Division #LC-DIG-jpd-01046*

Samurai, standing, facing left, wearing armor and holding a bow, also has arrows and a sword, c. 1878. Is he wearing knitted socks and carrying a knitted sword bag? *Library of Congress Prints and Photographs Division #LC-DIG-jpd-01047*

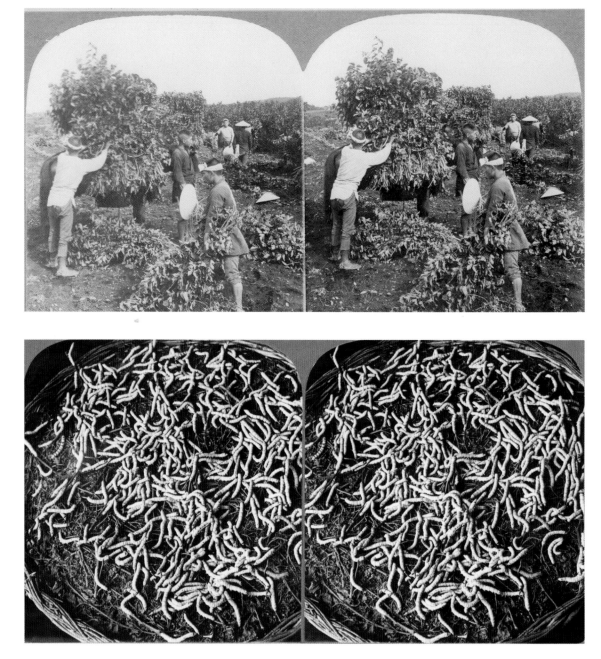

❋ Japan, a nation without sheep, has a long tradition of silk manufacturing: Gathering mulberry leaves for the silk worms, right, workers load bundles of mulberry leaves onto horses. Below, a basket full of wriggling silk worms hungry for the morning meal. *Library of Congress Prints and Photographs Division, Stereograph Cards Collection: # LC-USZ62-134389; LC-DIG-ppmsca-10719*

"Japanese women, just like their counterparts in many other countries around the world, knitted socks and underwear to send to the front," writes Kihara of the role knitting played during World War I. Its popularity continued in the 1920s, as did other needlecrafts, and soon enough, Japanese spinning companies were manufacturing their own hand-knitting woolen yarns (made with imported roving, of course).

Until World War I, yarn imported into Japan came mainly from Germany, England, and France, but when war broke out, Europe prohibited the export of goods, including yarn. At the same time, Japanese yarn had begun production and was exported not only to Asian countries (including China), but also to Africa and England. Its quality was not as high as those that had once been imported, but it consistently gained market share.

The following report on Japanese knitting in the aftermath of World War I comes from Japanese knitting correspondent Jun Miyamoto:

A depression hit Japan. The economy tanked, and the wool market dropped along with all the others. However, depression brought more interest to knitting, as the deflated price of yarn meant it was affordable for everyone.

In 1923, there was a large earthquake in the Kanto area that devastated the wool industry. But it also accelerated the transition from Japanese-style dress to a more western style as the region was reconstructed. At this time, a huge wave of yarn and knitting began and spread rapidly; shawls especially were big fashion. As knitting became hot, the value of yarn, and its variety, skyrocketed. As before, imported yarns were high quality and pricey; domestic yarns were more accessibly priced.

Domestic yarn companies advertised frequently in women's magazines. These magazines of course had written about knitting, and appended knitting pattern cards as supplements, which became very popular. Also, the magazines organized many classes and exhibitions with prizes.

Haruyo Eto, one authority in knitting and the education of women in handcraft at that time, created knitting chart symbols using examples from foreign knitting patterns. These chart symbols are the origin of current Japanese unified knitting symbols.

In the years before World War II, the Japanese yarn industry reached its first height of prosperity. Most yarns of this period were bulky, and were used mostly for knitting rather than crocheting. In the years leading up to and encompassing World War II, wool and other knitting yarns almost disappeared due to lack of source materials. Following government regulation, yarn companies tried to find other materials for making yarn, and these were very poor quality. But even this very poor, fake wool yarn was in short supply. Many yarn companies found their factories, storage facilities, and shops burned down in the bombings.

Five years after the ceasefire, wool could finally be imported again, as well as sold without any regulation. The domestic yarn industry regained its productivity, and the market increased rapidly. In the lifestyle arena, women's apparel changed drastically. Knitting was an easy way to make garments in those days of short supply, and even if yarn was still quite expensive, it was comparatively cheaper than buying ready-made clothes. Before the war, most knitted garments were for children, and some socks, gloves, and items for cold weather were also made; but beginning in the 1950s, knitting became popular predominantly for women's wear. Accordingly, yarn migrated to a finer weight, especially fingering.

The quality of yarn improved spectacularly. Not only the quality of material itself, but the colors, the variety, dyeing methods, colorfastness, toughness, and functional development, such as washability and moth-proofing. Yarn companies took to fierce competition in their advertising. Theme songs were written, actresses and Miss Universe prizewinners appeared on posters, billboards were erected alongside railways. Knitwear shows and knitting contests were organized. In 1954, Nihon Vogue-sha was established, not only to publish knitting books but also to provide handcraft education and to organize knitting-related associations.

In the 1950s and 1960s, Japanese in big cities made the shift to fashionable ready-made garments and gave up their knitting needles. Even yarn shops began to sell ready-made sweaters. The gloves, socks, and underwear that were mainstays of hand knitting before World War II were replaced by ready-made synthetics. In these days, "hand-knit" meant only sweaters and cardigans.

Competition between yarn companies became very keen, and many yarn companies went out of business. The survivors began to compete to develop new products. Acrylic yarn became popular, and there was a renaissance for all things

Japanese instructions for how to cast on.

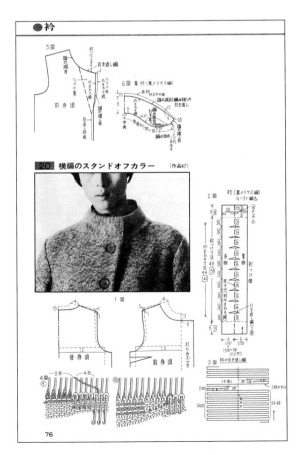

衿●

＊衿巾 6cm。裏メリヤス編横編、裏衿もいっしょに編みます。
＊製図…1・2図参照。衿つけ寸法は前後衿ぐり寸法をはかり、外まわり（折り山）寸法はその10%減にし、図のように等分の位置で減らすよう製図します（引き返し）
＊ゲージ…メリヤス編 23×32（極太毛糸）
＊編み方要点…後衿りは1段ごとの引き返し編、前衿ぐりは1段ごとの引き返し編と端の減目を編みます。衿は表と裏をいっしょに作り出し、ゲージを3目盛りつめて表裏交互に1段と2図の引き返しを入れながら編みますが（2・3図参照）引き返し編の渡り糸は4図のように編み地の下側に入れ替えます。下前の位置でボタンホールを作ります。
＊仕上げ方…前後衿ぐりの引き返しの部分は割り糸で巻きどめします。衿は折り山から2つに折って左右の端を裏メリヤスはぎます。衿の両端から前衿ぐり寸法をはかって印をつけ、衿と身頃の裏をみてN・Pと合わせ、その間でも2箇所位仮りにとめて1目中を すくいとじします。裏衿は衿つけ線のめと代々割り糸でまつりとじします。下前のボタンホールの始末をし、上前の裏にボタンをつけます。

＊1段ごとの引き返し編 181頁
＊端の減目 179頁
＊ボタンホール 100頁
＊割り糸 88頁
＊すくいとじ 95頁
＊裏メリヤスはぎ 107頁
＊まつりとじ 125頁

21 鈎針編のきもの衿 （作品48）

＊衿巾 4cm。身頃衿ぐり線でやわらかいカーブを出し、鈎針編でレース風の味を出した直線の衿です。
＊製図…1～3図を参照して実寸大の製図をし、衿を4図の編み方向に描きなおします。
＊割り出しの要点…衿ぐり線は編み目グラフで割り出します。後衿ぐりは約10%伸ばして19cmに仕上るよう後衿つけ線の目数を計算します。（自然の伸びの状態にする）衿の肩線の減目は後衿だけでします。（4図）
＊編み方要点…身頃衿ぐりに地糸で細編1段編みます。4図を参照して所定の数を前は1目ず、後は休ませてある目に針を入れます。2段めから配色糸にします。2段め全体細編1段、つぎから模様になります。後のN・Pの内側で模様から減目しながら編み、後衿の外まわりが13cmになるようにします。
＊仕上げ方…身頃の衿さがりの部分の取り出しは引きぬき

Two examples of Japanese knitting patterns: short and to the point.

した、ぬき計算、つかいやすく編みます。編み方99頁、デザイ

ディールウラー（フランス）使用

29 30

ジャケット

のゆったりとしたかぎ編みにしました。縁回りの大きなスカラップで女らしさを。編み方98頁　デザイン　市田和子　パピー毛糸使用

22

⌗ Stylish cardigans,
featured in a 1960s Japanese
knitting magazine.

The industry tried to woo them back with hand-knitting renaissance events here and there. As a result, another boom occurred around imported hand-knitting yarns, many of which arrived on the market at this time. Yarn companies undertook awareness campaigns by making patterns, organizing classes, and advertising in magazines.

In the 1980s, there was another hand-knitting renaissance. This was partly triggered by yarn companies offering gifts to knitters who bought more than five hundred grams of yarn. Cowichan sweaters became especially popular, and Japanese hand knitters embraced a variety of global traditional hand-knitting styles and techniques.

Today, things are different again. Every year with the winter season's arrival, several knitting books appear on the shelves of bookstores. For the most part, they are for beginners, and until recently you would have found a monopoly of the knitting magazine *Keitodama*, which introduces exquisite, but complicated patterns that require high knowledge and technique, so that people who already know how to knit a little and want to try something new have a difficult time finding patterns that are appropriate and "cool." That was all we had, until 2000.

Since then, there has been a website that is sought out and loved by a new generation of knitters in Japan. This site provides careful and detailed basic knitting instructions, as well as niche and traditional ethnic knitting techniques, such as Sanquhar. The most important feature of this site is that it shows knitters how to read patterns written in English, and how beautiful and high-quality imported yarn is, and as a result it has opened a window for Japanese knitters into knitting in Anglophone countries. It is called "Tata and Tata's Husband's Amimono ABC."

For Japanese knitters, language is always a big wall standing between us and overseas cultures. But thanks to this site, many knitters have found the courage to try world knitting techniques and styles. Tata's site has covered the importance of EZ (the late, great Elizabeth Zimmermann) to U.S. knitting,

handmade. Knitting held its renewed popularity for small garments until the early 1970s. Its popularity during these years was estimated to be around twenty or thirty million hand knitters.

After the energy crisis of 1973, the wool industry began to downsize. People's interest in hand knitting diminished at the same time that they were putting home knitting machines—once popular bridal gifts—back in the closet.

⌗ A meeting of Tokyo's
Stitch 'n' Bitch, spring 2010.
Photo by Jun Miyamoto

the exquisite coloring beauty of Alice Starmore, as well as the vogue for sock knitting sweeping North America. Conversely, the site's English page gives a rare opportunity for Anglophone knitters to learn how to read Japanese charts and symbols, understand needle size differences, and interact with Japanese culture. This site truly took on a missionary role for stray knitters.

The current generation of knitters born in Japan have had their eyes opened to overseas knitting by Tata's site, Amazon's foreign knitting book section, and Rowan's patterns. Some knitters have started *amimono* (which basically means any needlecraft, including knitting and crochet) blogs and groups to exchange information about which books are cool, which sites look nice, which online shops are cheaper, how to purchase yarn from overseas, and so on. Until very recently, Japan didn't have sock yarn; later, only one or two imported brands were available, but yarn shop owners remained clueless about it. Some self-patterning sweaters seen as shop samples were actually, accidentally, knitted with sock yarn.

A Stitch 'n Bitch group has been started in Tokyo and is conducted by Anglophone knitters, and the concepts of knit-outs and knit cafés have finally arrived here. This latest knitting generation knows how to read knitting abbreviations in English, and what Knitty and Ravelry are. Japanese knitters have finally joined the global knitting scene.

What most clearly separates the new generation of knitters from the old is the discovery of the

Japanese yarn advertisement.

"amateur" knitters' techniques introduced in this exhibition were stunning and incredible. Japanese knitters' standard levels are quite high, which we were unaware of for many years due to a lack of comparison. Still, our knitting and crocheting has been guided by strict methods that we have followed blindly; this practice removes flexibility and individual discretion. If you could follow the instructions perfectly, you would get a professional outcome; if you could not, it was as if someone whispered in your ear, "You are not good enough. Discipline!" If you knit in your own original way, someone would point it out and give you advice on how to correct it. High standards require high obedience, no freedom permitted.

This description might sound exaggerated, but this characteristic works in two directions. The advantage of it is that a good portion of the population of Japanese knitters is highly qualified. The disadvantage is that this skill level narrows the entrance for newcomers interested in knitting. Here in Tokyo, you do not normally find novice knitters on the street. When you confess, "I knit" to someone, you must already be highly proficient. People admire knitters because they are proficient enough to call themselves knitters.

So when we encountered EZ's pronouncement, "Actually, there is no wrong way to knit," it sounded incredible to us, and we sensed that there was no similar EZ in Japan. We wondered whether the absence of this sentiment in Japanese knitting might be one of reasons knitting doesn't spread as easily here.

However, the new generation can read EZ's words for themselves and see how contemporary knitting goes far beyond what Japanese culture has to offer, from Nora Gauhgan's newest stunning designs, to Dave Cole's American flag swatch made with gigantic needles and a pair of excavators. Now we can freely combine dignified, stringent chart knitting techniques and relaxed, unconfined knitting methods, right alongside our computer screens.

freedom of knitting and the release if offers from the curse of discipline. In the 1960s, the president of Tokio Hamanaka, one of Japan's surviving yarn companies, came up with a motto: "(Knitting as handcraft) is something anyone can try; but the garment must be exquisite like the professionally made, and have perspective and depth." This concept was evident in two exhibitions in London that were organized by Yoshimi Kihara. The

Teaching Knitting, Japanese Style: Jean Wong

The Nihon Amimono Culture Association (NAC) is the teaching arm of Nihon Vogue, esteemed publishers of Japanese knitting books. It first opened the doors of its flagship, thirteen-story crafts-education building (one floor per discipline offered) in the 1950s, and in 1961, it was accredited by the Japanese Ministry of Culture. Now it boasts outposts all over the world, and to date has graduated fifty thousand instructors, who have spent between seven and nine years mastering all disciplines of handcraft.

Known for its extremely exacting methods, the NAC teaches things like using different shaping for the front and back of a sweater's armhole; drafting patterns to fit your own body using the metric system, graph paper, and a nifty tool called a gauge ruler; and blocking—yes, blocking—your gauge swatches.

Jean Wong was certified through the NAC in Taipei and now teaches throughout Vancouver, Canada (her current hometown), and the United States.

"I first learned to knit when I was in elementary school from my neighbor who lived across the street. She taught me how to knit baby hats, booties, and straight scarves—I wouldn't really call it 'learning' so much as following along with her instructions. My mother wasn't a knitter herself, so I believe that was when I was first hooked onto knitting. When I was pregnant with my eldest son, I picked up knitting again so I could make things for my baby, and I joined a private tutoring school that offered classes. I was disappointed, though, since they taught only knitting techniques, and none of the design and calculation skills I was looking for. When my son turned two, I saw an ad in the paper that was recruiting students for a newly established NAC course in Taiwan, and it instantly convinced me to sign up. I was an accountant at the time, so I could only go to night classes. Since the teacher was Japanese, living in Taiwan (costing a lot), we went twice the speed as usual, doing classes twice a week instead of the usual once. Because of this, after about two months, I had to quit my full-time job to focus on knitting.

⚏ This vest features a large number of angular arrangements, each piece of which needs to align perfectly with the other. All the measurements are personalized to the wearer. *Jean Wong, knittingwithjean. com NAC (Nihon Amimono Culture Association www. nac-web.org), certified Nihon Vogue Knitting trainer*

"I quickly found that the NAC course was exactly what I was looking for. They encouraged tailored knitting, instead of the usual follow-the-pattern classes that I'd been exposed to in the past. There was also a lot of focus on fine finishing—in fact, the fine finishing techniques are very detail-oriented, which creates works that stand up to the strictest scrutiny—and I felt that it gave my work a much more professional feel. Also, there was a tremendous amount of freedom—a student could use any yarn and any stitch pattern to make their work truly unique.

"My husband worked for an American multinational company in their Taipei office, frequently went on business trips to the United States, and interacted frequently with Westerners. My younger son also had a severe allergy problem that was made much worse because of Taiwan's tropical climate; his doctor jokingly suggested that the only solution to it was to move to a drier area, say Australia or North America. Given that my husband's dealings were primarily in the United States, we decided that North America would be a less startling change.

"I had no idea about the knitting scene in Vancouver prior to moving here, and in fact did not

Kazekobo

Kazekobo is the trade name of Japanese knitwear designer Yoko Hatta. For more than thirty years, in a fickle and ever-changing industry, Kazekobo has been a knitting force to be reckoned with. In the 1960s and 1970s, she was part of a wave known as the "Mansion Makers," in which young designers established their own micro-brands of clothing and supplied them to boutiques. Today she publishes books; the morning we met in New York City, where she was visiting, she showed me galleys of her latest book on Fair Isle knitting, which featured a distinctly wonderful and commonsensically Japanese group of full-color knitting charts. She also creates patterns for magazines, appears on television to discuss clothing, lectures, teaches, contributes articles on all manner of crafts, and designs collections for yarn companies eager to showcase their wares at important trade shows.

Kazekobo's style has been defined as simple, with "subtle hints of contemporary detailing as well as, by contrast, making rather complex designs appear disarmingly simple." But the designer herself is too modest to make these pronouncements about her work, insisting instead that she merely knits what she is asked to. (She will admit, however, that she enjoys almost complete freedom in her designing, a privilege that comes only with prestige.) For all her hard work over the years, Kazekobo's place in the Japanese knitting pantheon is also, at least in some tiny measure, her heritage. Her mother was a crafts editor for the publisher Kodansya; at the end of our interview, when I showed her a book of Japanese knitwear designs from the 1960s, hoping to get her to identify an over-arching Japanese "style," she looked at the cover briefly and remarked: "I think my mother edited that book."

"I don't have children, so I've been working all my life. That is pretty rare in this field. Some designers became popular in a short time and became known for a style, then faded out. We designers are very flexible when it comes to what we do. I don't categorize myself. As I get older, I understand what editors and yarn companies want. What I do reflects the lifestyle and dress style of the time.

"I can do what I want," says Hatta of the incredibly detailed and skillful designs she stitches up for yarn companies, which are shown at trade shows to promote the yarn to retailers. "The director of the company makes the theme," (pictured left, above, and on facing page, "Ballets Russes" and "African Rhapsody.") "Then I work my understanding of the theme."
Photos by Yoko Hatta

"My mother was an editor. She worked for Kodansya before World War II. There were only a few women editors working for publishers. She grew up and got married. My father was in southern Manchuria running a company when Japan was [colonized]. I was born in Manchuria—we couldn't come back. My father lost everything; he had to give it all back to China. He was already sixty years old. When we finally came back to Japan, my mother started working. We had no toys, we had crochet books. We were unbelievably poor.

"My mother had to practice knitting and crochet because she worked in that department. She did it for her work, to understand. I read pattern books and had a do-it-yourself spirit—I made toys. I made lace in junior high, but I still couldn't knit—crochet was easier. I wanted to make some garments, so in high school I ripped out a sweater, steamed the yarn, and made a vest. It seems strange now to think how important this event became in my life.

"I wanted to work in stage design. I took a course, but I was not good at space designing. And I was not patient for working with directors—they are really difficult people. I couldn't take it; I decided to do something else. By now I could knit, so I started making garments and brought them to boutiques; there were not many people knitting in the 1970s in Tokyo. I was making something interesting. I didn't have any money, and I liked to make clothes. If we saw Pierre Cardin designs, we couldn't afford to buy them, but we could copy them.

"Women older than my generation, many of those women started working before they got married, and they knew sewing, knitting, crocheting—that was in most women's background. Now, many housewives don't work compared to the Western world. Women in Japan, if they don't need to work, they don't work. They have hobbies and they cook food for their husbands. Young women's interest is not anymore in handicraft. At one time in the 1980s, knitting was popular. Almost all women made sweaters for their boyfriends. Then one day it ended, because not that many women could knit nicely, and their boyfriends didn't want to wear these sweaters. For a while, people looked down on knitting. Recently, crochet especially has been coming back; with crochet you can make smaller things, very beautiful and up-to-date. A lot of young designers are using it. In Japan we don't ask why we knit *and* crochet, we ask why Westerners don't do both. The word *amimono* means to work with yarn, even lace making, netting, embroidery. There is no boundary. To a Japanese, knitting and crochet are the same. They both became popular here at the same time.

"I work for different yarn companies, using their yarn. I sell designs to the yarn companies. They give me a theme for the season, and I can do what I want. The director of the yarn company makes the theme—one fall's concept had to do with the anniversary of Darwin, and another theme was "Ballet Russes." Then I work my understanding of the theme. I make designs, swatches, patterns, check the finishing. Most Japanese handicraft designers do the same, although some work for the fashion industry. My designs are shown at yarn trade shows to promote the yarn to retailers. Also, if you buy a pattern magazine or book, my name is in it.

"I think in my field, what I do might give some influence to the knitting and handicraft field. I stay in my studio to do work. These days, the Prince of Knitting [Mitsuharu Hirose (*see page* 195)] comes on channel three to teach knitting. One designer has a yarn store called Victory, and her patterns—maybe from a Western perspective—they look like they have a Japanese style: kind of simple, using natural, thin yarn. I think most designers don't think of 'Japanese style.' But if there is one, maybe it has to do with materials; Japan is good at bamboo and silk."

get involved in the local knitting community for some time. After about two years of life in Canada, I wanted to kill some time while waiting for my sons' English tutoring classes to finish, so I went to the mall. I was wearing one of my own somewhat complicated patterns, and a lady approached me in a shoe store. She invited me to join the West Coast Knitters' Guild; that was my first step back into the knitting community. The same lady opened a yarn store some years later, and invited me to teach some of my techniques in her store.

"I think that one of the most fundamental philosophies in the NAC course is that there's no reason why a student can't make professional-quality work without being a professional, and no reason why students cannot make a work truly their own. I believe that this sort of thought can be applied to regular knitting classes as well, with a stronger focus on tailoring and much more detail-oriented teaching. I generally offer fine finishing courses because it is the least time-consuming for

students, and it allows them to quickly learn some techniques that can dramatically improve the feel of their work.

"I feel like Western knitters generally do not have a huge amount of trouble adapting to Japanese knitting techniques. There is certainly some difficulty in the beginning stages, since the topics addressed are almost entirely foreign to what students have learned in the past. I hope they will demand more from themselves after taking my classes. The many techniques I teach all add a tremendous amount of polish to one's work. I feel that I need to pass on the notion that everyone can create professional works that unleash their creativity, and that students can become more than knitters, but artists with their own freedom. This I think is incredibly important; so many of my students have spent time creating works that they are then dissatisfied with. I feel that the NAC program, with its focus on customization and detail, allows students to really gain a sense of accomplishment when they finish."

"The Prince of Knitting:"

Matsuharu Hirose

By Jun Miyamoto

The Prince of Knitting, replete in one of his signature "precise" crocheted jackets.
Photo courtesy of Matsuharu Hirose

Matsuharu Hirose is an icon of old-school Japanese knitting, with his own television show (Oshare-Koho, which means "Fashionable Atelier"), a fan club, and even a museum devoted to his creations. Jun Miyamoto interviewed him at the tail end of a day he'd spent teaching at Nihon Vogue. "After that interview with Mr. Hirose, I found an appropriate way to describe him," writes Miyamoto. "It must be 'missionary of amimono (needlecraft).' He loves creating with yarn so much, this makes him happy to be a missionary."

When Matsuharu Hirose was kid, his grandmother worked at ripping out old sweaters for neighbors, and there was always yarn around him. He was a boy who loved handcrafts like sewing, and when he was in elementary school, his teacher praised his handcraft skill and his open mind, which gave him confidence that he was good at what he loved to do.

As for knitting and crochet, surprisingly, these he learned from books. His mother didn't knit, nor did his grandmother. But with that confidence gained through his teacher, he gave them a try. And, there was a lot of yarn at home. When Hirose was in junior high school, he made mittens and scarves in crocheting, and in high school, he knitted up his first sweater.

Since Hirose's first appearance on TV in 1993, he has been teaching knitting and crochet all over Japan, always wearing his own crocheted jacket. His style is quite clear: feminine with a flowery motif and frill, a lacy, delicate texture, a body-conscious style, all of which require very good skills. He believes his approaches are original to knitting. Generally, in his opinion, the image of knitting is casual and something just to keep you warm—rather unsophisticated, mundane items. But by revising your view, you can use a knitted garment to be original and to be fashionable. He wanted to transform knitting into a gorgeous party dress.

Hirose developed his knitting skill in knitting school, and by teaching knitting classes at the NAC (*see page 191*). He also worked for several years at Nihon Vogue as a knitting book editor. With these technical capabilities in his background, he believes that he can get knitters to like his style. He has a clear consciousness of being eye-catching as a male knitting teacher and designer in a female-dominated knitting world. He thinks it's good to command attention, which is very important for him. He hopes that people who have seen him on TV or on the covers of his knitting books will study this lacy-crochet-jacket-wearing man and be interested, not only in him, but also in knitting.

His approach to fashioning garments comes from his admiration for women; that is to say, he wants women to wear feminine, elegant clothing rather than manly, casual items. He thinks feminine dress makes women look beautiful and elegant. And, of course, he offers a precise technique to make it real.

In Hirose's opinion, typical Japanese knitters are married women, aged forty to sixty, with a few in their thirties—housewives who are free of taking care of kids, and can afford yarn and classes on their husbands' income. Most of them have no ambition to be professional knitters or teachers, but like to knit for their own pleasure. In his opinion, only about 1 percent of Japanese knitters are in their teens and twenties, and even schools that have homecraft teachers rarely pass on the knitting technique to their students. Watching this sad occurrence around the younger generation, Hirose would like to be a catalyst to attract interest to his craft. These days he's traveling all over Japan, teaching kids' knitting classes in addition to classes and lectures for adults.

When Hirose traveled to the United States with Japanese knitters to watch the knitting boom, what he found were people who loved knitting simple, endless, stockinette and garter-stitch garments. He felt at the moment that what Japanese knitters wanted and what U.S. knitters wanted were quite different, although he guesses that now Japanese knitters, like U.S. knitters, are also looking for healing from the craft. In recent years, the idea of the knit café was imported from the United States into Japan, and it was welcomed. Getting together to knit and crochet, chatting, and drinking coffee, means the craft is considered a tool of communication, rather than a means to make something useful and beautiful.

Hirose considers it his role in the Japanese knitting world to get people's attention in order to save the future of knitting in this country. Younger knitting generations seem to prefer small, easy, fast, and pretty items like hats and scarves over challenging, complicated, time-consuming garments. Still, if after making several simple hats and scarves, young knitters one day find Hirose's delicate and challenging knitting to be interesting, he would be very happy to be there to act as a navigator.

Habu Textiles

Habu Textiles is a shop in New York City that specializes in unusual yarns from Japan, some of which are never otherwise seen outside that country, or by anyone other than the rare breed of Japanese fashion designer. Founded in 1999 by Takako Ueki as a weaving studio, the shop currently carries three hundred fifty types of yarn—such as bamboo, soy, silk-wrapped stainless steel, hemp bark—and has become a Mecca for yarn enthusiasts of every variety. Not to be confused with the Japanese luxury yarn manufacturer known as Habu in the United States and Avril in Japan, this unique and lovely outpost derives its name from a poisonous snake indigenous to the region of Okinawa. Explains Ueki, "I wanted to have a name related to those islands. 'Ha' means 'wave.' 'Bu' means 'fabric.' We chose a different character for 'ha' for our name, which means 'number eight.' Because of its bottom-wide shape, this number is believed to bring a life which will slowly . . . open up for you." Following is a small tour led by Ueki to open up the world of rare and gorgeous Japanese yarns.

The yarn at Habu Textiles—most of it cast off from the Japanese fashion industry—is tucked into every available space in the small Manhattan shop.
Photo by Veda Alban

"Japan has no natural resources. Even with silk, Japan produces a very small amount, not enough to make an industry. Silk is imported from China and Vietnam, and the quality has gotten quite good. Nothing is produced in Japan; they are experts at processing—taking other people's materials and making them better.

"Usually the fashion industry goes into the mills, then the factories to try to make what they want. Hand knitting and weaving come next. Yarns are used by the fashion industry and are discontinued within a year. I push the mills to keep making some of these yarns for me. Some of the smaller ones are willing to do it. Some of the yarns are imported from Italy or China, then dyed in Japan.

"Our yarns show a mixture of many different techniques—printing, dyeing, and also painting —some of which are unique to Japan. About one-third of our yarn comes from Habu in Japan, but I work with six or seven suppliers. I go to Japan one or two times a year to look for new yarn.

"Japanese love cables and Fair Isle. Anything complicated. Maybe because we are conscious of what we use for materials. We are a big textile culture, especially kimono culture; older people grew up touching fabric—maybe that is kind of ingrained. Yarns from Japan tend to have a little more texture; they're thinner. That's not necessarily true of all yarns from Japan, like Noro. I just wanted to offer beautiful yarns that didn't fit into a category. Because so many of these yarns are so thin, it is more interesting and easier to mix several yarns to come up with a yarn that is your own. We always make suggestions of how to put two or three together—that makes a huge difference in what comes out in the end."

Knitted mohair: "This yarn is already knitted into a multicolored tube on a knitting Nancy. You can knit with it as is or stuff fiber inside and felt it. A few yards could create a wild-looking scarf or necklace."

Soy yarn: "This probably came from China. Soy whey left over from making tofu is processed, sprayed through a nozzle, then spun into fiber. It is very soft."

Printed *gima* cotton: "When I started, people didn't know about this yarn. *Gima* literally means 'fake linen.' It is made to feel like linen, but is 100 percent cotton (there is a silk *gima* too). It's flat and it's made by lining up strands of fine cotton and gluing them together with a kind of sizing. Flat yarn shows off certain patterns well, like herringbone and simple stockinette, but it's also great in seed stitch or garter stitch—very three-dimensional."

Stainless-steel yarn: "A 40-micron stainless-steel core is wrapped with a fine yarnlike silk, linen, or cotton. It's high-tech. The original invention of this was not from the yarn mill but from industry—it was created to make oil filters. Because of the stainless steel, there is a memory in the yarn. It's good for making 3-D fabric. Twist it around—it will stay in that shape unless you straighten it out. It is easiest if you knit this yarn in two strands; however, a lace stitch in a single strand is beautiful."

Silk and fiddlehead fern cotton: "This is a very traditional yarn from the north of Japan—Niigata—made from an old technique and originally used for weaving kimonos. It is such a soft silk with a kind of rustic look."

Processed bamboo fiber: "Bamboo fiber is liquefied using a rayon technique and formed into tape. It is extremely soft—much softer than spun bamboo—and the sheen is gorgeous. It also dyes very well."

Spun bamboo: "This is very fine, flat, and stiff. Unlike a bamboo yarn made like rayon, this one is spun, and then processed to get its particular pearly sheen."

Pompon *moiré*: "Pompons are attached to two-ply nylon, but this yarn came from a mistake. The yarn was supposed to be chenille spaced with pompons, but the machine malfunctioned and the balls were shot in in tighter configuration. The company looked at it and thought it made a good yarn. Really cute, with little pompons everywhere."

Paper yarn: "This is very particular to mills in Japan. It can only be made by a small manufacturer, as it needs a lot of sizing, since otherwise it is too brittle. It's not cost effective, so many large mills don't want to bother. For one of the yarns we carry, linen pulp is made into paper and shredded. For another, small pieces of linen paper are sandwiched between the nylon core; this is a very strong, yet adorable yarn. It looks like snowflakes knitted on large needles.

Pine: "This is a recycled yarn from pine. It is usually used to create the *obi* sash for kimonos in Japan. It is very sturdy. You can use it to make great sculptural pieces in knitting."

Tsumugi silk combination: "This is an unusual silk yarn, originally made for kimonos. It has so many colors within a strand! Silk yarn is wrapped in silk cord, which is an ordinary idea, but the cord is wrapped horizontally to give it a new look."

Pineapple: "This yarn is made from pineapple and ramie. The pineapple fiber is taken out from the vein of the pineapple leaves. Ramie is added for additional strength. You can knit a very light garment from this yarn."

Dyed paper/silk: "This is a paper yarn with a raw silk (for additional strength). It has been dyed by an indigo dyer in Japan without any synthetic chemicals in the vat. The green is achieved by overdyeing the indigo with a natural yellow dye called *kihada*. Naturally dyed indigo yarns need to 'age.' The darker-colored indigo, especially, will dye your hands at first as you work with it. This is because indigo never penetrates into the fiber, but simply sits on the surface of the yarn. After letting it sit for several months and also washing repeatedly, the color will settle. The blue will simply get better from then on."

China

A scant amount of information is available concerning hand knitting in China. Still, what little literature exists about the matter is eye-opening and certainly shows how thoroughly universal the craft is and has been throughout time.

Owen Lattimore, professor of Chinese studies and once-advisor to Chiang Kai-shek, posits that there was no real hand knitting in China until after World War II—this despite a rich textile trade that he dates, possibly, as far back as 2000 BC. But he does offer this interesting tidbit in his book *The Desert Road to Turkistan*:

> After defeat of the White Army during Russian Civil War in 1923, monarchists retreated to China where they were transported eastward by camel. To pass time, Russian soldiers taught Chinese camel pullers to knit. They would reach back to the first camel of the file they were leading, pluck a handful from the neck, and roll it in their palms into the beginning of a length of yarn; a weight was attached to this, and given a twist to start it spinning, and the man went on feeding wool into the thread until he had spun enough yarn to continue his knitting.

Antonia Finnane, in her book *Changing Clothes in China*, finds evidence of a cottage industry in China in the early 1910s, albeit surrounding home knitting machines that could be purchased outright or rented on a monthly basis, by one family or a group of families pooling their resources. During World War I, "as European imports dried up, small factories and cottage industries mushroomed and demand for the hand knitting machine soared," she writes. A 1912 advertisement pitched to Shanghai residents claims, "The only machine capable of increasing your income! . . . You can also earn up to three dollars a day by instructing others!"

Hand knitting was still in its infancy at the beginning of World War II, although Finnane quotes a fashion feature from 1924 claiming that knitted woolen garments, including children's socks and hats, women's scarves, tops, and vests, "have become very popular." She finds hand-knitted garments being mass-produced at schools for the deaf in the 1930s. By the end of World War II, knitting had taken off. Finnane takes a stab at pinpointing the swiftness of its spread: "It is possible that European handicrafts had an impact in Shanghai during the war through the agency of thousands of Jewish refugees, who unlike the average expatriate lived among poor Chinese and had to make a living in humble ways."

By the mid- to late 1960s, Mao Zedong was sending educated urban youth to the countryside for reeducation. Finnane offers this story about one girl's experience:

> Mu Aiping ended up in an isolated corner of Shanxi, where the Beijing sent-downers found themselves scratching for roots to eat during the annual spring famine. They were astonished to find that knitting—from home-made, poor quality wool—was seen as a man's job, while shoes were not bought in a store but hand-made by women . . . She presented her host family with some green knitting yarn, which was used to make a jumper for their future daughter-in-law. More than twenty-two years later she returned to the village for a visit, and found that the garment was still being worn.

Pattern books, where they exist, follow the Japanese example, "most obvious in the preference for diagrams rather than verbal instructions as the normal form of recipes," says Richard Rutt.

✳ Chinese Zodiac
Tabi socks, designed by
Pinpilan Wangsai. *Photo by
Sue Flanders and Janine Kosel*

✳ Good Fortune Scarf,
designed by Lily Chin.
*Photo by Sue Flanders and
Janine Kosel*

❖ *Bed of Wool Skeins*, Xian,
1997, watercolor on paper,
by David Paskett.
Bridgeman Art Library

Bhotia female, Buddhist, near Lhassa, knitting (1865–1875). *Courtesy of New York Public Library Photography Collection, Miriam and Ira D. Wallach Division of Art, Prints, and Photographs #1125289*

India

"Knitting has never been important to the people of India," writes Richard Rutt, "but there seem to be traces of knitting traditions entering the sub-continent from the Middle East as well as from Europe." In his 1903 book *Indian Art at Delhi*, Sir George Watt remarked that knitting was unknown in the country "prior to the efforts of the missionaries. It is called *jorab-bunna*," he writes, "and is taught in most female schools."

Rutt itemizes several hand-knitted articles that bear out his assertion of both Eastern and Western influence. First is a pair of socks in the Victoria & Albert Museum in London, "made of Chaddar floss rough silk in Shahpore jail in the mid-nineteenth century. They are knitted from top to toe and have grafting under the heel."

Another example is a white cap, also owned by the Victoria & Albert, "covered with the typical *botch* or 'Paisley' pattern, well-known in Kashmir shawls, knitted in black, blue, and red . . . Bands of flowers, in red, yellow, blue, and green on a black ground, surround the rim and the crown . . . [This piece is] known to have come from Ludhiana in the Punjab, where a colony of Punjabis settled in 1833 after they had left their homeland because of famine."

There is also a certain slipper from the 1960s, possessed of patterns that can "nearly all be found in the Turkish designs recorded by Betsy Harrell and Kenan Ozbel."

And finally, there's a piece that is a testament to the way knitting can arrive in a culture, then be embraced by it: another pair of stockings, "these long in red with black, yellow, white, and green sprays. 'Knee guards' are attached to the front, pointing upwards. The knitting is done from the toe to top. These appear to be entirely Indian." All in all, though, concludes Rutt, "The whole picture is far from clear."

✳ Mid-nineteenth-century nightcap (probably), knitted wool lined with a coarser layer of undyed knitting. According to the Victoria & Albert Museum, "Knitting is not a craft traditional to India, but was introduced by Europeans, probably in the late eighteenth century. This piece was probably knitted by the Kashmiri immigrants who created the woolen shawls. Kashmiris left their homes because of a famine and settled in Ludhiana in 1833, where the piece originates. The knitted hats are strongly reminiscent of Kashmir shawls in their use of the 'boteh' or paisley motif. It is most likely that the shawls and knitted items found a market in Simla, the summer hill station of the British administration." *Courtesy of Victoria & Albert Museum #2006AH2069*

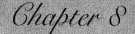

Chapter 8

AUSTRALIA AND NEW ZEALAND

An Australian volunteer driver knits while waiting for U.S. officers to finish eating
lunch at Menzies Hotel. Photo by Wallace Kirland, January 1, 1942.
Time & Life Pictures/Getty Images

A T TIMES IN AUSTRALIA'S HISTORY it was said that 'Australia rode on the sheep's back,'" claims a textbook called *Society and Environment*. In fact, since 1796, when the first small colony of merinos was introduced to the continent, wool has been an integral part of the Australian national psyche. That continues to be true today, with more than 95 percent of the wool produced in Australia sold for export.

As for what Australians knit with this wool and other materials, it did not vary much at first from what was knit by British and other original European settlers, who brought their own traditions to these new shores. However, through the generations, distinctly Australian forms of knitting began to emerge—a testament to the ways in which this ancient craft is ever evolving.

Knitting in New Zealand tells a similar tale, with early European settlers bringing their knitting with them and using it as you might expect: to knit up garb for their families and decorations for their homes. Some items were highly practical; others fell into the realm of parlor knitting. As Heather Nicholson reports in her excellent history, *The Loving Stitch*, when immigrant "gentlewomen" finally arrived on New Zealand's shores in the late nineteenth century, they brought English pattern books containing "recipes for lace edgings, beaded purses, collars, trims, gloves, pin cushions, window curtains, fringes, bags, various sorts of wraps such as mantles, clouds, boas, fascinators . . . and scarves, along with cloths and runners." A sort of desperation tinged the craft on and off throughout the years, as many rural settlers struggled with crushing poverty and were forced to make all manner of everything.

English "gentlewomen" arriving on New Zealand's shores brought with them a fondness for posh knitting—such as for bead-knit bags—that was assuredly challenged by the poverty they encountered in their new lives. *Museum of Fine Arts, Boston*

Madame Weigel

Born in erstwhile Prussia in 1847, Johanna Weigel arrived in Melbourne in 1877 and very quickly became a beloved arbiter—and enabler—of homemade fashion for several generations of Australian women. In these late years of the nineteenth century, many rural homemakers had no access to store-bought clothing for themselves or their families, and to them, Madame Weigel opened up a brand-new world of professionally tailored patterns for dresses and pretty much everything else under the sun.

In the 1880s, Weigel and her husband Oscar began publishing the *Journal of Fashion*—in subsequent decades retitled *Madame Weigel's Journal of Fashions*. According to the Powerhouse Museum in Sydney, until mass-produced and inexpensive pattern books became more prevalent, this was "the primary local source for needlework patterns for clothes" of the era and included, of course, plenty of patterns for things knitted. They included the Smart Slipover, described thusly: "Worn over a skirt blouse . . . this little slipover is the essence of chic." And this somewhat ingenious offering for Spiral Bedsocks: "being heel-less, these socks give double wear as they may be continuously turned and still fit well."

By the 1930s, Madame Weigel was putting out some of those mass-produced, inexpensive knitting pattern books of her own. They were, says Heather Nicholson in *The Loving Stitch*, "probably the most popular knitting recipe books ever published in Australasia." How many were eventually published, exactly, remains a bit of a muddle; the Powerhouse Museum owns a copy of *Cosies, Afghans, Cushions, Wool Novelties* "Series #1" from 1935; an extant edition of *Cushions & Cosies* from 1937 is identified as Volume 6. But no record remains of how many series, or volumes, ever emerged to dazzle the knitting public.

For however few or many of these fifteen- and sixteen-page pattern booklets there were, they

Australia went mad for Madame Weigel and her pamphlets on tea cosy knitting. Here, a booklet from the mid- to late 1930s features a pattern for a cosy knit in Daffodil Stitch (*see page 208*). *Collection, Powerhouse Museum, Sydney*

Madame Weigel's Cosy Knitted in Daffodil Stitch

If desired it may be carried out in one colour, with edgings of contrasting, or a charming idea is to commence at the lower edge with a darker shade, and work each four succeeding lines of daffodil pattern in a shade lighter, i.e.–The lower line, Orange, 2nd line, Burnt Orange, 3rd line, Gold, 4th line, Daffodil Yellow, 5th line Primrose, edging each line with one row of green, and finishing the top with green. The following are directions for a five-cup teapot. Should a larger or smaller cosy be required, add or subtract 13 stitches for every ½ inch larger or smaller in circumference. The cosy is worked in two halves, and is finished at top with a cluster of green leaves.

MATERIALS REQUIRED

For cosy in one colour with contrasting edges–

2 oz. 4-ply with ½ oz. contrasting for edges and leaves at top.

For cosy with five colours–

five ½ oz. skeins of 4-ply, with 1/2 oz. of contrasting for edges and leaves at top.

1 pair No. 11 knitting needles.

Commencing at lower edge cast on 159 stitches in green (or colour used for edging the lines of the daffodils). Break off and join in main colour. Work as follows:–

1st Row.–* P. 3, K. 10, repeat from * throughout ending P. 3.

2nd Row.–K. 3, * P. 10, K. 3, repeat from *.

3rd Row.–* P. 3, K. 2 tog., K. 6, K. 2 tog., repeat from *, ending P. 3.

4th Row.–K. 3, * P. 8, K. 3, repeat from *.

5th Row.–* P. 3, K. 2 tog., K. 4, K. 2 tog., repeat from * ending P. 3.

6th Row.–K. 3. * P. 6, K. 3; repeat from *.

7th Row.– P. 3, K. 2 tog., K. 2, K. 2 tog., repeat from *, ending P. 3.

8th Row.–K. 3, * P. 4, K. 3; repeat from *.

9th Row.–* P. 3, K. 2 tog., K. 2 tog.; repeat from *, ending P. 3.

10th Row.–K. 3, * P. 2, K. 3; repeat from *.

11th Row.–* P. 3, K. 2 tog.; repeat from *, ending P. 3.

12th Row. –K. 3, * P. 1, K. 3; repeat from *.

13th Row. –* P. 2, P. 2 tog. (of which 1 is a purl st. and 1 a knit st.); repeat from *, ending P. 3.

14th Row. –Knit.

These 14 rows make 1 line of daffodil stitch. Break off.

Join in green for the second line of daffodils.

Next Row.– * K. 3. Cast on 10 stitches *. Repeat from * to * to end of row (159 stitches).

Break off green and join in main colour.

Repeat from 2nd to 14th row.

Continue in this manner until 5 rows of daffodils are worked (or required depth), then cast off as follows:–

slip 1, knit 2 tog., pass slip st. over *. Repeat to end of row.

Work another side to correspond.

Neaten the edges and sew together, allowing an opening for spout and handle. Draw top in a little and finish with a cluster of green leaves.

To Knit Leaf.–

Cast on 1 stitch and knit in garter stitch as follows :–

1st, 2nd, 3rd, 4th, and 5th rows, K. twice into 1st then knit straight on 6 stitches for 10 rows.

In next 5 rows decrease by knitting first 2 stitches together.

Work about 8 leaves and arrange in pretty cluster at top.

If a lining is desired cast on 50 stitches and knit in garter stitch for depth of 4 lines of daffodils, then decrease by knitting 2 stitches together in every second row at three regular intervals for the remainder. Cast off. Knit corresponding side and slipstitch inside of cosy.

—From *Cushions & Cosies,* Madame Weigel, c. 1937

caused a great sensation, particularly over their offerings for tea cosies. *Cosies, Afghans, Cushions, Wool Novelties* alone offered, in addition to patterns for afghans, egg cozies, and pillows, the Dutch Girl Tea Cosy; Basket Tea Cosy; Early Victorian Tea Cosy; Vandyke Crocheted Tea Cosy; Tea Cosy in Fancy Knitting; Honeycomb Cosy in Crochet; Honeycomb Cosy in Knitting; Crocheted Tea Cosy in Tricot Stitch; and the Knitted Berry and Bell Stitch Cosy.

Clearly, Madame Weigel was all too familiar with the crafty wants and desires of a nation of tea drinkers. However, according to Nicholson, "A pattern book full of patterns for remarkably ruffled bedjackets and capes" was a close runner-up in the popularity department. It's decidedly fitting that Madame Weigel's *pièce de résistance* in the cozy department was her whimsical pattern for a koala. How Australian can you get?

"Australiana"

Beginning in the mid-1970s and continuing on throughout the 1980s came the fervent embracing in Australia of all things, well, Australian: from natural motifs like kangaroos to the translating of aboriginal designs to fashion. Along with this came a reclaiming of Australia's great asset, an industry that had seen decline off and on through the years: wool.

One of the pioneers of this reclamation was Jenny Kee, who opened a boutique called Flamingo Park in Sydney in 1973. With her "first winter season looming," curator Glynis Jones wrote for the Powerhouse Museum, "she decided to create a garment that was distinctly Australian combining wool 'our greatest export' with the traditional craft of knitting with 'purely Australian imagery.'" The result? A koala jumper, the likes of which Kee was to design and redesign for almost two decades (*see page* 210). One was even given to Princess Diana in 1981 as a wedding gift; she was photographed wearing it a year later at a polo match—which, of course, resulted in an international tumult. Orders poured in, a special pattern for the koala sweater was commissioned by an Australian women's magazine, and Jenny Kee and her version of knitted Australiana were on the map. "There's a new Nationalism taking over the Australian fashion industry," reported the *Daily Telegraph*. "Imported goods are strictly taboo."

Jenny Kee Winter Knits, published in 1988, made much of this phenomenon. It featured twenty-five patterns for dresses, sweaters, and cardigans, in bright geometrics of cockatoos, emus, and "Oz Flora" that fairly scream "1980s!" Her 1990s follow-up, *Knits from Nature*, continued the theme, with bold, bulky knits featuring dolphins, stingrays, and kangaroos, along with a plethora of global peace and nature-loving symbols.

Concurrent to all this, two art teachers giving classes in Fremantle Prison started Desert Designs, a company meant to offer a commercial outlet for indigenous artisans—one in particular named Jummy Pike, who'd been their student. This idea had been raging around Australia for a few years already, with aboriginal designs turning up on batiks and other fabrics. Its applications to knitwear culminated in Desert Designs' 1990 book (titled, aptly, *Desert Designs*), which featured twenty-six knits with aboriginal designs by Pike and two others: Deagidditt, a silk-screener from the western desert; and Doris Gingingara, a self-taught naturalist artist from the Northern Territory.

While the Desert Designs sweaters are clearly of their era—with strong design elements in bright colors or highly contrasting black and white—they offer an interesting glimpse of aboriginal life. Each sweater is accompanied by a photograph of the original artwork that inspired it, depicting things like sand hills and desert flowers, birds from the Dreaming of aboriginal mythology, outlines of legends, and artifacts important to aboriginal life. A few paragraphs explain the images. For one, by Deagidditt, of large hands splattered onto the body of the sweater, the book relates: "'To the north of my country, the people make these hand prints on rock walls. Sometimes you might see a hand with one or two fingers missing.' If you visit the sites of cave paintings virtually anywhere in Aboriginal Australia you will often see 'stencils' made by people placing their hands on the cave wall and spraying white ocher from their mouths over their hands creating silhouettes. This ancient form of art is the inspiration for this design."

Accompanying another, with a freeform design at the shoulder by Gingingara, is this description: "'These men are sitting down making rainstorm magic. They bring storm clouds and lightning over, bringing the rain.' The rainy season in the north brings new growth, new foods, and tells the people that it is time to move on in their seasonal nomadic migrations. Rainmaking is an important ritual in a dry country like Australia, and certain clever people, tribal 'doctors,' have the ceremonial

A Koala "jumper" knit by Jenny Kee was presented to Princess Diana as a wedding gift; a year later, she was photographed wearing it, and Kee was bombarded with orders for her knits, most of which featured bold designs that were unmistakably "Australian." *Collection, Powerhouse Museum, Sydney and Jenny Kee; photo by Marinco Kojdanovski*

knowledge to bring rain, to summon the wrath of the Rainbow Serpent, an ancestral being who often dwells in waterholes and attracts rainclouds."

Australiana knitting, then, proves itself broad enough in focus and context to show the country as it truly is. On one hand, the knitting of Jenny Kee shows the obvious things we associate with Australia, like koalas; on the other, Desert Designs shows the sacred side, providing a glimpse of Australiana's more mystical thinking and spirituality.

Peggy Squares

What to do with leftover yarn is surely a question that has plagued knitters since there's been knitting. And for many, many generations, the answer has been granny squares, or something like them: swatches of mismatched yarn and patterns that can be assembled into blankets and coverlets of all sizes. In New Zealand, they call them Peggy squares, and their story adds a bit of a twist to an otherwise humdrum tale.

With rough times hitting New Zealand during the Depression, knitting meant salvation in more ways than one. Unemployed women could knit for money and to clothe their families. Beginning in 1930, children could knit to help keep each other warm. As Heather Nicholson tells it, four-year-old Peggy Huse, having just learned to knit squares that her mother had fashioned into a doll's blanket for her, was "discovered" by a woman named Muriel Lewis, who, as the "Wool Woman," contributed to a weekly children's radio show broadcast by "Aunt Molly" on station 2YA. Lewis suggested that Aunt Molly tell her child listeners that they could "knit squares with leftovers from their mothers' knitting bags," according to Nicholson, and then she asked little Peggy to come up with instructions for number of stitches necessary to make a six-inch square. The concept was a huge hit.

Writes Nicholson: "Aunt Molly described Peggy and told her listeners how to make 'Peggy squares' . . . The Sunbeams, who sang at Aunt Molly's sessions, started knitting, and Aunt Molly organized the 2YA staff, including some of the men, into knitting Peggy squares. Soon, the idea spread all over New Zealand. Petone Mills even gave the name Peggy to a line of knitting wool . . . Quantities of squares were sent in, along with contributions from children's pocket money to pay for the fabric to line the blankets. Aunt Molly then arranged for volunteers to take on the huge task of sewing the squares together and lining the blankets."

Curiously, the whole concept, and even the name, of Peggy squares was presaged by this entry in an American magazine for children called *Little Folks*, from 1918:

"What's that you have sticking out of your pocket, Peggy?" asked Hugh, pointing to a bumpy place in Peggy's pocket.

"That's my knitting," answered Peggy, bringing out a gay piece of work. "See, it's a Red, White, and Blue square, I'm knitting for the AFGHAN CLUB!"

"What's the AFGHAN CLUB?" asked Hugh.

"Haven't you read about it in LITTLE FOLKS MAGAZINE?" asked Peggy. "It's just great; we all knit squares—nine inch squares—of wool and send them to the editor and she is going to put the squares together for us to make a beautiful AFGHAN."

There's no record of how many blankets were eventually fashioned from the squares Peggy Huse inspired. But it was certainly enough to make the moniker, writes Nicholson, "part of our indigenous vocabulary," with its own entry in the *Dictionary of New Zealand English*.

Kiwicraft

In among the first wave of white settlers to reach the island group, missionaries helped usher in a tradition that came to be known as Kiwicraft. They sought to teach indigenous Maori how to knit (they were already accomplished weavers, of mats and other things, for which they used the harakeke [*Phormium tenax*], or New Zealand flax, indigenous to Norfolk Island and the Chatham Islands). "The prevailing belief," writes Nicholson, "was that lay missionaries skilled in crafts should be used to introduce the 'Arts of Civilized Life' and then lead the people to Christianity by example." The Maori also proved to be excellent sheep shearers—a not insignificant skill in a country newly bustling with ovines (the first sheep were introduced in New Zealand around 1814).

As in Australia, knitting books and magazines came largely from abroad until 1915, when *Her Excellency's Knitting Book* became the first New Zealand-published collection of patterns, including "recipes" for socks, balaclavas, and gloves, sized specifically to fit inside a knitting bag. In addition, as in other countries including Australia, New Zealand knitters did their part knitting during the two World Wars, and knitting to make a (very) little extra money during the Great Depression.

In those lean years, a cottage industry sprang up around the spinning of unsold and otherwise worthless fleeces—a cottage industry of and for men, as it happened. As Nicholson reports, to take advantage of this fleece surplus, certain handy men figured out how to fashion homemade spinning machines; in one instance, "Enormous ingenuity, scrap timber, brass shoe nails and part of a bicycle pump were assembled to a spinning head" and bolted to a sewing machine. One Commander R. R. Beauchamp set up a small business to provide a bit of income for unemployed male university students—spinning local wool, which they then wove into Mackenzie tweed fabric. An interesting

Prudence Mapstone

Prudence Mapstone is an Australian knitter who has gained worldwide renown for her freewheeling style of freeform knitting. To date, she's self-published four enormously popular books on freeform knitting and what you can make with it, and she's recently coauthored a fifth (with Jonelle Raffino). She's a much-beloved teacher whenever and wherever she sets up (work)shop.

"In the very early 1980s, I discovered intarsia-style knitting, and right from the start I graphed out my own complex picture-knit designs. As well as knitting for myself and my family, I created many one-off garments each year for fundraisers at the primary school my daughter attended, and also for the art show at the high school where my husband taught. After a while I was knitting complex, multicolored overcoats, often all in one piece, increasing, decreasing, and working short rows to shape the garments as I knitted. Unfortunately, so much heavy knitting eventually took its toll on my hands. I thought for a while that I was going to have to give up my favorite craft, but after a short break from knitting, I began again in a small way, working with only a few stitches at a time and sometimes combining them with some basic embroidery and crocheting, so that my hands were switching between different ranges of movement.

"About that time, I was told about two creative crocheters from the United Kingdom who worked a form of unusual patchwork crochet; discovering that they created amazing art garments from their random crochet patches led me to more experimentation. The idea of working smallish patches as they did certainly appealed to me, because I had been having the most problems with my hands. So, still combining knitting and crochet together, I continued to play around as my own style developed.

"The two crocheters I refer to are James Walters and the late Sylvia Cosh. They wrote a number of books, both together and separately, which I finally managed to hunt down—notably *The Crochet Workbook*. I believe they belonged to the Knitting Craft Group, which was set up by the British Hand Knitting Association in the 1980s, and their work also appeared in *Wool 'n Magic* by Jan Messent, who was a fellow member of that group. They were certainly at the forefront of creative crochet in the United Kingdom at the time, and coincidentally, around the same time, a number of girls who studied at the Pratt Institute in New York City also started creating amazing artwork with crochet. Perhaps at that time knitting remained more mainstream, as crochet began to move toward the concept of fiber art. I have managed to get copies of most of the more creative, 'no-pattern' crochet books from that time, but just a couple of knitting ones. Many of these early craft books are now beginning to command rather high prices. When James and Sylvia visited Australia in the late 1990s, I was lucky enough take a weekend class with them. Their creations were always totally in crochet, and seeing some of the 'fancy' stitches they used inspired me to experiment even more with crochet, and I soon began to add more than just the plainer stitches I had already been playing with onto my knitting.

One of the "scrumbled" creations of Prudence Mapstone: "Canaray," a freeform knit and crochet sleeveless V-neck top made of cotton, silk, and manmade fibers. *Photo by Prudence Mapstone*

"With freeform, it is sometimes hard to see exactly where you could be heading until each piece starts to develop its own personality, but if you work with a range of colors that go together well, and don't try to work with too many stitches or rows at a time, then it is amazing how well everything just 'grows.' I feel that anything not done to an exact pattern is freeform, but the word *scrumble* came about when I was asked to give a title to my workshop (it had a better ring to it than 'crazy woman's knitting'!). James and Sylvia came up with the term *scrumble* to refer to their approach to freeform crochet. In James' words, 'the crochet pieces, or scrumbles, are made separately and joined, a bit like traditional motifs, into a patchwork, except scrumbles are all different in size, shape and stitch detail, so the patchwork is "organic" with no formal plan.'

"It is definitely possible to create complex freeform garments all in one piece, but as the work gets bigger, it will take more and more concentration to get the piece to do exactly what you wish it to do, and especially when you are making a somewhat solid fabric for a jacket or coat as opposed to a more loose and drapy type of fabric for a shawl.

Working with patches certainly keeps the whole process more enjoyable. Creating smaller pieces that you can arrange later gives you a better opportunity to achieve an overall balance to all of the different colors and textures that you may be using. It is also much easier to create a 'flat' fabric this way. Flat certainly may not be important if you are freeforming for a rug, cushion, or wall hanging . . . but most of us don't want our clothing to stack on the extra inches, so unintentional lumps, bumps, and bulges are generally best avoided for freeform garments. Also, working with many small scrumbles to ultimately create the fabric for larger items will ease the potential strain on your hands, which could happen as the piece becomes progressively heavier.

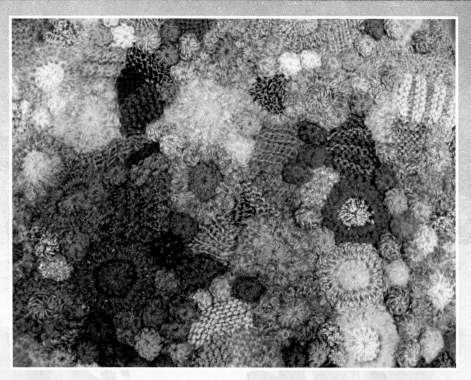

Close-up of "Midnight to First Light," a dramatic full-length cape made of wool, mohair, rayon ribbon, and Lurex thread. *Photo by Prudence Mapstone*

"I love natural fibers, but am also drawn to glitz, and I definitely prefer quality yarns. Knitters are extremely lucky that at present there are so many well-made yarns on the market. But having said that, sometimes I will work with anything that wraps around my needles or hooks so long as it is in a color or texture that I think will work well in the piece I am creating. I sometimes split or combine yarns to give varying effects, and have often over-dyed various pastels to give a more subtle blend within the same color range, but with so much wonderful yarn available commercially I haven't yet been prompted to take up spinning.

"When I teach a workshop, I generally throw people in at the deep end, getting them started first with a few small areas of multidirectional knitting, explaining the process as the work progresses. Generally I give everyone a set of guidelines and patterns for a range of stitches that they might like to use, just in case they feel the need for written notes, but I tell them they don't really need to take notice of the notes during the workshop. As each person's work begins to develop, my goal is to guide them in directions that will work for them, and get them to explore the possibilities. Most people are happy to plunge in and experiment, in which case the notes will just act as a reminder, or maybe inspire them to try a few more techniques after the class.

"I don't know that we have an actual Aussie style. When I was growing up, most of the patterns we saw here, if not local, had originated in the United Kingdom. As a teen, probably the last time I followed a pattern was to knit myself a couple of mohair jackets from a knitting book by a mainstream Australian fashion designer (I still remember the photos in the pattern book—very mod, 1960s après-ski!). During the 1980s, Sydney designer Jenny Kee started a trend for 'Australiana' knits (*see page* 209)—oversized picture-knit jumpers depicting our native flora and fauna. It is strange that, since a large part our country experiences fairly mild temperatures, even though we still often knit heavy-ish garments, we really don't have a great need for many of them. So sometimes hand knits tend to last quite a while here, as they usually aren't worn all that often. Perhaps, in the past, this has made some people consider hand knitting to be something that is slightly out of date.

"We might produce some of the best and softest wool in the world, but our relatively small population and the fact that the weather in much of the country doesn't really warrant the wearing of 'woolies' has taken its toll on our spinning mills over the years, so unfortunately there aren't many still in operation here. Much of our best wool is sent overseas for processing, and some of it comes back to us as knitting yarn, spun in places like Italy. Our 'wool shops' are few and far between now, unlike when I was growing up, when it seemed that every other suburb and most of the larger towns always had their own.

"We may have been a country of knitters in the past, but for a few years it was definitely on the wane here, and younger people weren't taking up the craft. When I moved from Sydney to Brisbane in the early 1980s I felt that I was one of the few people knitting in the sub-tropics. When I heard about a faraway knitting guild, I joined just to receive their newsletter, so that I could convince myself that other people were still practicing the craft farther south. But knitting is again on the rise here, partly due to the fact that there are such wonderful yarns and books available at present, and also because of the worldwide interest about knitting on the Internet. Perhaps our knitting habits have been somewhat different to other parts of the world. We have never been as big on making afghans here as they are in the United States, and sock knitting was practically unheard of here since the 1950s, but things are changing. Many of the new knitters now are coping with extremely complicated projects, so not only the number of knitters, but perhaps also the skill level, is improving."

Merino

Just as with Australia, when it comes to New Zealand, the knitter's mind turns almost immediately to wool, although the beginnings of the wool trade here did not get off to an auspicious beginning. "In May 1773, Captain James Cook set a pair of sheep ashore in Queen Charlotte Sound, where they promptly died," writes Heather Nicholson. The first sheep (Merinos, of course) to be successfully introduced to New Zealand were brought from Sydney, Australia, in 1814, and from this time on, they were an enormously important component of Kiwi life. However, trouble brewed again from time to time; sheep and cattle brought to Waitangi to graze had all been eaten by the Maori by 1817.

Two men shearing sheep, with flock of sheep behind them, c. 1919. *Library of Congress Prints and Photographs Division, Farm Security Administration Collection; # LC-USZ62-77805*

Merino is defined as a short-wool sheep bred primarily for wool, as its mutton is said to be of poor quality. "The wool is close and wavy in staple, reaching four inches in length, and surpasses that of all other sheep in fineness," says Britannica's dictionary of arts and sciences. "[I]t is so abundant that little but the muzzle, which should be of an orange tint, and hoofs, are left uncovered."

By some accounts, the first commercial sheep farming transaction took place in 1835, when John Bell sold some of his merino back to Sydney. Nicholson reports early shearing with scissors in some instances, and references to "surplus" wool, which to her mind means that "wool was used domestically from the earliest days of European settlement in New Zealand." In the 1850s, much wool was exported to the textile mills of Yorkshire (England), and to keep up with the demand, forests were cleared and grasslands planted as pasture for sheep.

However, there are a couple of cruel ironies for knitters: By the time woolen mills went into operation in the 1870s, the vast majority of New Zealand wool was being exported. Hand knitters in the 1950s and 1960s actually had to purchase imported yarn, although even these began to grow scarce. Writes Nicholson:

> In 1961, 340,000 pounds of yarn were imported, but local manufacturers made 1.5 million pounds. Hand-knitting yarn imports continued to drop and, in 1963, amounted to only 73,085 pounds . . . All these years, our best hand-knitting yarns had been spun from fine Merino wool tops imported from Australia . . . Eventually, our own wool tops industry

got under way in 1964. With protection, imported skills, and new technology, Mosgiel, Alliance, Kaiapoi, and Holeproof began to make top-quality, world-class, plain double knitting, and double crepe yarns. Much of this yarn was exported, mainly to Australia and South Africa.

Still, today, there are an average of twelve sheep in New Zealand to every person, although Merinos hardly dominate anymore—Romneys, Drysdales, and Perendales have all been added to the mix over the decades. There's also a new fiber on the New Zealand market: Merino Possum. As described by Clara Parkes in *The Knitter's Book of Yarn*: "This cat-sized marsupial is trapped as a predator, and its fur is shaved and dehaired to obtain the soft undercoat."

Thoroughbred Merino sheep, 1930–1940. *Library of Congress Prints and Photographs Division, Farm Security Administration Collection, #LC-USW33-024201*

side note to this story is that thirty years later, Beauchamp's son John took up spinning himself and eventually began to design and sell his own spinning wheels.

A technique akin to knitting from the fleece (unspun fiber), Kiwicraft originated in New Zealand's wool sheds, with Maori women working as wool handlers (known as "fleecos"). According to Jean Abbot and Shirley Bourke, they took it upon themselves to rescue waste wool during their breaks, which they then rolled into thread—a technique they originally used in preparing flax fiber for *taaniko* and other forms of weaving. Heather Nicholson sees the technique as sort of a hybrid. "High-country memories tell how Scots shepherds, complete with plaids and dogs, gathered locks of fleece wool caught on scrub, fences, and matagouri bushes," she writes in *The Loving Stitch*. "They drew the fibres out and rolled the resulting loose strand between their hands to make a yarn to be knitted into socks. Perhaps it was Scottish missionaries who taught the Maori how to hand roll unspun wool; they combined it with the traditional technique where flax fibres are rolled and twisted on the thigh."

Techniques for Kiwicraft originally differed from community to community. "The oldest and commonest," according to S. M. Perry in the *Web Quarterly Journal of New Zealand Spinning*, "was for women to collect rain-washed wool from the barbed wire fences or to pluck it from dead sheep (an unpleasant job unless the carcass was well rotted) and then to comb it and tease and knit it on short, sharpened scraps of number eight fencing wire." Luckily, times are not nearly so dire of late, to the extent that, quips Perry, "farmers will now give their wives freshly shorn fleece for their knitting." The method used at the National Kiwicraft Competition (whose first organizer gave the craft its name), is described by Perry thusly: "The tips of the locks of [good quality] wool [with little or no weathering at the tips] are combed or flick-carded (the tips are flicked briskly on to the teeth of a small carder and pulled sharply away). Thread of required thickness is drawn from this fluffed up wool into the palm of the hand, given a squeeze to 'set' it and shaken loose. Then this thread is more firmly 'set' by being rolled firmly between the palm of the hand and a sacking apron wrapped tightly over the thigh. Rolled into a ball, the wool is now ready to knit. Notice that it is not spun. It has no twist in it."

This is in contrast to several other techniques, which Perry likens to European techniques of spinning scrap wool on a spindle. She remarks, "In true Kiwicraft, the wool is drawn out in a straight thread—never twisted—and it is this that gives softness to articles knitted from it."

To knit it, instructs Perry: Hold the fragile thread "between the index and middle finger, not wound around the little finger. Adjust the gauge of the thread by pulling it gently if too thick. Where it is too thin, pull it apart completely, lay ends together and roll them before knitting. When the knitting of a Kiwicraft garment is finished, it is washed well and carefully and dried flat, being careful not to stretch the ribbing." It's all the perfect way to occupy your children during school holidays, say Joyce Fraser and Beverley Horn, teaching them "to use their hands in a creative and quiet fashion."

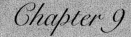

Chapter 9

THE UNITED STATES AND CANADA

Magdeline Whea-kadim, a Pacific Northwest Tulalip Indian, knits in 1906.
Photograph by Norman Edson, University of Washington Libraries

*W*HAT DISTINGUISHES THE KNITTING of North America? What makes the knitting of the United States distinctly American, or of Canada, Canadian? It's a tough question to answer, even for inveterate historians of the craft. The history of knitting in these parts begins with the knitting of other places—the United Kingdom, the Netherlands, Germany—and for many years, it was simply an offshoot of that craft in those places, in those times.

But knitting is as much a cultural melting pot as New York City is, merging the textile crafts of one people with the skills of another to emerge as something new and unexpected, in ways great and small. Eventually, traditions that were distinctly North American began to take shape.

In the Pacific Northwest and Canada, European settlers brought sheep and knitting to their new home. Before long, native populations took up knitting needles themselves, creating their own unique style of sweater called Cowichan, after the Cowichan Valley in which they lived. The thick, warm sweaters, knit using natural tones, feature symbols from the area culture.

Across the continent in the province of Newfoundland, the first thrummed mittens were knit to warm hands during the region's cold, damp winters. In the United States, American Virginia Woods Bellamy would register a patent in 1948 for her one-of-a-kind knitting style: Domino knitting. And a little less than thirty years later, Barbara G. Walker, a trailblazer in the knitting realm if there ever was one, embraced and popularized the technique of mosaic knitting. These distinctly North American knitting traditions mark the beginning of what has become a thriving and inventive knitting culture.

✳ Woman Knitting with Family—family around table in yard, with woman knitting and dog nearby, c. 1876, Town of Newark, Wisconsin. *Photo by Andreas Larsen Dahl, courtesy of Wisconsin Historical Society, #27101*

✳ Full-length portrait of a man with a fringed, knitted bag across his chest, posed as if shooting a rifle, (1880–1910). *Library of Congress Prints and Photographs Division # LC-USZ62-136949*

✳ Family group in living room on Broad Channel Island, Jamaica Bay, New York City, 1915. *Bain Collection, Library of Congress Prints and Photographs Division #LC-USZ62-98903*

Native American Knitting of the Southwest

Textile crafts were certainly not unknown to the indigenous people of the American Southwest, weaving in particular. As for knitting, it was "learned from the whites, at what period is difficult to ascertain," according to Walter Hough in his 1918 report on the Hopi Indian Collection at the United States National Museum. And by "whites," he meant, of course, the Spanish, who arrived in the mid-sixteenth century and brought *churro* sheep with them, which resulted in a change of Native American materials from wild cotton to wool. "Many of the Hopi, in common with the Navajo, Zuni, and other Pueblo tribes, are familiar with the art of knitting, but usually practice it only in the making of leggings of blue yarn," said Hough. According to Scholar Dorothy Koster Washburn, these leggings would have been twelve to fourteen inches long, and held up with red garters. They were used for dance ceremonies, although Susan Strawn identifies them as knitted long, in white wool, and short, in black.

Raymond Friday Locke found a history of Navajo men knitting leggings too, for his 1976 *Book of the Navajo*. He quotes the *Ethnologic Dictionary of the Navaho Language*, written by Franciscan missionaries in 1910, about the practice:

> At present only steel needles are used in knitting, which are either purchased at the trading post, or made of wire or the ribs of an umbrella. These are broken to the proper length and slightly rubbed on a stone to obtain a smooth blunt point.

Visions of America, knitting, and with knitwear: Woman's National Service School Under Woman's Section, Navy League Knitting, 1916. *Harris & Ewing photographer, Harris & Ewing Collection Library of Congress Prints and Photographs Division #LC-DIG-hec-01918*

Leggings consist of long footless stockings, encasing the leg from the kneecap to instep. At the top end a raised rim . . . is knitted by using *left* stitches, that is, the yarn is passed from left to right instead of the usual way. This rim affords a hand grip, and also adds to the wear and tear in pulling on the legging. To distinguish the right from the left legging, and the inside from the outside, a line or ridge is knitted down along the outside of the leggings in relief, like a raised seam, by using *left* stitches at this point. At the lower end of the leggings a knitted or plaited wool cord is fastened, which passes under the foot below the instep, and to keep the legging form working upward. The foot and lower legging is covered by the moccasin . . .

Since leggings were always considered part of the male attire (women have begun to wear them only in recent years) knitting was and still is mostly done by the men.

Additionally, the dictionary made some interesting references to Navajo words and phrases for knitting, showing that the craft became an accepted part of the culture. The Navajo had words for knitting leggings, stockings, handbags, gloves, and mittens; blue, black, and white leggings, a finished knitted rim; the knitted ridge along the side of the legging; the fringed rib at the top of a legging; and knitting needles. In her book, *Knitting America*, author Susan Strawn finds evidence of at least one pair of Navajo leggings knit with a red and white zigzag on a blue background. Locke concludes: "W. W. H. Davis observed that Navajo men were wearing the knitted leggings in 1855."

The Zuni tribe of New Mexico wore knitted leggings as well, as a pair in the collection of the Brooklyn Museum attests. These were picked up by the museum's first curator of ethnography, Stewart Culin, on a 1903 collecting expedition among

Before steel and iron was available, knitting needles were made of wood, for which the slender twigs of . . . *Findlera rupicola*, or of . . . black greasewood, were used . . .

For knitting, blue, white, and black yarns are used, and the present output of the knitting industry is limited to leggings and gloves. The latter is made with a separate thumb, although in late years some have also been knitted with all five fingers separate.

the Indians of New Mexico. He purchased them, according to the museum, "from the silversmith, along with a white cotton shirt and pants." The museum catalog continues, "In a report on Zuni dress in 1879, Matilda Coxe Stevenson noted that the men wore a 'footless stocking knit of native blue yarn' with their buckskin moccasins. In cold weather, the foot was 'wrapped in old cloth' for additional warmth. When Culin arrived in 1903, the footless stockings were still in fashion but were worn with 'American clothes' . . . Culin also acquired a hank of indigo-dyed yarn and five wooden knitting needles with a partially knit stocking so that he could document the knitting process."

Like the Navajo, the Zuni also knitted gloves (none of which Culin collected). Unlike the Navajo, they also apparently knitted footed socks. The nineteenth-century pair in the Brooklyn Museum collection come just above the ankle, are striped orange and white with an orange band at the top that ties and a pattern of checkerboard at the toes (also in orange and white). Such socks were said to be a specialty of the Zuni and were not produced in other pueblos.

A Tigua knitting, New Mexico, c. 1890. *Library of Congress Prints and Photographs Division # LC-USZ62-79651*

Native American Knitting of the Pacific Northwest and Alaska

The Cowichan sweater is by now so famous that many knitters know at least a few of the details of its history: European settlers to Vancouver Island, British Columbia, in the mid-nineteenth century brought domestic sheep and a tradition of hand knitting with them and introduced these to an indigenous population of weavers. Native craftspeople transformed both simple knit-purl techniques and later, Fair Isle patterning, into the classic natural-colored, weather-proof sweaters so familiar today, and a cottage industry was born.

A few details about the process still bear noting. It's been remarked that the Sisters of St. Ann, who arrived in the Cowichan Valley in 1864 to begin a school for Native Americans, were among the most diligent teachers of the craft. They taught students first how to knit socks and mittens, then knee-length underwear and sweaters, the latter of which began as simple knit-in-the-round turtlenecks of one color. However, as Margaret Meikele notes in her monograph *Cowichan Indian Knitting*, "Similar instruction was occurring in other mission schools throughout the province . . . Settlers who became their neighbors shared skills, and, with samples of knitting available to copy, native women skilled in other handwork most likely could teach themselves to knit."

Fair Isle patterning became popular in Cowichan knitting around 1910, and its introduction is generally credited to a settler from the Shetland Islands named Jeremima Colvin, who settled at Cowichan Station in 1885. Patterns, though, were (and remain) highly personal affairs: deer, moose, eagles, and all manner of animals; old weaving patterns or motifs from newspaper graphics; flowers, leaves, geometrics. Explains Meikele, "Characteristically, [designs] are placed horizontally on the mid-portion of the body of the sweater. If the design in this portion of the sweater is geometric, it is laid out in a broad band and repeated on the sleeves. If the main design is representational, it is usually centered on the back, with the same design on the front of a pullover, or two smaller versions of the same representation on either side of the front on a cardigan. There are usually geometric motif bands above and below the representational figure, motifs which are also repeated on the sleeves." The shape of the sweater, which includes a shawl collar, is usually boxy (thick yarns are used, after all)

A fascinating side note to this tradition popped up in the "Virtual Museum" of the Emily Carr University of Art and Design, whose "BC150 Applied Arts Project" catalogs fifteen decades of British Columbia applied arts. It's manifested in two pairs of socks, hand knit by a Japanese Canadian in the late 1930s, about sixty years after the first impoverished Japanese immigrants arrived in Canada and found work mostly in British Columbia's fishing, mining, and forestry industries, and about fifty years after the arrival of the first Japanese women (their wives). The socks are knit of cream-colored wool, with colored bands around the toes and cuffs, and simple geometric motifs circling their upper portions.

The accompanying text reads as follows:

These *Saiwashi kutsushiita* (socks) are another great example of the kind of cultural fusion that figures so prominently in Canadian material culture. Hand knit by Japanese Canadian Shio Yabuno, the socks mimic Salish knitting, subtly reinterpreting forms and motifs. Notably, Salish knitting techniques are themselves a fusion of First Nations weaving skills and European knitting, which quickly evolved into a new and important cultural tradition. 'Saiwashi' is the word used by Japanese Canadians to refer to local First Nations, from whom they bought handmade socks and jackets. Japanese Canadian women

eventually started making socks on their own, using the technique they learned from the First Nation knitters. Those socks were knee-high and very thick—suitable for fishermen to keep themselves warm on the sea.

Yarn for these sweaters (and the socks too) is and always has been wool, shorn from downy breeds such as the Dorset, Hampshire, and Suffolk. The yarn is characterized by Meikele as "thick, handspun, one-ply, [and] natural-coloured," yielding garments that are "characterized by their

⁜ Two pairs of *Saiwashi kutsushiita*, knit by Shio Yabuno in the late 1930s, inspired by Cowichan sweater designs. *Photo courtesy of the Japanese Canadian National Museum*

uneven texture, their warmth and their lightness relative to overall bulk."

In stark contrast to such descriptions are those pertaining to qiviut, yarn made from the downy underwool of the Arctic musk ox. It's softer than cashmere, eight times warmer than wool, and extremely lightweight. Of it, Schoolhouse Press publisher (and knitting royalty) Meg Swansen has made this compelling comparison: "You know that fluffy spot behind a cat's ear? Where the fur is so soft you can hardly tell you're touching it? That is the closest I can come to describing the feel of Qiviut."

Qiviut, like Cowichan sweaters, is another North American success story well known by now to many knitters. The extinct Arctic musk ox was reintroduced to Alaska in the 1930s from still-extant herds in Greenland. A group of them were set loose on Nunivak Island, and from these wild herds the anthropologist John J. Teal Jr. managed to begin a farm, where musk ox were raised for their fiber: qiviut. A cottage industry was established to assist impoverished Native Alaskans living in remote locations; in the late 1960s, they were organized into a cooperative to produce fine, lacy scarves, stoles, and cowl-like *nachaqs*. Today, the Oominmak co-op is about 250 members strong.

Patterns for this knitting are largely derived from motifs and implements traditional to Native life. Harpoon Pattern, from the village of Mekoryuk, is taken from an ancient ivory harpoon head. Wolverine Mask Pattern, as its name suggests, was taken from a wolverine mask worn for festival dances. Several other patterns, from various villages around Alaska, derive from motifs found on the trim of parkas. "The basic lace design," says Donna Druchunas, quoting from a written report by Ann Shell of a lace-knitting workshop taught by Dorothy Reade in 1968, "is 'drawn' on a background of stockinette stitch with yarnovers. On the right side row following each purl row, the stitches above yarnovers are knit through the back loop. This creates a very strong outline and accentuates the 'drawing' much more than using a standard knit stitch."

✻ An adult Arctic musk ox will shed up to an incredible six pounds of fiber a year, but the yarn spun from it is still scarce and in great demand. *Photo by Carl Johnson*

Newfoundland and Canada's Eastern Coast

People in frigid climates have been innovating for generations to make warm clothing even warmer. Thick knit-purl patterning, extra sleeves and socks, inserts for shoes, and felting all have contributed to the coziness (and bulkiness) of honest working folks out in the frosty regions of the world. In Newfoundland and Labrador on Canada's east coast, knitters have long cottoned to a little fleecing technique called "thrumming," to keep hands extra-toasty. Fishermen in particular used thrummed mittens "as a wet mitten for hauling nets in winter," according to mitten historian Robin Hansen in *Favorite Mittens*.

According to knitter Adrian Bizilia, who offers a thrumming tutorial on her blog, helloyarn. com, *thrum* refers to yarn left over after cutting woven cloth from the loom. The word makes an appearance in 1887's *Etymological Dictionary of the Scottish Language*—and so many settlers in Newfoundland and Labrador were of Scottish extraction. According to the dictionary, *thrummed* meant "Covered with small tufts . . . applied to knitted or woven woollen stuffs which have been dressed with a rough, shaggy, or tufted surface." As many native crafters of the Newfoundland/Labrador region were dedicated hand spinners, this "waste" was originally mostly natural-colored, although today, pretty much any color goes. Sandi Wiseheart, writing about thrumming on knittingdaily.com, *Interweave Knits'* blog, mentions that these thrums were used in a variety of ways, including as stuffing for pillows and mattresses. Resourceful knitters also eventually hit upon the idea of knitting them right into the fabric of their mittens—or cuffs, or thumbies, as they're sometimes called, according to Hansen—making a cushy double layer of fabric.

Alice Earle Morse, in *Costumes of Colonial Times*, sheds a bit of light on the climate of the times in which thrummed mittens were coming to the fore, in this instance in New England: "Wadmoll mittens were among the supplies furnished to the Bay planters. Knit mittens and those made of heavy cloth and fur were constantly worn . . . The knitting of mittens was for many years a lucrative household industry, and much ingenuity was displayed in the various ornamental stitches employed and pride in the short time employed in knitting. Many girls could knit a pair of double mittens in a day. Thrummed mitens were knit from the thrums of wool and were much cheaper." In coastal Canada, according to Hansen, mittens had a distinct front and back and were meant particularly for either the right hand or the left hand—no ambidextrous mittens in these parts.

✳ Thrummed mittens.

Spectrum Photofile

Eventually, thrums developed from their origins of waste yarn to something a bit softer, namely roving. These days, bits of roving are torn into thin strips and folded, then worked into the body of the knitting at regular intervals. The closer together the thrums are, the warmer the garment and, arguably, the more lovely. The pattern that emerges on the outside of the work when a contrasting color is used is none other than our old friend the louse; thanks to roving's puffy nature, though, the lice look more like hearts. On the inside of the work, where their ends dangle, they eventually mat together, making a thick, delightful liner.

Other Newfoundland mitten traditions also center around the ever-prevalent fishing industry, which led to an uber-specialization in garment specifics. Writes Shirley Scott in *Canada Knits*, "In Newfoundland, where cod fishing was dominant," a fingerless glove called a header's mitt "was worn when cleaning fish and protected the palm of the hand, which was pushed against the backbone of the fish again and again during endless hours of repetitive work." In the work of salting and drying fish, headers were second in line at the processing table, just after cutthroats, who slashed the fish from throat to belly. Headers then removed and saved the liver, pulled out the fish guts, then yanked the head off "with one quick, clean snap." Splitters, who were responsible for actually splitting the fish in half "with two swift cuts . . . down to the tail [and] up" then cutting out the backbone prior to drying or salting them, also required a mitten of their own. The more generally useful wet mittens were on fishing boats in Maine, Newfoundland, and Nova Scotia. They were knitted up extra-large, boiled once or twice to shrink them, then actually dipped into the briny deep each time before using. As a fisherman wore them, "wetting them in salt water each time," writes Hansen, "they shrank even more, became even more matted, until they were molded to his hands and quite stiff when dry."

Craft display by Grenfell Labrador Work and NONIA Newfoundland, including seal skins, knitted goods, and wood crafts, at Piccadilly Circus, London, 1931. *Courtesy of the Rooms, Newfoundland & Labrador Provincial Archives Division—VA 93-174*

NONIA

Knitting to pay for nurses: It's not an idea that surfaced in any recent rounds of the U.S. debate on health care. But in the outports of Newfoundland in the early years of the twentieth century, that's just what folks were doing.

The fishing industry at the turn of the century throughout this former colony of the United Kingdom comprised a series of isolated communities along the coast, first in Newfoundland, then later in Labrador as well, some of which could be reached only by boat. Many had been founded in the sixteenth century by Basque, Portuguese, Spanish, and English fishermen and whalers, with little infrastructure to support them due to the fact that England's parliament had originally decreed permanent settlement of Newfoundland illegal. Not surprisingly, these outports were lacking plenty of goods and services. One of the greatest was medical care, and one of the ways two wives of the governors of Newfoundland thought

in his *Twentieth-Century Newfoundland*. "The whole scheme was . . . an attempt to provide minimal health services in rural areas without any cost to the government. The idea was to establish local committees to oversee the provision of nursing services. These committees would be responsible for looking after the salaries and welfare of nurses." And these salaries were raised by knitting.

According to the Canadian government's own "heritage" site dedicated to NONIA and similar organizations, heritage.nf.ca, the government actually "agreed to pay for half of all nurses' salaries if the committee could finance the rest through its various fundraising efforts." So, Lady Elsie Allardyce, the second of two governors' wives who threw herself into this task, hired "outport women to knit sweaters and other goods, which [NONIA] in turn sold to the public and used the profits to pay for nurses' salaries. It formed local committees across the island to organize knitting and weaving efforts, distribute wool, and pay workers," says the site. The site additionally claims that the association raised the quality of life of those it employed to make handcrafts by paying them in cash during the Depression: "Reverend Hugh MacDermott writes of NONIA's impact on one knitter in his book, *MacDermott of Fortune Bay*: 'When I gave payment to the first knitter she looked at the amount of money—ten dollars—with eyes that sparkled and then were filled with tears. Next day I met her on the road and said, "Were you satisfied yesterday with your pay?" She replied, "I don't know how I got home, whether on my head or on my heels. We had nothing in the house . . . I bought flour and other things we sorely needed."

Though the Canadian government took over healthcare for Newfoundland in 1934, NONIA continues today as a cottage industry, still employing about 175 Newfoundlanders to knit sweaters, socks, mitts, and hats, which it sells though its website and shop.

to address this was through an organization that would in 1924 come to be known as the Newfoundland Outport Nursing and Industrial Association, or NONIA.

"NONIA's purpose was to send fully trained nurses to live in the outports," says James Hiller

Utopian Knitting: The Shakers and the Mormons

Writes Richard Rutt in A *History of Hand Knitting* of the Shakers, an odd group of religious devotees who eventually died out (in fairness there are three members left, in Maine) due to their strict adherence to celibacy: "Knitting was an integral part of the lives of Shaker sisters. They worked on fine needles, less than 2mm thick. They made circular rugs and chair seat 'cushions' by sewing together flat spirals of tubular knitting [*see French knitting, page 26*] . . . Chair seat covers could be trapezoidal in stockinette, bordered with a doubled strip of knitting. They also made the usual plain stockings, gloves, shawls, sweaters, 'gaiters' (actually a form of spats), men's neckties, afghans, and [circular] washcloths . . . made of sixteen segments of garter stitch, arranged in alternating colors. The rows ran radially, decreasing from the centre in alternate shortened rows."

Historian Beverly Gordon has this to add in her book, *Shaker Textile Arts*:

> In later years . . . washcloths, facecloths, sweaters, potholders, toys, rugs, and other items were also knitted and sold in Shaker stores . . . [B]y any standards Shaker hand knitting was exceptionally fine. Knitting needles, or 'pins,' were purchased locally, and all were less than size 00 in the measuring system we use today . . . At least some, and possibly most, of the Shaker communities [eventually] purchased knitting machines and put them to heavy use. Canterbury had a special knitting shop where the machines were kept. Great quantities of sweaters and stockings were turned out by machine, but all were finished by hand. Sweater sleeves and bodices, for example, were machine-knit, but cuffs and edgings were hand-knit. Stockings were knitted as tubes on the machines, but footings were knitted by hand.

Stockings featured a particular detail called a gusset, which was appropriated by many knitters outside the Shaker communities.

Elsewhere on the utopian landscape, in the mid-nineteenth century, a group of Mormons began their trek westward, ultimately to Utah, in an attempt to escape religious persecution. As much as possible, independence from the outside

❋ Eldress Fannie Estabrook, full-length portrait, sitting, facing left, knitting, at the Hancock Shaker village near Pittsfield, Massachusetts. *Photo by Samuel Kravitt, Library of Congress Prints and Photographs Division #LC-DIG-ppmsca-07484*

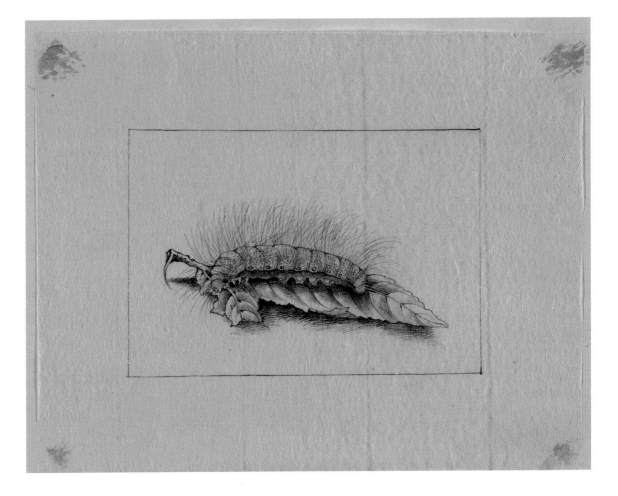

world was seen as the ultimate way to achieve this, and knitting was seen as providing an exemplary means to that end. Brigham Young himself advised his followers to "[w]ear the good cloth manufactured in your own mills," and, somewhat hilariously, "[T]he art of knitting stockings is not near so generally understood among the ladies as it should be. I would tell you how it should be done had I time and knew how myself."

His (female) followers dove headlong into the craft of knitting. Knitting had its own "division," with supervisors who taught girls to knit and also assisted them in finding markets for their goods. As Anne Macdonald writes in her encompassing history *No Idle Hands*, "when knitwear was turned into ready cash, workers were praised for keeping the money in the territory." Most knitting was accomplished with wool; but sericulture—the raising of silkworms—was mandated by the end

of the nineteenth century, and the community's Desert Silk Association saw to the tedious, back-breaking work of raising, harvesting, spinning, and knitting up silk. Fine silk was doubled and twisted by respinning, then used to stitch up stockings and bags, an assortment of which were exhibited at the great fair in Chicago in 1893.

"[I]ndustry is the source of wealth," Macdonald quotes from one Electra Bullock; and indeed, this Mormon propensity for constant work may have been seen as a means to achieve this both literally and figuratively. How industrious were they? Again, Macdonald quotes a Mormon girl: "The girls knit the stockings, and helped with the sewing. Aunt Sally's oldest girl used to spin and weave. We younger ones helped to card the wool bats and to put in quilts. I would take my knitting and run into Aunt Sally's of an afternoon. We did not like to knit alone."

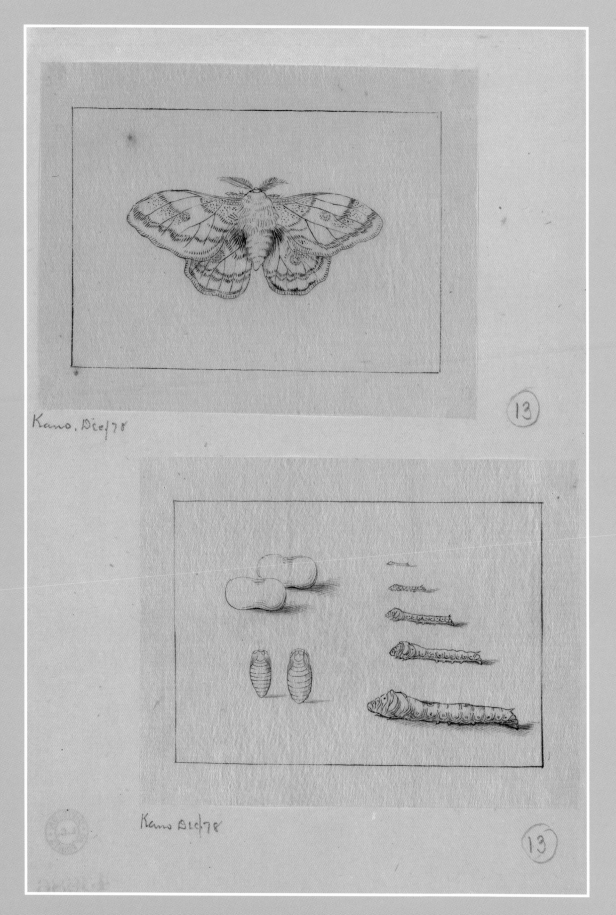

Kano, Dic/78

Kano Dic/78

Argyle Redux: Intarsia

Intarsia is a technique of color-block knitting that derives its name from an Italian method of inlaying decoration into wood. In intarsia knitting, a new color of yarn is drawn over the previously used yarn in every row, in order to prevent gaps in the work. The motif is knitted back and forth, so that yarn strands do not wind up on the wrong side of the color block. Yarn is wound onto bobbins for ease of color changing. The oldest known example of instarsia dates from the fourteenth century, on a pair of Egyptian socks. Mary Thomas in her *Knitting Book* calls the technique "geometric knitting," of which the argyle pattern is a prime example.

The originally Scottish argyle patterning using intarsia was adopted post–World War II by knitting co-eds weary of the mandates for Army khaki and Navy blue, and became a distinctly American craze. Anne MacDonald has devoted several full pages to it in *No Idle Hands*.

It began as a mania for socks—socks for boyfriends, primarily, knitted up by a stereotype of the bridge-playing, chain-smoking college girl intent on "knocking his socks off." Even beginner knitters took to their needles with zeal, resulting in a panoply of inventions to assist those tangled up in strands: Line Reels, Yarn O'Bobbins, Stitchexes, Rispindles, Colorpluses, and Argyle Boxes, as McDonald reports.

Socks for him quickly turned into socks for her, and matching sweaters, vests, hats, and mittens for everyone. Writes Susan Strawn in *Knitting America*, "Nearly every knitting pattern book included the mandatory argyle or a variation of argyle for men, women, babies, children, and teenagers."

Even by the early 1950s, when the fad had largely dissipated, "Argylers," writes McDonald, "were still in full cry, elaborating on 'traditional' Scottish patterns by knitting diamonds within diamonds and combining diamonds with plaids and stripes. Argyles were so popular with high school cheerleaders that the going rate was $20 a pair for handknit ones. They were equally popular on college campuses, and Virginia Williams, of Omaha, Nebraska, who earlier made them in high school, bargained with matriculating G.I.s to knit two pairs of socks in exchange for the loan of a full set of textbooks."

✳ This pattern book, published by Bucilla in 1950, features several patterns to feed the craze for for argyle socks.

BUCILLA
Hand Knit Socks
for Men, Women, Children

VOL. 340 $3.50

PATTERN

Men's Argyle Socks and Anklets

Instructions are for socks, changes for anklets are in parentheses.

MATERIALS

Fleisher's Super-Spun Nylon, Main Color A, 2 skeins; Contrasting Colors Band C, 1 skein each.

Budlla Wonderized Handi-Wool, Art. 026, Colors D and E, 1 card each; or Fleisher's Wonderized De Luxe Sock and Sport Yarn, Main Color A, 2 skeins; Contrasting Colors Band C, 1 skein each.

Bucilla Wonderized Handi-Wool, Art. 026, Colors D and E, 1 card each.

Budlla Nylon. "Heel 'n Toe" Yarn, 1 card; use with De Luxe Sock and Sport Yarn.

Budlla Aluminum Sock Needles, 1 set Size 12 (1)

Budlla Yarn Bobbins, 1 set.

GAUGE

9 sts=1 inch   13 rows or rounds=1 inch

Note: Chart and instructions call for cross lines to be knitted in. Cross lines may be embroidered in duplicate st after sock is completed, in which case diamonds are worked in solid color and cross lines are embroidered after sock is completed.

CUFF—With color A, cast on 68 sts loosely. Using 2 needles only, work k 2, P 2 ribbing back and forth for 3 ins.

Inc. row—Work ribbing, increasing 1 st in every 9th st 7 times, finish row; 75 sts. Now wind 2 bobbins of each color, or use color A from skeins.

Use separate bobbin for each change of color. Do not carry colors across on wrong side of work, except across single st of cross lines. Begin pat.

SOCK-LEG-Row 1—Join C, k 1; with A, k 17; join D, k 1; join E, k 1; with A, k 17; join B, k 1; join 2nd strand of A, k 17; join D, k 1; join E, k 1; with A, k 17; join C, k 1. To prevent a hole when changing colors, always bring color to be used under last color used.

Row 2—P 2 C, 15 A, 1 E, 2 A, 1 D, 15 A, 3 B, 15 A, 1 E, 2 A, 1 D, 15 A, 2 C.

ANKLET-LEG-Row 1—Join B, pl; with A, p 17; join E, pl; join D, p 1; with A, p 17; join C, p 1; join 2nd strand of A, p 17; join E, pl; join D, p 1; with A, p 17; join B, p 1. To prevent a hole when changing colors, always bring color to be used under last color used.

Row 2—K 2 B, 15 A, 1 D, 2 A, 1 E, 15 A, 3 C, 15 A, 1 D, 2 A, 1 E, 15 A, 2 B.

Continue pat. in stockinette st-k 1 row, p 1 row, following chart until 74 (37) pat. rows.

Next row—With A, k 19 sts, slip on holder for heel; work next 37 sts in pat. as on chart; slip remaining 19 sts on holder for other half of heel. Continue pat. on 37 sts to end of chart, working 1 complete B diamond (Anklet-work t B and C diamond). Break off.

Take up 38 sts from holders to 1 needle with side edges at center of needle. Join wool and "Heel 'n Toe" Yarn on wrong side; omit "Heel 'n Toe" Yarn on Nylon Socks.

HEEL-Row 1—Slip 1 st as to p, p to end.

Row 2—* Holding both strands at back of work, slip 1 st as to p, k 1; repeat from * to end. Repeat last 2 rows until there are 36 rows on heel, end with row 2.

Turn heel follows: Wrong side-Slip 1, p 20, p 2 tog., P 1, turn. Slip 1, k 5, slip, k and pass, k 1, turn. Slip 1, p 6, p 2 tog., p 1, turn. Slip 1, k 7, slip, k and pass, k 1, turn. Slip 1, p 8, p 2 tog., P 1, turn.

Continue to work toward sides of heel, having 1 st more before dec. on each row until 22 sts remain. Break off "Heel 'n Toe" Yam.

GUSSETS AND FOOT—With free needle and A, from right side, pick up and k 18 sts on side of heel, k 11 sts of heel to same needle; with another needle k remaining 11 heel sts, pick up and k 18 sts on other side of heel to same needle; 58 sts. Turn, p back across sts on 2 needles. Turn, k 1, slip, k and pass, k to end of first needle; k to within 3 sts of end of 2nd needle, k 2 tog., k 1. Repeat last 2 rows 10 times; 36 sts.

Place all sts on 1 needle for sole. P 1 row, k 1 row until 37 (74) rows from where sts were picked up on sides of heel.

Place 18 sole sts on each of 2 needles and 37 instep sts on 1 needle. Join; k 1 round decreasing 1 st at center of instep.

K around on these 72 sts until foot measures 2 ins. less than desired finished length from tip of heel, allowing the 2 ins. for the toe.

Join "Heel 'n Toe" Yarn; omit "Heel 'n Toe" Yarn on Nylon Socks.

TOE—Begin at center of sole. Round I-K to within 3 sts of end of first needle, k 2 tog., k 1; on 2nd needle, k 1, slip, k and pass, k to within 3 sts of end, k 2 tog., k 1; on 3rd needle, k 1, slip, k and pass, k to end. K 1 round even.

Repeat last 2 rounds until 20 sts remain. K 5 sts of first needle and slip to 3rd needle. Break off, leaving end for weaving. Weave sole and instep sts tog., see page 30.

FINISHING—Sew back seam, matching pats. Sew seams at each side of foot. Steam wool socks, see page 31. Super-Spun Nylon does not require steaming.

—Pattern from Fleisher's, circa 1950

Lady's Modernistic Sport Ensemble

Sweater-Minerva Shetland Floss-7 Balls Honeydew, 1 Ball Tangerine, 1 Ball Marigold, 2 Balls Wood Brown, I Pro Each M. M. No.4 and No.3 Needles.

Size 36 to 38

Front. With No.4 needles cast on 15 sts. of Honeydew, 60 sts. of Marigold, and 35 sts. of Wood Brown. (110 sts.) The entire sweater is worked in Stockinette Stitch (K 1 row, P 1 row). Work 8 rows even, twisting the yarn when changing colors, but do not carry yarn; K 2 rows plain for turn of hem. Now follow chart (on inside of front cover) to shoulder, using a separate ball of yarn for each color being used.

Back. With Honeydew, K. across left shoulder, cast on 26 sts., and K. across right shoulder. Continue down back, increasing at armholes same as decreased at front. When back measures same length as front, K 2 rows for turn of hem, work 8 rows, bind off.

Sleeves. With Honeydew pick up 78 sts. around armhole, work even for 2 inches, then decrease 1st. at each end every 8th row 13 times. When sleeve measures 17 inches, change to Tangerine and No.3 needles, work 1 inch, change to Wood Brown, work 2 inches, then K 2 rows plain for turn of hem, work even for 6 rows, bind off.

Neck. With Honeydew and No.3 needles pick up sts. across front of neck line, K 1 row, P 1 row, for 4 rows, K 2 rows for turn of hem, work 4 rows, bind off. Repeat at back of neck, sew at shoulder, fold, and sew down on wrong side.

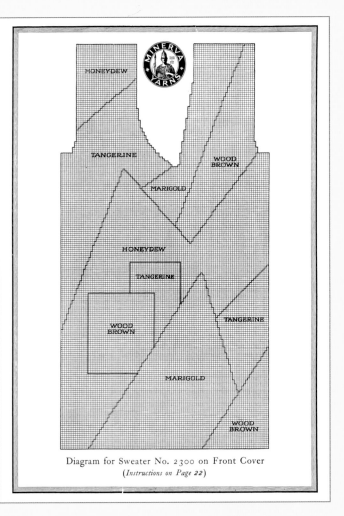

Diagram for Sweater No. 2300 on Front Cover
(*Instructions on Page 22*)

Elizabeth Zimmermann's Knitting Camp

Is there anyone more relevant to American knitting than the great (British-born) Elizabeth Zimmermann (EZ)? The point is hardly even worth debating.

In addition to her lifetime of service to "unventing" patterns, creating ingenious yarn structures (like the two-needle I-cord), publishing books, making TV shows, and generally turning the old knitterly ways of doing things on their ear, EZ created what has truly become an American icon equal to herself: Knitting Camp.

Long before there were ubiquitous knitting retreats, knitting cruises, and knitting blogs—even before these things were seriously thought of— in 1974 there was a weeklong session for about a dozen students on the finer points of knitting, at the University of Wisconsin Extension Shell Lake campus, led by EZ herself. In the early years, students could get college credit for Camp, and the majority of them stayed in student dormitories. These days, four consecutive days of action all happen within the walls of a Holiday Inn in Marshfield, Wisconsin.

No one's complaining about the change of venue (they have better, woolier things on their minds), least of all Lois Young, who has attended every session of Camp since its inception. In her second year, she opted for college credit in order to maintain her teaching certification. But what has kept her going back, and back, and back, for more than thirty-five summers? Says EZ's daughter, Meg Swansen, "For the attendees who have returned every year, it is like a family reunion; they come back to spend time with their like-minded friends, share

techniques, and discuss their knitting experiences during the preceding year." And as Young herself wrote for an EZ tribute in the essay collection *For the Love of Knitting*, "Elizabeth Zimmermann was funny, feisty, and a fabulous source of freedom to knit what you wanted without having to follow someone else's rules."

Which certainly does not mean that there was not, and is not, work. There are all-day sessions, with breaks for meals. There is knitting into the wee hours of the morning. There are "group discussions dwell[ing] on the latest techniques, designs, materials, and assorted other minutiae," according to Swansen. There are projects to complete, each with its own set of very particlar parameters: anything that can be worn on the head; gloves knitted sideways; anything incorporating color changes, a cable, a circular start, increasing and decreasing, an I-cord, and a buttonhole; and perhaps most famously, something that will cover a toilet paper roll (the last instigated by Swansen, who's been teaching at Camp, too, since 1975).

Is Camp still relevant in the digital age? Says Swansen, "The level of knowledge of 'beginners' continues to leap forward geometrically; the Internet has changed everything. It is possible that—even though knitters are now instantly in touch with each other around the world and every conceivable question is answered immediately— there is a nostalgia for personal interaction; to see garments in person; to feel the wool, to see it being worn and get eye-contact feedback from other knitters. Afterwards, the two hundred-plus Campers return to their local knitting communities, full of new ideas to share with their guilds and knitting buddies."

Karen Alfke

Karen Alfke. *Photo by Keith Brofsky*

Karen Alfke is a knitting teacher extraordinaire. Following in the tradition of Elizabeth Zimmermann (who instructed her students to "unvent" their projects), Alfke promotes a strong urgency in her students to become independent knitters, able to knit simple garments they are thrilled to wear over and over, without the use of patterns. Toward this end, she calls her "unpatterns" design tools for the independent knitter.

"Although I must have knit and crocheted with my mom and aunt and cousins when I was little, I don't remember specifics. The first project I knit and completed was a turquoise mohair vest (hey—it was the 1980s!), basically two rectangles, sewn together at sides and shoulders, leaving a slash neck opening. My aunt and cousins knit a lot with that same brand of mohair (I remember its name, too, to this day: "Sympathie"). I was sixteen. I think I went straight from that one to a wine-colored mohair blend sweater, with reverse-stockinette diamonds around the bottom hem.

"My challenges were pretty clear from the beginning, and some of them persist to this day: I am easily distracted by new projects, and always want to start more than I can finish. And, I always pick projects that are either far too challenging for my skill level (I think I wanted to do a stranded-colorwork Greek-key motif around the bottom edge of a fingering-weight cotton sweater as my fourth or fifth project), or pick things with an epic scope (later on that first year, my cousin and I knit floor-length dresses out of black sock yarn.) Glutton for punishment, that's me.

"I can't say that my aunt helped me overcome these challenges, but even now, when an idea is getting the better of me, I do recall her gentle reminders not to take on too much. She also taught me by example very well: For one design, she spent nearly an entire ball of yarn working up a long sampler swatch with several stitch patterns she wanted to incorporate. I watched her swatch and realized: *I can plan this stuff out in advance before I cast on the several hundred stitches I would need to start the sweater in the round.*

"I am adamant that we shouldn't apply labels to how we knit, especially if those labels are just meant to make someone feel bad about how they work. I see so many different ways to knit and purl in my classes that it's clear you can't single out one way as right and one way as wrong: it's what works for the individual, and what gives them joy in their craft. But having said that, there are some ways that create a fabric that looks like what most of us out there create, and knowing how to recreate that fabric reliably, without having to do too much mental work in reversing instructions, et cetera, is a great thing. (I am adamant that left-handers like me shouldn't be singled out to knit differently from everyone else. I'd even go so far as to say that it's 'wrong' to make them do so.)

"I know that from my own experience, learning more ways to knit simply opens the doors to more ways to have fun with yarn. When I learned to hold the yarn in my right hand in the British method, I could do stranded colorwork more efficiently. And when I learned to knit backward (working from left to right, as many left-handers are taught to do), sock heels and bobbles became a breeze. As in most things in life, knowing more than one way to do something is a gift.

"I help individual knitters find what works best for them by staying tuned to how their brains and hands work. I love to point out in classes that we all have our own strengths when it comes to remembering a pattern: Do you visualize it? Do you say it out loud to yourself like a mantra? Do you feel your hands and notice the rhythm of making the stitches? Each knitter I work with has their own way of approaching new information, and I find it very helpful to work with their natural learning types. The visual knitters want me to write it out or give them a chart to see. For the auditory learners, I talk them through the pattern and try to find the set of words that works with their brains, and so on.

"I never set out to do this for a living, but in retrospect, it seems like every single one of my former jobs gave me a skill that's essential to what I do in knitting. However, if you'd sat me down when I was eighteen and told me I'd be working as a knitting designer and teacher, I would have asked you what you'd been drinking. My career as a knitting teacher just started with an innocent trip to my local yarn store. I had recently moved to the Pacific Northwest, to a new town, and had found a lot of community on the Internet, in the early days of the KnitList. I was knitting like a fiend, checking out books from the library. Up until the mid-1990s, knitting was this strange European thing that I did and none of my other friends understood. A fellow KnitLister in my little town took me to the local yarn store, and I started adding to my stash. Then I started playing with linen stitch after running across it in a pattern in the Fall 1997 issue of *Family Circle Easy Knitting*—I still have the issue, and the first swatch I ever made in linen stitch. I started showing off linen-stitch projects at the Seattle Knitters' Guild, in the show-and-tell portions of their meetings, and someone asked if I would give a presentation on it. So in the spring of 1999, I stood in front of a hundred or so massively talented knitters and just shared what I'd been playing with.

"Afterward, I mentioned my presentation in a conversation with my yarn store owners, and they asked me if I would be interested in teaching beginning knitting and some other classes in their little shop. A knitting buddy of mine had coincidentally mentioned that the Fiber Trends Felted Slipper pattern would make an ideal project for teaching someone to knit, and that's how it all started.

"A few months later, a friend from the Seattle Knitters' Guild had an article in *Vogue Knitting*, where they mentioned she was opening a shop an hour south of me. And thus was Churchmouse born! I called her up, congratulated her on her opening, and offered to take names and numbers if she wanted to start up some knitting classes. I've been instrumental in their curriculum from the first day they opened, and that's one of my proudest achievements in this industry. It's been almost ten years now, and I figured at one point I'd taught almost 500 people to knit.

"My approach to sweater knitting gained a whole new dimension when I read Barbara Walker's *Knitting from the Top*. I joke in my Top-Down Unpattern workshop that I checked the book out from the library, started reading, got through chapter one (on raglan-sleeved garments), and stopped right there. It's only been lately, as I recognized the supreme wearability of set-in sleeve sweaters, that I picked up the book again and kept reading.

"I continue to be influenced and inspired by the amazing work my fellow designers are putting out. It seems like every time I turn around, someone's issued another great book with gorgeous designs. And after feeling intimidated by the exquisitely complex designs some people are able to generate, I have a little lie-down and remember what it is that I'm good at doing, and what I feel I was put on the planet to do: to help knitters make great, basic, wearable garments in the yarn they love, in a size and style that flatters them. So I leave the crazy cables and lace and complicated structural stuff to those who do it very well. But I find I take away inspiration from other designs—maybe an edging from something in *Twist Collective* or a cable that Jared Flood used in his latest book—and those pieces might inspire an element in something I knit next.

"As far as teaching goes, I was lucky to have training in graduate school, when I taught introductory German. The department I was working for gave us teacher training intensives, and then paired us up with a professor for guidance. So after three years of university-level teaching, I was comfortable designing courses, writing syllabi, and easing students into material in a variety of ways. And along with

Some of Alfke's Unpatterns, ready to wear. © 2010 A. Karen Alfke/Unpatterns.

that professional training, I've built my teaching style around good experiences I've taken from courses at knitting events. I have also been actively mentored by a few fellow knitting professionals, namely Susanna Hansson: She has given me quite a few tips that proved essential in running a happy classroom. My favorite: Bring a few extra sets of materials for your class, because there will always be one student who forgot them at home or left them in the car, and having them on hand ensures that everyone has a great class experience.

"I feel like I came late to the EZ fan club. Not having learned to knit in this country, I wasn't steeped in the classics of American knitting literature and had to find them myself after I got back from Germany. For years, I knit my sweaters my way, foraged for yarn at the (few and far between) local yarn shops when I needed a new project, and thought I was outside the norm in America. Then came the KnitList, which my sister-in-law turned me on to in 1996, and the rest, as they say, is history. Suddenly, I didn't feel alone as a knitter, and I realized there were mad, raving, rabid knitters all over the States. I started checking books out of the library, and that was when I discovered EZ. So maybe I would say that rather than influencing or inspiring me, she's been a reassurance and a reinforcement that North American knitters might appreciate what I bring to the table.

"Reading her books was a head-nodding experience: 'Well, yes, of course. Of course you can do that!' At the time, I was a hopeless garter-stitch snob (as in: I wouldn't knit it if you paid me), so I didn't knit my first Baby Surprise Jacket until years later. But I loved her memoirs, and her no-nonsense, matter-of-fact, don't-fear-your-knitting message felt like home.

"My main philosophy can be summed up thusly: There are no 'rights' and 'wrongs' in knitting, there is only what you want to make and how you can make that happen, and, knitting is meant to be fun, as well as productive."

Ravelry

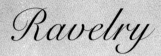

Ravelry is an online knitting community that provides a forum for every knit-related topic under the sun. Ravelry came to be when Jess, a longtime knitter and blogger, became frustrated by how difficult it was to access the wealth of knitting information available on the web. Her husband Casey thought that he would be able to build a website that would act as a resource hub for knitters, collecting all the great yarn and pattern information available online in one organized, central location. They started working on the site together, introducing it to a few friends at a time.

"The goal with Ravelry was to create an online knitting and crochet community—a personal organizer (for your projects, yarn stash, books and patterns, and more), with a rich pattern and yarn database and a vibrant forums area to meet and connect with other users around the world. We do feel that we have accomplished this, both in ways that we planned and that we could never imagine.

"We have a small staff: Casey and Jess, the cofounders (Casey is the Codemonkey and Jessica is Mama Rav); Mary-Heather, VP of Operations/Do-Gooder; Sarah, Community Support Specialist/Hostess with the Mostest.

"Jess and Casey worked on Ravelry nonstop on their own for almost a year. Both Sarah and Mary-Heather were very early and active Ravelry users (Sarah actually was a friend of Jess' through blogging, and she was the one who came up with the name Ravelry).

"Right now, there are such wonderful yarns to work with, such talented designers, and such a great fiber community in local stores and online, it's really easy for this hobby to become an obsession, or even a lifestyle. As Ravelry has grown (and grown, and grown) and a larger cross-section of people have joined, we have seen that there is a huge number of people at all skill levels and with all sorts of interests who love knitting and crocheting. While the Internet hasn't changed the actual physical act of knitting or crocheting, it is such an amazing resource—there is so much information, and so many people with similar interests to connect with—it does make our world of yarn lovers seem quite a bit smaller. Computers and yarn may not seem to mix, but they do go quite well together.

"We have no shortage of ideas. And if we haven't thought of something, our users have—that is really the key to Ravelry. Ravelry users have contributed the pattern and yarn information and photos, and they make up our amazing community on the forums. Our users are really educated and empowered and can be fearless knitters and crocheters, knowing that they have a great resource they can turn to. The site couldn't exist without the dedicated users that we are so lucky to have."

The whole Ravelry crew: from left to right, Sarah Bible, Mary-Heather Cogar, Jessica Marshall Forbes, and Casey Forbes, at TNNA 2009. *Photo courtesy of Ravelry*

Domino Knitting

These days, domino knitting—also called mitered knitting, modular knitting, patchwork knitting, and number knitting—is known to most contemporary crafters as the glorious domain of Dane Vivian Høxbro (*see page* 92). But she by no means lays claim to the technique; indeed, its origins stretch back at least a generation or two.

The book *Patchwork Knitting* was published in 1988 by German Horst Schulz—this is the man Høxbro credits with introducing her to the infinitely dazzling method in which knitted geometric shapes are joined by picking up stitches from previously knit shapes. Praise for Schulz and his intricate patterns fashioned from adjoined circles and chevrons, often with boggling optical effects, has not diminished over time. A Ravelry group called Horst Schulz Fans, for example, exists to assist and encourage knitters in the creation of his undulous, vibrantly colored patchwork quilt "An Africa Adventure."

But who is the true originator of the method? Legally, it is American Virginia Woods Bellamy. Legally, that is, because she patented what she termed Number Knitting in 1948 with the U.S. Patent Office. It holds (or held; the patent expired in 1965) U.S. Patent No. 2,435,068, and a Google search on the subject will yield a fascinating account of the matter by an avid knitter and copyright attorney known online as the Girl from Auntie. Apparently, Bellamy obtained a patent for a version of the technique in which only garter stitch is used (although plenty of knitters these days use other stitch patterns to interesting effect). She was highly organized in her explanation of the method, and she identified six modules as acceptable to it: the square, the right triangle, the oblique angled parallelogram, the rectangle, a square divided in half horizontally, and the double parallelogram. The patent included a graph of numbers and corresponding letters, along with a

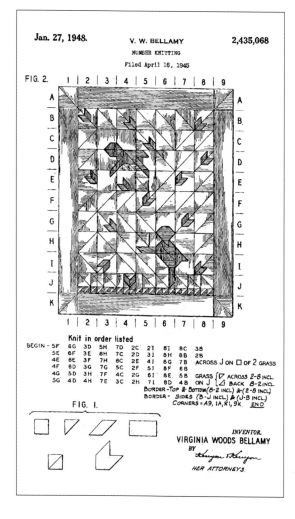

Virginia Bellamy's drawing of "Number Knitting," submitted with her patent claim in 1945. Follow if you dare!
U.S. Patent Office

sort of bingo call list of the order in which each square was to be knitted.

And rules—so many rules! Some are straightforward enough, like "Do not break the yarn unless (or until) necessary" and "Slip the first stitch and purl the last stitch of every row." Then there's "The number of stitches for each new unit must equal a multiple of the basic square which is the smallest square of the graph paper used for the diagram, and always equals the same number of stitches wide as ridges high." No wonder Schulz and Høxbro's comparatively humane instructions, enhanced by the possibility of in-person workshops, are now thought to encompass the origins of domino (or patchwork, or modular, or mitered) knitting. A knitter cannot recognize that which he or she cannot comprehend.

Barbara G. Walker and Her Treasuries of Knitting Patterns

Where would American knitting be today without the intervention of the inimitable Barbara G. Walker? Meg Swansen traced the origins of Walker's contribution to knitting in the reissue of *Mosaic Knitting* (the fourth of Walker's pattern books) in 1997: "As a wife and mother wanting to knit for her family—but never having held a knitting needle—Barbara taught herself the rudiments of knitting, then went in search of interesting patterns. At that time, all the books she found were full of plain stocking stitch garments; not nearly challenging enough to capture and keep her imagination and interest. So after a period of intense research, in 1968 she wrote one herself!"

In total, she wrote not just one, but four pattern collections (and in all, seven books about knitting). First came A *Treasury of Knitting Patterns* in 1968, with its almost six hundred entries, including one for King Charles Brocade, whose compelling introduction proves that Walker's appeal wasn't just in rote assembly: "This elegant version of Diamond Brocade carries a historical footnote of rather a gruesome nature. It is one of the patterns in a vest worn by King Charles I of England on the day of his execution in 1649. This vest, a marvelous piece of master knitting of the period, was worked in blue silk. It was preserved in the London Museum."

Two years later there came A *Second Treasury of Knitting Patterns* with seven hundred patterns, some of which Walker plumbed from vintage sources, as she did with the first treasury. Some were sent to her by a growing and enthusiastic readership—and she was diligent in crediting them—and a few she created herself. These last she called "contemporary originals, representing the constant and continuous flow of creative ideas in knitting," adding, "There is literally no end to this flow. It goes on forever because new ideas are always possible."

She really let loose with *Charted Knitting Designs: A Third Treasury of Knitting Patterns* (1972): 392 patterns and variations, almost all of her own devising, along with brand new techniques—"That is to say," she wrote, "certain knitting operations are combined in unusual ways, to make shapes that have never before translated themselves into a knitted fabric." A prime example of this is her twist-stitch Spider, with all eight legs clearly defined in wooliness. Said Walker about it, "The pattern techniques that make her in yarn . . . have much to teach you. As twist-stitch patterns go, this one is fairly complex. It has been chosen deliberately as an example to show you almost every kind of knitting operation that you might encounter in a twist-stitch design." In a few short years, she had gone from a barely knitting archivist to an advanced teacher.

Mosaic Knitting, published in 1976, was another instant and important classic. For in this book, Walker basically gave free reign to her imagination, inventing 157 mosaic patterns—she also coined the term—as well as 116 "Magic Mosaics," so named, she wrote," because of their four-way symmetry which resembles ancient magic symbols that presented the same face to all four directions."

The Fourth Treasury of Knitting Patterns was actually not part of the original "set," as Walker's first compendiums have come to be thought of. Published in 2000, it reintroduced a book titled *Sampler Knitting*, along with eighty-some new patterns by Walker.

Meg Swansen was certainly correct when she wrote of Walker's continuing relevance to the world of knitting design, "It is unlikely that you will be able to find a single knitting designer who does not know of, and use, the work of Barbara G. Walker." But for the rest of us less professionally oriented crafters, Walker's own words ring loud

and strong, as a sort of manifesto for all those who love to create: "To learn the techniques of pattern stitches is not only exciting, but it is to learn also that knitting can be almost anything, from the most cobwebby lace to the sturdiest blankets . . . In learning various pattern stitches, you can raise what is otherwise a mere craft to the height of a real art . . . Some patterns seem to cry out to be used. They say, 'don't just knit something—knit something beautiful!'"

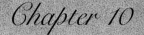

Chapter 10

SOUTH AND CENTRAL AMERICA

Man knitting *ch'ullu*, incorporating the handmade bobble yarns as he knits.

His village sits at 13,000 feet altitude. *Cynthia LeCount Samaké—*

Behind the Scenes Adventures: www.btsadventures.com

THE WEALTH OF INFORMATION WE now have at our disposal about knitting in the Andes—the epicenter of knitting in South America—can be largely attributed to the intrepid exploits of Cynthia LeCount Samaké. She wrote the seminal book on the subject in 1990, *Andean Folk Knitting*, after years of field research that found her hiking for days and hitching rides in trucks over the high terrain of Bolivia and Peru, in search of endangered folk knitting traditions. What she turned up was a goldmine of techniques and highly individualized styles. The fact that today, urban American schoolchildren can be found sporting cheap, machine-made knockoffs of the Andean knit cap called the *ch'ullu* (in Quechua, the language of much of the Andean highlands), or *ch'ullu* (Spanish) must owe at least a small debt to LeCount Samaké and the chain reaction of interest she set off for Andean knitting, by sheer virtue of her own keen curiosity.

The old, pre-Hispanic, pre-knitting method of making fabric in this region of the world is today known as crossed looping.

Cactus thorns and fishbones were often used as needles. Today, both men and women knit with five thin needles, often fashioned from bicycle spokes, hooked at one end. The yarn is tensioned around the neck, and it is these details of needles and tensioning that make clear to historians that knitting was brought to the Andes by the Portuguese and Spanish sailors who arrived in the mid-1500s. Settlers' wives began to arrive in the late seventeenth century, and as they were often knitters too, the new-to-the-Andes skill was further reinforced. Another interesting detail is that the knitting, almost always done in the round, is often only purled here rather than knit.

Ch'ullus of the Andes

Traditionally, the most common and important item knit in the Andes is the *ch'ullu*. It is the antecedent to the ancient and highly skilled knotting and crossed looping traditions (scholars Nilda Callañaupa and Ann Pollard Rowe in their article, "Men's Knitted Caps from Chincerro" in the *Textile Museum Journal*, report that looped caps are sometimes found in pre-Hispanic gravesites). *Ch'ullus* today are knit by boys as soon as they are able, and by men for themselves and their small sons and sometimes daughters. In some areas, women knit *ch'ullus* for the men and children; in some places, girls wear a feminine version of a *ch'ullu* for festive occasions, until they're married. In tradition-bound regions, young people of marriageable age still check out the knitting and weaving skills of potential partners. They believe that any person who perseveres until he or she perfects complex textile techniques, who can create an intricately patterned *ch'ullu*, for instance, is apt to be a patient and hardworking spouse.

Ch'ullu shapes and styles vary between Bolivia and Peru, as well as within individual communities, with differences in color, knit-in patterning, size, height, and pointy-ness. But the men's caps feature earflaps in all but a few areas. Sometimes there's a tassel or pompom at the peak, sometimes the cap is domed rather than pointed, sometimes there's a ruffle around the brim (on *ch'ullus* for girls), and sometimes the whole is embellished with hundreds of bobbles or buttons.

A *ch'ullu* imparts all sorts of information about its wearer. It can tell where he comes from, indicated by the cap's specific regional characteristics. In some

✳ Alpacas, in their variety of coat colors. *Cynthia LeCount Samaké— Behind the Scenes Adventures: www.btsadventures.com*

regions, the knitter works his name, age, birthday, and village in neat stockinette stitches right into the fabric. On Taquile Island, Peru, the color of an islander's *ch'ullu* shows whether or not he's married. Some caps are known as bachelor caps and are swapped for married caps on the wedding day.

Traveler and knitter Catherine Vardy reports an amusing and accidental side effect of her visit to Potosi, Bolivia, to collect regional *ch'ullus*, where she resorted to bartering with men wearing excellent examples when she found no interesting specimens for sale in the market. She writes in her online accounting of the incident, "Poosi Ch'ullus": "[W]hen a young woman is interested in a man, she steals his *ch'ullu* as a sign of interest in him as a potential husband. When a young man is interested in a woman, he will give his *ch'ullu* to [her] . . . I had wondered why everyone laughed when a young porter refused to take off his hat and give it to me, after I had bought it . . . Egads! I'm engaged. To sixteen young men in Potosi!"

LeCount Samaké was told that a fine *ch'ullu* takes about a month to knit, and is usually accomplished "in the season between harvesting and the next planting, and then only during daylight hours, since the light in many homes is a single candle, or perhaps an alcohol lamp." Three or more colors are typically used. These days, exceedingly bright acrylic yarns are often favored, as they are inexpensive and impart color to an often monochromatic environment. Knitters respin or overspin these yarns "to ensure a tight twist which leaves no fibers to pill," writes LeCount Samaké. Motifs include everything from geometric patterns and stars—many originating with pre-Hispanic woven textiles—to snakes, condors, butterflies, and flowers.

Perhaps more than any other characteristic, the intricate patterning and fine gauge of Andean knitting are what make it so distinctive and astounding to us. LeCount Samaké recounts how she always tells the people traveling on her textile tours to bring a knitting project to show the

Rainbow Cap from Boliva

Bright rainbow earflaps and colorful little dancers decorate these cheerful caps. The stitches for the base of the cap are picked up from tops of the earflaps, with stitches for back and front cast on between them.

YARNS

Wools, Group B

Forest green or other base color, 1 (2) 50 gm. Balls

Yellow or other color, for stripe behind dancers, 20 gms.

8-10 yd. scraps of rainbow colors: white, wine, red, orange, yellow, chartreuse, kelly green, bright blue, turquoise, soft pink, bright pink, coral, magenta, or other hues as desired.

Colors for each graph are indicated in the instructions.

NEEDLES

one set of 5 double-pointed needles, size 2, or size to obtain gauge.

GAUGE

15 sts = 2 inches

SIZES

Small (1-6 years); Large (6 years to adult)

Instructions for large size appear in ( ); if only one number is shown, use it for both sizes.

Use the dancer motif given, or use any motif that is 20 sts wide and 13 sts tall for the pattern band.

Rainbow Garter Stitch Earflap Instructions

These earflaps are fun to make and look especially charming with the bright color squares.

You knit one half of the strip of little garter squares first, then use short rows to make the triangle at the point, then continue with the rest of the garter squares.

Use 2 dp ndls for the border strip; add a third ndl to finish the center area.

Outer strip: Cast on 6 sts with chartreuse. K 10 rows.

Change color and K 10 more rows. Continue color changes (10 rows per square, 6 sts wide) until there are 5 squares.

Center triangle: Change color, K 3 rows. Work triangle in short rows as follows:

K5, turn, Sl 1, K4

K4, turn, Sl 1, K3

K3, turn, Sl 1, K2

K2, turn, Sl 1, K1

K1, turn. Slide sts to other end of dp needle.

Change color; work 5 more squares in 5 more colors.

Center: With Forest Green (or base color) pick up 25 sts along one side of color strip. Place marker. Pick up 1 st each side of triangle point. Place marker. Pick up 25 sts along remaining side of strip (52 sts).

K 1 row (reverse/back side).

Change to chartreuse and knit, working a double decrease on each side of marker: Sl 1, K2 tog, PSSO, before 1st marker; K3 tog. after 2nd marker.

K 1 row.

Knit working colors in following sequence, making double decreases on right-side rows before and after markers.

2 rows white

2 rows coral

2 rows red

4 rows wine

6 rows forest green

Center seam: Work Knitted Seam from back side to close center, or bind off sts and sew center seam.

Make a second earflap.

With hat cast-on color, work 1 row single crochet around each earflap.

Cap Instructions

With forest green, and 4 dp ndls, pick up 34 (40) sts across the top of first earflap, cast on 26 (32) sts for front, pick up 34 (40) sts across top of second earflap, cast on 26 (32) sts for back. 120 (144) sts.

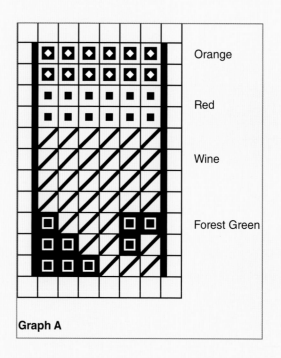

Graph A

Orange

Red

Wine

Forest Green

Join into a circle on 4 ndls and work with the 5th ndl with the face or outside of fabric toward you. Place marker at the join. Continue with forest green.

K 1 round. P 2 rounds. K 3 (5) rounds.

Work first 7 rows of Graph A with wine and forest green, then proceed with 2 rows red and 2 rows orange, as shown.

Small size: K 1 round yellow.

Large size: K 1 round yellow; dec 1 st at beg of each needle (140 sts).

Beginning at marker, work Graph B. See color notes on graph. (Small size: 12 people; large size 14 people.)

K 1 round yellow, then 2 rounds orange, 2 rounds bright red.

Small size: With wine, K 1 row decreasing 3 sts evenly along ea ndl. (108 sts).

K 1 round wine.

Large size: With wine, K 2 tog at beg of first and third ndls (138 sts)

K 2 rounds wine.

K another wine round, decreasing 3 sts evenly spaced along ea ndl. (126 sts).

Both sizes:

Work Graph C with wine and forest green. (Small size 18 waves; large size 21 waves.)

Break off wine.

Large size: K 1 round, decreasing 6 sts evenly spaced around the cap. (120 sts, 30 per needle.)

At this point, with 108 sts (small size) or 120 sts. (large size) begin rounded top with forest green or base color.

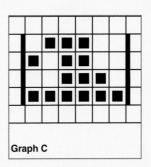

Graph C

SIZE LARGE, START HERE

Decrease round: Beginning at marker, *K8, K2 tog*; repeat * to * around to marker. (108 sts)

Continue both sizes, starting here with the 108 sts.

K 4 (8) rounds.

Decrease round: K7, K2 tog. (96 sts)

K 7 rounds.

Decrease round: K6, K2 tog. (84 sts)

K 6 rounds.

Decrease round: K5, K2 tog. (72 sts)

K 5 rounds.

Decrease round: K4, K2 tog. (60 sts)

K 4 rounds.

Decrease round: K3, K2 tog. (48 sts)

K 3 rounds.

Decrease round: K2, K2 tog. (36 sts)

K 2 rounds.

Decrease round: K1, K2 tog. (24 sts)

K 1 round.

Decrease round: K1, K2 tog. (16 sts)

Break yarn, draw end through last 16 sts, pull up snugly, and knot it securely to close the hole at the top.

CROCHETED OUTER EDGING

With any contrasting color, work 1 row single crochet around all edges, continuing around earflaps, etc. This unites the cap and makes it more solid.

—Pattern from Cynthia LeCount Samaké

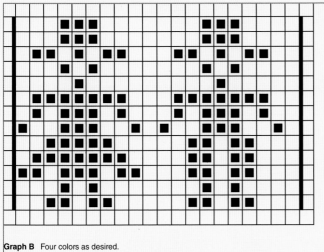

Graph B Four colors as desired.
Change colors for shoes, skirt/pants, faces & hats.

Cynthia LeCount Samaké's goddaughter Anita Coyla, wearing a typical little girl's ruffled bonnet on one of the Urus Islands—floating reed islands in Lake Titicaca. *Cynthia LeCount Samaké— Behind the Scenes Adventures: www.btsadventures.com*

later, a teenage girl came running up, waving the sock she had quickly finished, complete with perfect toe decreases!

LeCount Samaké discovered that Andean knitters "have adapted the intarsia method to their circular knitting in order to introduce many more colors into their work. Normally, if intarsia is worked in the round, the yarns end up on the opposite side of the motif, inaccessible for the next round." Andean knitters use an ingenious method of working around the *ch'ullu* in one direction, joining the yarn with one of two methods, then turning the piece and working around in the other direction (described below). Presto! The colors are in position to use in the next color motif.

The working yarn can be joined to knit back in the other direction either by interlocking the working yarn with the last color at the join, or with the more common "corded join" used in many places around Cuzco. For a corded join, the knitter saves a long strand or two from the beginning border at the cast-on bottom edge. He pulls this upward as he knits each round, and wraps the working yarn around it, turns the pieces, and continues around in the opposite direction.

Different techniques are used in other places. Sometimes knitters don't hesitate to bring the different colored yarns of an intarsia patttern across the back of the work from left to right, to place it into position to use on the next round. This creates floats on the back. LeCount Samaké calls this adaptation *zigzag intarsia*. In many areas, no matter the joining technique for the innovative circular knitting, knitters twist the working yarns of every stitch together; this is called "weaving in" but has no relation to an actual weaving technique.

In Bolivia, knitters often combine techniques, making intricate color motifs but carrying the colors all the way around in circular knitting, and twisting or "weaving" every stitch. With this spiral or circular method, the cap is quite thick and rigid, standing up in a point to impress the girls. The wrong side often looks as neat as the right.

knitters in the Peruvian highlands, because the village women love to see what they are working on, and with what interesting yarns. Melissa Drane, an American knitter, got a good laugh when she proudly showed off the chartreuse shawl she had made with very fine and costly mohair, in an openwork stitch. The villagers, who knit with size 000 needles and fourteen stitches to the inch, were dumbfounded, and asked Melissa if she were making a fishing net.

Another time, a traveler named Nancy Thomas was with LeCount Samaké in a village where she handed around a half-finished sock, begun with fine, space-dyed wool. The village women were fascinated, and Nancy lost track of her sock as it was passed around the group. About ten minutes

Other Andean Knitting Traditions

Like *ch'ullus*, coin purses (*monederos*), socks (*medias*), ceremonial masks, and festival leggings, some knit by men, some by women, are typical knitted items of the region. Knitted sleeves (*maquitos*) seem to have been a contribution of the Spanish, write Nilda Callañaupa and Ann Pollard Rowe in their study of men's knitted caps from Chincero: "Knitted sleeves provide a further clue about the Spanish source of this technique. The concept of separate sleeves is derived from Spanish costume. Women's dresses of the late fifteenth and early sixteenth centuries had detachable sleeves, and some of these were knitted. Detachable knitted sleeves with multicolored patterns survived as part of the traditional women's costume in Obrigo in León [northern Portugal], until early in the twentieth century." Curious that it should be the Andean men, then, who adopted the style.

The *maquitos* of the Chinchero region are commonly knit with black, white, and red patterning and are connected by a band to keep them from slipping off the arms. In other areas of Peru, such as Huancavelica, men wear brilliant multicolored sleeves over their jackets to keep warm.

LeCount Samaké speculates on the origins of the popular Bolivian and Peruvian *monederos*—coin purses fashioned in all sorts of whimsical animal shapes. Did Spanish ladies introduce figure-purse knitting to the Andes, or vice versa? She concludes that figure purses probably originated in the Andes, a spinoff of tiny, intricate, three-dimensional cross-looped figures made by the pre-Hispanic people of coastal Peru.

Although acrylic yarn is the fiber of choice for many Andean knitters these days, yarns from the native camelids (llamas, alpacas, and vicuñas) and from sheep introduced by the Spanish, were all once prominent. And of course, spinning and dyeing were also once part of traditional fiber production. In some regions, knitting cooperatives have been started and have successfully revived traditional textiles, producing both contemporary and traditional versions of typical garments for an appreciative tourist trade.

✳ A young knitter named Reuben. *Cynthia LeCount Samaké—Behind the Scenes Adventures: www. btsadventures.com*

An adolescent girl's ruffled bonnet, Lake Titicaca, Peru. According to LeCount Samaké, the girls knit these themselves and "although this is not verbalized, they are surely to attract boys. This is a totally new style of ruffled brim, very rigid with thick edging, although the cap itself is not new." *Cynthia LeCount Samaké—Behind the Scenes Adventures: www. btsadventures.com*

❊ Knitter in Pitumarca,
village near Cuzco.
Cynthia LeCount Samaké—
Behind the Scenes Adventures:
www.btsadventures.com

Guatemala

Knitting in Guatemala has been studied in the past decade and found to be a distinct form by textile scholar Ann Pollard Rowe. Investigating the large square wool bags of Sololå, Nahualá, and Zacualpa, she outlined some of the details: knitted top-down; worked in two colors, usually black and white or red and white; and, in most instances, had extra colors floated at the back of the work rather than "woven" in. Joaquin Munoz and Anna Bell Ward, in their 1940 book about the country, *Guatemala, Ancient & Modern*, were slightly more specific about bags from the village of Solola: men "knit a bag of about sixteen inches square of black and white wool with designs of horses or plain stripes, seldom names are knitted on them."

Though knitters in Guatemala seem to favor hooked needles, they accomplish their knitting working on the "right" side, or knit side, and they do not tension yarn around their necks.

Concludes Rowe, "The differences in the knitting techniques of the Andes and Guatemala suggests that knitting was introduced into these areas from different places in Spain, and that there was regional variation in knitting techniques within Spain. While crossed knitting has not previously been noted in Spain, there are in fact relatively few early examples of Spanish knitting that have been preserved and published, so a gap in our knowledge cannot be taken to be definitive. Crossed knitting is found in some Balkan and Turkish pieces . . . so it certainly was known in the Arab world."

✳ Dancer with knit mask at Virgin of Carmen celebration in Paucartambo, Peru. *Cynthia LeCount Samaké— Behind the Scenes Adventures: www.btsadventures.com*

WHERE TO FIND SOME OF THE ARTISTS, KNITTERS, AND HISTORIANS FEATURED IN THIS BOOK

Karen Alfke—2ndesign.com

Sigrid Briansdotter (Anne Marie Haymes)—*Nålbinding Made Easy*

Nancy Bush—woolywest.com

Annelies de Kort—anneliesdekort.nl

Donna Druchunas—sheeptoshawl.com (look for her upcoming book with June Hall at nomad-press.com)

Françoise Dupré—axisweb.org/seCVPG. aspx?ARTISTID=3684

Anke Grevers—geldersemutsen.nl

Habu Textiles—135 West 29th Street, Suite 804, New York, NY, 10001; habutextiles.com

Solveig Hisdal—oleana.no

Vivian Høxbro—viv.dk/English/default.htm

Susanna Hansson—oneofsusannas.com (also visit master dyer Gustafsson's website, solsilke.se)

Kazekobo—kazekobo.net

Elsebeth Lavold—ingenkonst.se/viking_e.htm

Hélène Magnússon—helenemagnusson.com

Prudence Mapstone—knotjustknitting.com

Sharon Miller—www.heirloom-knitting.co.uk

Veronika Persché—persche.com

Leena Riihelä and Riihivilla Natural Dyed Wool—riihivilla.blogspot.com

Cynthia LeCount Samaké—http://www.btsadventures.com

Annete Streyl—streyl.net

Annemor Sundbø—annemor.com/english.htm

Felieke van der Leest—www.feliekevanderleest. com/?l=en

Jean Wong—knittingwithjean.com

BIBLIOGRAPHY

Abbot, Jean and Shirley Bourke. *Spin a Yarn, Weave a Dream*: A History of the New Zealand Spinning, Weaving and Woolcrafts Society, 1969–1994. New Zealand: New Zealand Spinning, Weaving, and Woolcrafts Society, 1994.

"Ackworth Medallion Samplers." *Sampler & Antique Needlework Quarterly*. http://www.sanqmagazine. com/Story.htm. Accessed 6/12/09.

Allen, Larry. *The Encyclopedia of Money*. New York: Checkmark Books, 2001.

Bailey, Susan Strawn. "Knitting in the Amanas." *Piecework*, September/October 2007.

Baird, Catronia. "Fair Isle Knitting." http://scottishtextileheritage.org.uk/ onlineResources/articles/articlesTem2. asp?articleNo=17. Accessed on 5/13/09.

Barnes, Galer Britton. "A Tale of Scottish Kilt Hose." *Piecework*, September/October 1995.

Barnes, Galer Britton. "Amish Wedding Stockings of the Nineteenth Century." *Piecework*, March/ April 1997.

Barnes, Galer Britton. "Cowichan Sweaters." *Piecework*, July/August 1998.

Basset, Lynn Zacek. "Red Fezzes and Yellow Slippers: Mark Twain and Charlie Langdon in the Holy Land." *Piecework*, July/August 2004.

Berlo, Janet Catherine. "Oomingmak: Knitting Vision into Reality." *Piecework*, January/ February 1996.

Bizilia, Adrian. "How I Thrum." http://www. helloyarn.com/wp/?p=425. Accessed on 6/13/09.

Bliss, Debbie, ed. *Traditional Knitting from the Scottish and Irish Isles*. New York: Crown Publishers, 1991.

Bremner, David. *The Industries of Scotland: Their Rise, Progress, and Present Condition*. Edinburgh: Adam and Charles Black, 1869.

Bruzelius, Margaret. "Exploring a Knitted Pattern: Bohus Stickning sweater generates diverse designs knit with simple stitches." *Knitting Around the World from Threads*, edited by Threads Magazine, Newtown, CT: Taunton Press, 1993.

Bush, Nancy. *Folk Knitting in Estonia*. Loveland, CO: Interweave Press, 2000.

Bush, Nancy. "Gifts of Knitting." *Piecework*, March/ April 1998.

Bush, Nancy. "Knit Northland Mittens with the Two-End Knitting Technique." *Piecework*, January/February 2007.

Bush, Nancy. *Knitted Lace of Estonia*. Loveland, CO: Interweave Press, 2008.

Bush, Nancy. "Knitting in Estonia." *Piecework*, September/October 2008.

Bush, Nancy. "Knitting in Norway." *Piecework* May/ June 2007.

Bush, Nancy. "The Lace Knitting of Haapsalu." *Piecework*, July/August 2005.

Bush, Nancy. "*Nålbinding* From the Iron Age to Today." *Piecework* May/June 2001.

Bush, Nancy. "Riina Tomberg: Preserving Estonia's Knitting Traditions." *Piecework*, January/February 2009.

Bush, Nancy. "Special Knits for Special Occasions: Norwegian Wedding Gloves." *Piecework*, November/December 2008.

Bush, Nancy. "Tvåänsstickning: Sweden's Two-End Knitting." *Piecework*, January/February 2007.

Bush, Nancy with Maarja Vārv. "Aino Praakli: Carrying on Estonia's Knitted Mitten Tradition." *Piecework*, January/February 2007.

Callañaupa, Nilda and Ann Pollard Rowe. "Men's Knitted Caps from Chinchero." *Textile Museum Journal* (1999–2000): 69-80.

Carlson, Jennifer L. "A Short History of the Monmouth Cap." personal.utulsa.edu/~Marc-Carlson/jennifer/Monmouth.htm. Accessed on 4/20/09.

Compton, Rae. *The Complete Book of Guernsey and Jersey Knitting.* New York: Arco Publishing, Inc., 1985.

Cornell, Kari, ed. *For the Love of Knitting.* Minneapolis, MN: Voyageur Press, 2004.

Daly, Catherine M. "Anna Mizens, Latvian Mitten Knitter." In *Circles of Tradition: Folk Arts in Minnesota,* by Willard Burgess Moore, 80-87. Minneapolis: University of Minnesota Press, 1989.

Davies, Kate. "In the Steps of Jane Gaugain." *Twist Collective,* Spring 2009.

De Fairhurst, Rohese. "Project—Scoggers & Hoggers." *Fibre Guild of Lohac Newsletter* 5 (Midwinter) AS XXXIX. Accessed online 11/13/09.
sca.org.au/fibre/projects/scoggers-hoggers.php

De Master, Sandra Messinger. "Messages in Mittens: The Story of a Latvian Knitter." *Piecework,* November/December 1995.

Dexter, Janetta. *Nova Scotian Double-Knitting Patterns.* Nova Scotia: Nimbus Pub. Ltd, 1985.

Dominick, Sabine. *Cables, Diamonds, Herringbones: Secrets of Knitting Traditional Fishermen's Sweaters.* Camden, ME: Down East Books, 2007.

Druchunas, Donna. "Amish Knitting and Crochet: Preserving Time-honored Traditions." *Piecework,* March/April 2005.

Druchunas, Donna. "Knitting and Crochet: A Marriage Made in History." *Black Purl Magazine,* December 2009.

Druchunas, Donna. "Knitting from Norway." *Black Purl Magazine,* Summer 2007.

Druchunas, Donna. *The Knitted Rug: 21 Fantastic Designs.* Asheville, NC: Lark Books, 2005.

Druchunas, Donna. "The Tradition of Knitting in Lithuania." *Piecework,* December 2009.

Druchunas, Donna. "Turkish Delight for Knitters." *Black Purl Magazine,* Fall 2007.

Dumfries Museum. "A History of the Sanquhar Knitting Pattern." http://www.dumfriesmuseum.demon.co.uk/frames.html. Accessed on 4/20/09.

Earnshaw, Pat. *A Dictionary of Lace.* New York: Dover Publications, 1999.

Epstein, Nicky. *Knitting on Top of the World.* New York: Nicky Epstein Books, 2008.

Erlbacher, Maria. *Twisted-Stitch Knitting.* Pittsville, WI: Schoolhouse Press, 2009.

Falick, Melanie. "Cobwebs from the Steppes: Russian Lace-Knitted Shawls." *Piecework,* May/June 1995.

Fanderl, Lisl. *Bauerliches Stricken* 1& 2. Rosenheim, Germany: Rosenheimer Verlagshaus, 2001.

Fatelewitz, Madelynn. "Knitting in the North Atlantic." *Knitting Around the World from Threads,* edited by Threads Magazine, 73-77. Newton, CT: Taunton Press, 1993.

Finnane, Antonia. *Changing Clothes in China: Fashion, History, Nation.* New York: Columbia University Press, 2007.

Fraser, Joyce and Beverley Horne. "Kiwicraft." *Web Quarterly Journal of New Zealand Spinning, Weaving and Woolcraft Society* 4, No. 1 (March 1973): 7

Future Museum of Scotland. "Sanquhar Knitting." http://futuremuseum.co.uk/Collection.aspx/sanquhar_knitting/Description. Accessed on 5/7/09.

Garnett, Lucy Mary Jane. *Balkan Home Life.* New York: Dodd, Mead & Company, 1917.

Gaugain, Jane. *Lady's Assistant in Knitting, Netting, and Crochet,* London: Ackerman and Co., 1840.

Gibson-Roberts, Priscilla and Deborah Robson. *Knitting in the Old Way: Designs and Techniques from Ethnic Sweaters.* Fort Collins, CO: Nomad Press, 2005.

Gordon, Beverly. *Shaker Textile Arts.* Hanover, NH: University of New England, 1980.

Gottfridsson, Inger and Ingrid Gottfridsson. *The Swedish Mitten Book: Traditional Patterns from Gotland.* Asheville, NC: Lark Books, 1984.

Gravjord, Ingebjørg. *Votten I norsk tradisjon*, Bø Museum, 2007.

Guõojónsson, Elsa E. *Notes on Knitting in Iceland*. Reykjavik, Iceland: National Museum of Iceland, 1979.

Hale, Sarah Josepha Buell. "Ladies' Work Department—Knitting." *Godey's Lady's Book* magazine, 1847.

Hall, June. "Europe's Newest Guild 'The Unbroken Thread' in Lithuania." *Journal for Weavers, Spinners, and Dyers*, September 2006.

Halldórsdóttir, Sigridur. *Three-Cornered and Long Shawls*. Pittsville, WI: Schoolhouse Press, 2005.

Hansen, Robin. *Favorite Mittens: Best Traditional Mitten Patterns*. Camden, ME: Down East Books, 2006.

Harrell, Betsy. *Anatolian Knitting Designs: Sivas Stocking Patterns Collected in an Instanbul Shantytown*. Hopkins, MN: Redhouse Press, 1991.

Heite, Louise. "Icelandic Knitting." *Knitters* magazine, 2000.

Hiller, James and Peater Neary, eds. *Twentieth Century Newfoundland: Explorations*. St. John's, NF: Breakwater, 1994.

Higgins, Jenny with Luke Callanan. "Health-Care Organizations: The Commission of Government, 1934-1949."

http://www.heritage.nf.ca/law/health_care_org. html. Accessed 5/6/10.

"History of Orenburg Lace Shawls." http://macterica.ru/index. php?name=history&lang=en. Accessed 4/20/09.

Holligworth, Shelagh. *Complete Book of Traditional Aran Knitting*. New York: St. Martin's Press, 1983.

Hough, Walter. "The Hopi Indian Collection in the United States National Museum." From the Proceedings of the United States National Museum. Washington, D.C.: Government Printing Office, 1918.

Howitt, William. *The Rural Life of England*. London: Longman, Orme, Brown, Green, & Longmans, 1938.

Høxbro, Vivian. *Shadow Knitting*. Loveland, CO: Interweave Press, 2004.

Humphrey, Carol. *Quaker Schoolgirl Samplers from Ackworth, needleprint*. 2006.

Ivey, Kimberly Smith. *In the Neatest Manner: The Making of the Virginia Sampler Tradition*. Williamsburg, VA: Curious Works Press and the Colonial Williamsburg Foundation, 1997.

Jackson, Suzyn. *Knit it Together*. Minneapolis, MN: Voyageur Press, 2009.

Jurkuviene, Terese. *100 Emilijis Navickienes Pirstiniu*, Lithuanian Folk Culture Centre.

Kalsson, Gunnar. *History of Iceland*. London: C. Hurst & Co., 2000.

Karniemi-Alve, Leena. "From the Arctic Circle: Knitted Rovaniemi Mittens." *Piecework*, January/February 2008.

Kee, Jenny. *Knits from Nature*. New York: Prentice Hall Press, 1990.

Keele, Wendy. *Poems of Color*. Loveland, CO: Interweave Press, 1995.

Kihara, Yoshimi. "Beyond the Comfort Zone." http://www.knitjapan.co.uk/features/c_zone/ c_zone.htm. Accessed on 6/3/09.

Kihara, Yoshimi. "Knit Paintings: Beyond glorious color with Japanese knitting techniques." *Knitting Around the World from Threads*, edited by Threads Magazine. Newton, CT: Taunton Press, 1993.

Kihara, Yoshimi. "The Story of Knitting in Japan," Parts 1 and 2. http://www.knitjapan. co.uk/j_select/pages/japanknitting_pt1.php and http://www.knitjapan.co.uk/j_select/ pages/japanknitting_pt2_pg1.php. Accessed on 6/3/09.

King, P. G. "A Contribution to the History of Fine-Wolled Sheep to Australia." *Centennial Magazine*, 1 (1888).

Kinzel, Marianne. *First Book of Modern Art of Lace Knitting*. New York: Dover Books, 1972.

Kmeleva, Galina. "A Tribute to Lace-Knitting Legend Olga Alexandrovna Federova." *Piecework*, May/June 2009.

Kmeleva, Galina and Carol R. Noble. *Gossamer Webs: The History and Techniques of Orenburg Lace Shawls*. Loveland, CO: Interweave Press, 1998.

"Knitting: From Islam to the West." *Tournaments Illuminated*, 165. http://www.sca.org/ti/articles/2008/issue165/MedievalKnitting.pdf . Accessed online 6/12/09.

Korach, Alice. "Shetland Lace: These intricate shawls mark handknitting's finest hour." *Around the World from Threads*. Newtown, CT: Taunton Press, 1993.

Kosel, Janine and Sue Flanders. *Norwegian Handknits: Heirloom Designs from the Vesterheim Museum*. Minneapolis, MN: Voyageur Press, 2009.

Krogulski, Sandy. "Turning a Curse into a Blessing: Propaganda and the Emigration of British Single Women." *Concept: An Interdisciplinary Journal of Graduate Studies* 2010.

Ladies' Work-Book, The. John Cassell, La Belle Sauvage Yard, London, Project Gutenberg

Lambert, Miss. *My Knitting Book*. London: John Murray, 1943.

Lambert, Gail Ann. "The Taxonomy of Sweater Structures and Their Origins." Thesis, North Carolina State University, 2002.

Lambert, Miss F. *Handbook of Needlework*. New York: Wiley & Putnam, 1842.

Lattimore, Owen. *The Desert Road to Turkistan*. London: Methuen, 1928.

Lavold, Elsebeth. *Viking Patterns for Knitting*. Trafalgar Square Publishing, 2000

LeCount, Cynthia Gravelle. *Andean Folk Knitting*. Cambridge, MA: Adventure Publications, 1990.

LeCount, Cynthia Gravelle. "Andean Knitted Figure Purses: Mondeneros for Your Money." *Piecework*, January/February 2009.

Leighton-White, Sue. "The Needles' Music: Hand Knitters of the Dales." *Piecework*, January/February 1994.

Letoutchaia, Faina. "Estonian Lace." Paper presented at the Knitting Beyond the Hebrides Lace Symposium.

Lewandowski, Marcia. *Folk Mittens: Techniques and Patterns for Handknitted Mittens*. Loveland, CO: Interweave Press, 1997.

Lewis, Susanna E. "Knitting Lace." *Piecework*, May/June 1997.

Ligon, Linda. "Innovation in the Andes: Making Bobble Yarn." *Interweave Knits*, Winter 2006.

Lind, Vibeke. *Knitting in the Nordic Tradition*, New York: Sterling Publishers, 1998.

Locke, Raymond Friday. *Book of the Navajo*. Los Angeles: Mankind Pubishing Company, 2001.

Lovick, Elizabeth. "Gutter Ganseys." *Interweave Knits*, Winter 2006.

Lovick, Elizabeth. "The Same but Different: Shetland Lace in a Europen Context." Paper presented at the KBTH Lace Virtual Conference, March 2006.

Lovitch, Marcy. "Icelandic Wool." *Interweave Knits*, Winter 2003.

Luutonnen, Marketta. "Rustic Production as a conveyor of Meaning. A Study of Finnish Pullovers." Ph.D. dissertation.

Lyttle, Bethany. "Cowichan Sweaters: Durable & Enduring." *Interweave Knits*, Fall 2008.

MacDonald, Ann L. *No Idle Hands: The Social History of American Knitting*. New York: Ballantine Books, 1988.

Magnússon, Hélène. *Icelandic Knitting: Using Rose Patterns*. Tunbridge Wells, UK: Search Press, 2008.

McCormack, Mary A. *Spool Knitting*. New York: A.S. Barnes & Company, 1909.

McGregor, Sheila. *The Complete Book of Traditional Fair Isle Knitting*. New York: Scribners, 1981.

McGregor, Sheila. *Traditional Scandinavian Knitting*. Minneola, NY: Dover Press, 1984.

McLeod-Odell, Judith. *Heirloom Knits: 20 Classic Designs to Cherish*. New York: St. Martin's Press, 2007.

Meikele, Margaret. *Cowichan Indian Knitting*. CA: University of British Columbia Museum of Anthropology, 1987.

Merkiene, Irena and Marija Banionien. *Gloves of Lithuania Minor: At the Crossroads of Cultures*. Zara, 1998.

Morris, Fritz. "Stilt Walkers of Les Landes," *Technical World Magazine*.

Morse, Alice Earle. *Costume of Colonial Times*. Charleston, SC: BiblioBazaar, 2010.

Muecke, Stephen. *Desert Designs: 26 Knits by Aboriginal Artists*. New York: Prentice Hall Press, 1990.

Muñoz, Joachín and Anna Bell Ward. *Guatemala, Ancient & Modern*. Pyramid Press, 1940.

Newberry, Susette. *Knitting Letters: A to Z*, unionpurl@blogpot.com.

Nicholson, Heather. *The Loving Stitch*. Auckland, NZ: Auckland University Press, 1998.

Noble, Carol Rasmussen. "Lace and the Midnight Sun." *Piecework*, July/August 1996.

Norbury, James. *Traditional Knitting Patterns*. New York: Dover Publications, 1973.

Oberle, Cheryl. *Folk Shawls*. Loveland, CO: Interweave Press, 2000.

Olsen, Osva and Ingvar Svanberg. "Nålbinding in the Faroe Islands." *Annale Societatis Scientiarum Faroensis* 51 (2004), 193–197.

"Orenburg Shawls." geocities.com/jpotter49505/essays_files/orenburg.html. Accessed on 5/29/09.

Oomingmak Musk Ox Producers' Co-operative, qiviut.com.

Ozbel, Kenan. *Knitted Stockings from Turkish Villages*. Istanbul, Turkey: Is Bankasi Cultural Publications, 1981.

Pagoldh, Susanne. *Nordic Knitting: Thirty-One Patterns in the Scandinavian Tradition*. Loveland, CO: Interweave Press, 1997.

Paludan, Charlotte, and Lone De Hemmer Egelberg. 98 *Pattern Books for Embroidery, Lace and Knitting*. Copenhagen: Danske Kunstindustrimuseum, 1991.

Parkes, Clara. *The Knitter's Book of Yarn: The Ultimate Guide to Choosing, Using, and Enjoying Yarn*. New York: Potter Craft, 2007.

Patterson, Veronica. "Fancy Dress for Hands: The Rosesaum Mittens of Norway." *Piecework*, November/December 2006.

Patterson, Veronica. "The Land of Counterpane: Knitted Cotton Coverlets." *Piecework*, May/June 1996.

Perry, Mrs. S. M. "Kiwicraft," *Web Quarterly Journal of New Zealand Spinning, Weaving and Woolcraft Society* 3, No. 4 (November 1972): 4.

Pulliam, Deborah. "Early Silk Knitting." *Piecework*, March/April 2007.

Pulliam, Deborah. "Knitted Containers: Ubiquitous, Useful." *Piecework*, January/February 2007.

Quaker History, Vols. 7 and 8. Friends' Historical Society of Philadelphia, Ferris & Leach, 1916–1918.

Quimby, Vicki. "Gaels and the Knitting Tradition." *Am Foghar*, Autumn 2009.

Reid, Stuart. *Wellington's Highlanders*. Oxford: Osprey Publishing, 1992.

"The Renaissance of Latvia's Ethnographic Mittens." http://www.rigasummit.lv/en/id/cats/nid/698/. Accessed 4/20/09.

Rhoades, Carol Huebscher. "Bead-knitted Wrist Warmers: Beauty and Warmth." *Piecework*, January/Februay 2006.

Rhodes, Melody. "Cowichan Sweaters of the Coast Salish People: Traditional Woll Garments from the B.C. Cowichan Valley." December 13, 2009.

http://www.suite101.com/content/cowichan-sweaters-of-the-coast-salish-people-a172435. Accessed 6/23/09.

Rosing-Schow, Lita. "Danish Knitted Vests." *Piecework*, January/February 2005.

Rowe, Mary. *Knitted Tams*. Loveland, CO: Interweave Press, 1989.

Rutt, Richard. A *History of Hand Knitting*. Loveland, CO: Interweave Press, 2003.

Saliklis, Ruta. *A Wealth of Pattern: Northern European and Middle Eastern Folk Knitting in the Helen Allen Textile Collection.* Madison, WI: University of Wisconsin, 1990.

Samaké, Cynthia LeCount. "Andean Knitted Figure Purses: Monederos for Your Money." *Piecework,* January/February 2009.

Savage, Timothy. Japanese Canadian National Museum. bc150.ecuad.ca/museum/08_04. html. Accessed 3/10/10.

Schurch, Charlene Tompkins. "Christine Duchrow & Art Pattern Knitting." *Piecework,* January/February 1987.

Schurch, Charlene Tompkins. *Mostly Mittens.* Asheville, NC: Lark Books, 1998.

Scott, Shirley. *Canada Knits: Craft and Comfort in a Northern Land.* Ontario: McGraw-Hill Ryerson, 1990.

Shaw-Smith, David. *Traditional Crafts of Ireland.* London: Thames & Hudson, 2003.

Shell, Ann. "Report from Dorothy Reade's Lace Knitting Workshop, 1968." Coominmak Co-operative archives.

Sinclair, Sir John, ed. *The Statistical Accounts of Scotland.* London, 1793.

"So who invented modular knitting?" *The Girl from Auntie* (blog). http://www.girlfromauntie.com/journal/so-who-invented-modular-knitting/. Accessed 6/16/09.

Society and Environment. Western Australia: R.I.C. Publications, 2000.

Sokalski, Linda D. Y. "Colorful Tvåändsstickning." *Knitting Around the World from Threads,* edited by Threads Magazine, 26-28. Newton, CT: Taunton Press, 1993.

Sokalski, Linda D. Y. "Swedish Two-Strand Knitting." *Knitting Around the World from Threads,* edited by Threads Magazine, 50-53. Newton, CT: Taunton Press, 1993.

Stanley, Montse, "Knit Lace." *Knitting Around the World from Threads,* edited by Threads Magazine, 67-70. Newton, CT: Taunton Press, 1993.

Starmore, Alice. *Alice Starmore's Book of Fair Isle Knitting.* Newtown, CT: Taunton Press, 1988.

Starmore, Alice. "Fair Isle Knitting: The versatile, traditional methods of stranded-color knitting in the round." *Knitting Around the World from Threads,* edited by Threads Magazine, 31-32. Newton, CT: Taunton Press, 1993.

Starmore, Alice. "Unraveling the Myths of Shetland Lace: Learning to create openwork motifs." *Knitting Around the World from Threads,* edited by Threads Magazine, 55-57. Newton, CT: Taunton Press, 1993.

Starmore, Alice and Anne Matheson. *Knitting from the British Isles: 30 Original Designs from Traditional Patterns.* New York: St. Martin's Press, 1983.

"Stilt Walking—A Sketch, with engraving, of Sylvain Dornon, the Stilt Walker of Landes." *Scientific American Supplement* 821 (September 26, 1891).

Strawn, Susan M. *Knitting America:* Minneapolis, MN: Voyageur Press, 2007.

Strawn, Susan M. "Traveling Stitches." *Piecework,* September/October 2008.

Sundbø, Annemor. *Everyday Knitting: Treasures from a Ragpile.* Torridal, Norway: Torridal Tweed, 2000.

Sundbø, Annemor. *Setesdal Sweaters: The History of the Norwegian Lice Pattern.* Torridal, Norway: Torridal Tweed, 2001.

Sundbø, Annemor. *Invisible Threads in Knitting.* Torridal, Norway: Torridal Tweed, 2007.

Swansen, Meg. "The Etymology of the I-Cord." *Piecework,* September/October 2008

Thomas, Clarissa. "Knitting and Knitwear in the Stuart Period." *Orders of the Day* 32, No. 5 (September 2000). Accessed online 6/13/09.

Thomas, Mary. *Mary Thomas's Knitting Book.* New York: Dover Publications, 1972.

Turnau, Irena. *History of Knitting Before Mass Production.* Institute of the History of Material Culture, Polish Academy of Sciences, 1991.

Turnau, Irena. "The Knitting Crafts in Europe from the Thirteenth to the Eighteenth

Century." *Bulletin of the Needle and Bobbin Club* 65, no. 1 and 2 (1982): 20-28.

Vogue Knitting. *The Ultimate Sock Book*. New York: Vogue Knitting, Soho Press, 2007.

Upitis, Lizbeth. *Latvian Mittens*. Pittsville, WI: Schoolhouse Press, 1997.

Uten, Erica. "Tokens of Love: Quaker Pinballs." *Piecework*, September/October 2009.

van der Klift-Tellegen, Henriette. *Knitting from the Netherlands: Traditional Dutch Fishermen's Sweaters*. Asheville, NC: Lark Books, 1985.

Van Tuyl, Laura. "Folklore in the Palm of Your Hand: Mittens with a Past." *Christian Science Monitor*, January 26, 1989.

Vardy, Catherine. "Potosi Ch'ullus." http://needleartsbookshop.com/attic/aecvhats.html. Accessed 4/20/09.

Walker, Barbara. *A Second Treasury of Knitting Patterns*. Pittsville, WI: Schoolhouse Press, 1998.

Walker, Barbara. *A Treasury of Knitting Patterns*. Pittsville, WI: Schoolhouse Press, 1998.

Walker, Barbara. *Charted Knitting Designs: A Third Treasury of Knitting Patterns*. Pittsville, WI: Schoolhouse Press, 1998.

Walker, Barbara. *Mosaic Knitting*. Pittsville, WI: Schoolhouse Press, 1997.

Watt, Sir George. *Indian Art at Delhi* 1903. Delhi: Motilal Banarsidas, 1987.

Weston, Madeleine. *Classic British Knits*. New York: Crown Publishers, 1986.

Wiseheart, Sandi. "What is a Thrum and Why Is It in My Mitten." *Knitting Daily*, February 2009. http://www.knittingdaily.com/blogs/daily/archive/2009/02/02/how-to-thrum-a-mitten.aspx. Accessed 6/13/10.

Wiseman, Nancie M. "A Collection of Knitted Lace Edgings." *Piecework*, July/August 2005.

Wogec, Mary Frances. "A Miniature Lace Tablecloth to Knit for Tatiana's Tea Table." *Piecework*, September/October 2009.

Wong, Andrea. "The Portuguese Style of Knitting." *Piecework*, January/February 2009.

Wright, Mary. *Cornish Guernseys and Knit Frocks*. London: Ethnographica, 1983.

Wright, Mary. *Cornish Guernseys & Knit Frocks*. London: Ethnographica, 1985.

Zilboorg, Anna. *Simply Socks: 45 Traditional Turkish Patterns to Knit*. New York: Lark Books, 2001.

ACKNOWLEDGMENTS

A monumental undertaking such as this one you now hold in your hands could not possibly come to fruition without the help, guidance, and input of many, many fine and talented people. I am unspeakably grateful to all the knitters, historians, and photographers whose work and words grace these pages; and to the various museum professionals around the world who helped me unearth just the right image, just the perfect kernel of information.

A few exceptionally wonderful people went far beyond what is reasonable in the service of a mere book (someone else's book at that):

Jun Miyamoto, Clara Parkes, Hélène Magnússon, Nancy Bush, Tuulia Salmela, Annemor Sundbo, Lizbeth Upitis, Donna Druchunas, Carla Meijsen, Anna Maija Bäckman, Vivian Høxbro, Susette Newberry, Meg Swansen, and Cynthia LeCount Samaké. I humbly thank these goddesses of yarn for all they contributed to this tome.

Finally, thanks to my editor Kari Cornell, who is always kind enough to think of me, and tireless in her efforts to see these books come to light. And to Ada and Rob, who never complain overly much about sacrificing our weekends together to all my myriad projects.